SNAKE DANCE

Patrick Marnham is a biographer and travel writer. He began his career as a reporter on *Private Eye* and has written for many newspapers including the *Daily Telegraph*, the *Guardian*, the *New York Times* and *Libération*. He has worked as a BBC script writer and a special correspondent in Africa, the Middle East and Central America. He has been literary editor of the *Spectator* and was the first Paris Correspondent of the *Independent*. He has written lives of Diego Rivera, Georges Simenon, Jean Moulin and Mary Wesley. His books have won the Thomas Cook Travel Book Award and the Marsh Biography Award. To accompany this book Marnham has written the prize-winning documentary film *Snake Dance*, directed by Manu Riche, the Belgian film maker. Patrick Marnham lives with his family in Oxfordshire.

ALSO BY PATRICK MARNHAM

Road to Katmandu

Fantastic Invasion: Dispatches from Africa

So Far from God: A Journey to Central America

*The Man Who Wasn't Maigret: A Portrait of
Georges Simenon*

Crime and the Académie Française

*Dreaming with His Eyes Open: A Life of
Diego Rivera*

The Death of Jean Moulin: Biography of a Ghost

Wild Mary: A Life of Mary Wesley

PATRICK MARNHAM

Snake Dance

Journeys Beneath a Nuclear Sky

VINTAGE BOOKS
London

Published by Vintage 2014

2 4 6 8 10 9 7 5 3 1

Copyright © Patrick Marnham 2013

Patrick Marnham has asserted his right under the Copyright, Designs
and Patents Act 1988 to be identified as the author of this work

First published in Great Britain in 2013 by Chatto & Windus

Vintage
Random House, 20 Vauxhall Bridge Road,
London SW1V 2SA

www.vintage-books.co.uk

Addresses for companies within The Random House Group Limited
can be found at: www.randomhouse.co.uk/offices

The Random House Group Limited Reg. No. 954009

A CIP catalogue record for this book
is available from the British Library

ISBN 9780099542247

The Random House Group Limited supports the Forest
Stewardship Council® (FSC®), the leading international
forest-certification organisation. Our books carrying the
FSC label are printed on FSC®-certified paper.

To John Coulson and Illtyd Trethowan,
who shared with us their love of words

CONTENTS

PART IV: OPPENHEIMER'S JOURNEY

PART V: THE PEOPLE FROM HELL

'The tranquil waterway leading to the uttermost ends of the earth flowed sombre under an overcast sky – seemed to lead into the heart of an immense darkness.'

The final sentence from *Heart of Darkness* (1902) by Joseph Conrad

AUTHOR'S NOTE

Snake Dance is also the title of a prize-winning documentary. The journeys described in this book were made in the company of my friend Manu Riche, who introduced me to the work of Aby Warburg, suggested the title and directed the film.

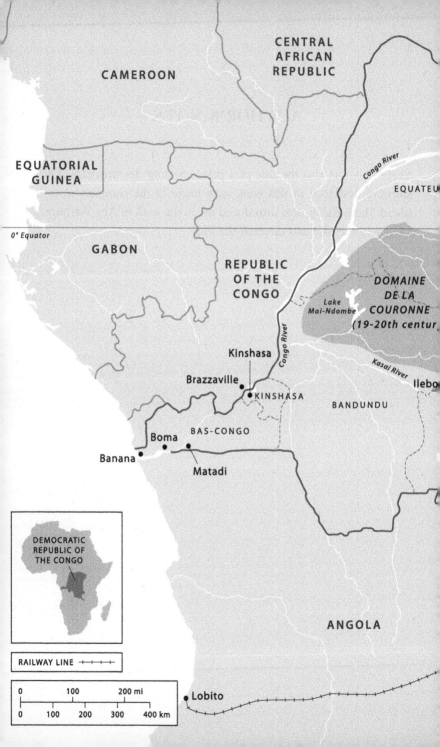

CAMEROON

CENTRAL
AFRICAN
REPUBLIC

EQUATORIAL
GUINEA

Congo River

EQUATEU

0° Equator

GABON

REPUBLIC
OF THE
CONGO

DOMAINE
DE LA
COURONNE
(19-20th centur

Lake
Mai-Ndombe

Congo River

Kasai River

Kinshasa

Ilebo

Brazzaville

KINSHASA

BANDUNDU

Boma

BAS-CONGO

Banana

Matadi

DEMOCRATIC
REPUBLIC OF
THE CONGO

ANGOLA

RAILWAY LINE ┼┼┼┼

0   100   200 mi

0   100   200   300   400 km

Lobito

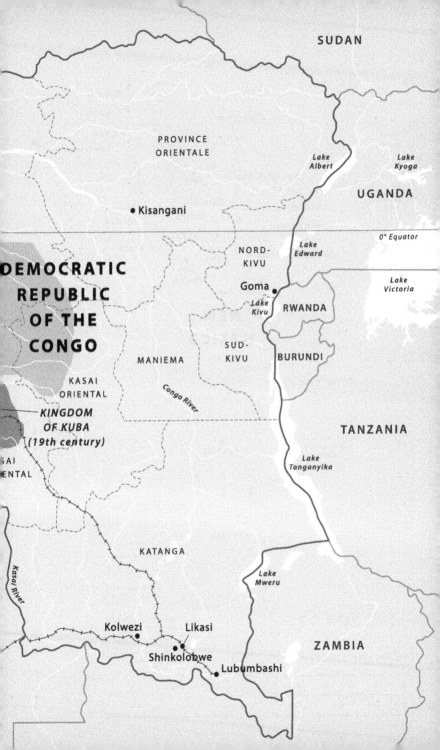

COLORADO

Mesa Verde

Four Corners

San Juan River

Antonito •

Rio Grande

To Hopi →

San Ildefonso
Los Alamos
Valle Grande
Jemez Springs •
Jemez Mountains
San Felipe Pueblo •

Taos •

Espanola
Terrero
Santa Fe •

Lamy •

Las Vegas

San Jose River

Albuquerque •

NEW MEXICO

Rio Grande

Sangre de Cristo Mountains

To Denver →
Trinidad •
Raton •
To Independence →

Mountain Route

Cimarron Route

Route of Santa Fe Trail

Wagon Mound •

San Miguel •

Canadian River

Pecos River

34°

• Socorro

Bosque del Apache

Sierra Oscura

Trinity Site

• Carizzozo

San Andres Mountains

33°

Jornada del Muerto

Gila River

Tularosa •

Pecos River

32°

• El Paso

Rio Grande

TEXAS

MEXICO

RAILWAY LINE +++++

0   25   50   75   100 mi
0   50   100   150 km

THE LOST STATES OF OLD MEXICO

NEVADA
CALIFORNIA
UTAH
WYOMING
COLORADO
KANSAS
ARIZONA
NEW MEXICO
OKLAHOMA
TEXAS

MEXICO

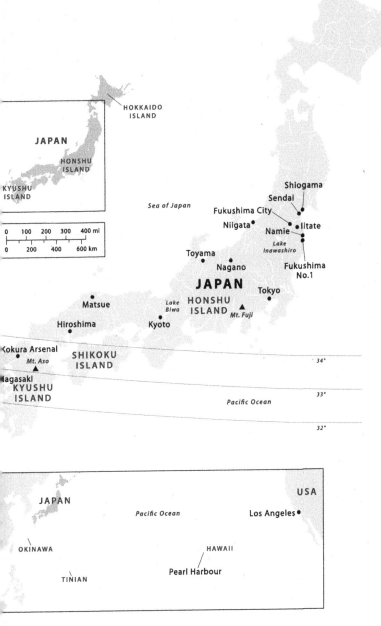

HOKKAIDO
ISLAND

JAPAN

HONSHU
ISLAND

KYUSHU
ISLAND

0   100   200   300   400 mi
0   200   400   600 km

Sea of Japan

Shiogama
Sendai
Fukushima City
Niigata
Namie
Iitate
Toyama
Lake
Inawashiro
Nagano
Fukushima
No.1
JAPAN
Tokyo
HONSHU
ISLAND
Lake
Biwa
Matsue
Mt. Fuji
Hiroshima
Kyoto
Kokura Arsenal
Mt. Aso
SHIKOKU
ISLAND
34°
Nagasaki
KYUSHU
ISLAND
33°
Pacific Ocean
32°

JAPAN
USA
Pacific Ocean
Los Angeles
OKINAWA
HAWAII
TINIAN
Pearl Harbour

Foreword

In 1890 the novelist Joseph Conrad spent six months in 'the Congo Free State', a huge area of central Africa that had become the private property of King Leopold II of the Belgians. What he discovered horrified him. A brutal campaign of enslavement and mass murder was being presented as a civilising and scientific mission.

In December of the same year Sioux Indians of Pine Ridge, South Dakota, started to dance the Ghost Dance. They believed that this ritual would bring back to life all the warriors who had died fighting the White Man. The White Man would cease to exist and the 60 million buffalo exterminated by the repeating rifle would return to the plains. Their Ghost Dance ended in 'the last battle', the Massacre of Wounded Knee.

Conrad saw the outrages being committed against the people of the forest, in secret, as more than the criminal enterprise of one ruthless regime. In his subsequent novel, based on his experience, *Heart of Darkness*, he portrayed those crimes as an emblem of the future decline of his civilisation.

Fifty years after Conrad's voyage up the Congo River, uranium mined in the Belgian Congo by the same company that had employed Conrad was secretly shipped to New Mexico where it was used in the construction of the atomic bombs that devastated Hiroshima and Nagasaki in 1945.

The direct link between the novelist's dark vision and the construction of a weapon that could destroy our world was the inspiration for this story.

Snake Dance is the account of a journey made in three stages. It tracks the path taken by the uranium, from the Congo via New Mexico to Japan, and follows the long chain of mischance and ambition that led from mass destruction to the Cold War and the growth of American Empire.

It is the story of an onward voyage, downstream, along Conrad's tranquil waterway, the river that flowed sombre under an overcast sky, out of Africa – and into the heart of an immense darkness.

July 2013

PART I

JOURNEY TO A RUINED COLONY

PART I

JOURNEY TO A RUINED COLONY

CHAPTER ONE

The Edge of Darkness

Uncle Norman died on 8 March 1906. He died at the breakfast table in Helderfontein House, Stellenbosch, Cape Province. He was two years old and his morning porridge had been laced with arsenic. The breakfast room at Helderfontein was a long, sunny room that looked out on to the flower garden. At that time of the morning in March the flowerbeds were still being irrigated; the entire garden could be irrigated from one tap by an ingenious system of stone water-channels and wooden barriers. When Norman died my grandmother was pregnant with the third of her six children.

The intended victim of the arsenic attack had been my father, then aged four. The breakfast room was at one end of the house. The nursery and the children's bedrooms were at the other. My father had a strong sense of hierarchy and of his proper position in the world of Helderfontein, and this saved his life. Having taken his time about coming to the breakfast table – he was normally the first there – he entered the room to find Norman being violently sick. 'I am not sitting at table with a child who is being sick,' my father announced and left the room with his porridge untouched. When my grandmother arrived she noticed, while trying to calm the little boy, that several flies which had landed in a pool of spilt milk were dead. The jug of milk was removed and later that day, after Norman had died, it was sent for analysis.

My grandmother was a devout Christian, so Norman was buried on a hillside close to the house since he had not been baptised. The land was part of the farm and to reach it you had to pass the fruit store and cross a bridge over the stream. She marked the grave with a little stone and forbade anyone in the family ever to mention Norman in her hearing.

The chief suspect was a man called Wilson who had been my grandfather's coachman. Wilson was a man of mixed race, later classified in the days of apartheid as 'Cape Coloured'. He had been dismissed a few weeks earlier for theft and had been heard swearing his revenge. He knew the morning routine at Helderfontein, knew when the cows were milked and where the breakfast milk was kept. He knew the best time to enter the dairy unseen and knew that the first person to taste the milk would be his employer's older son. But the police enquiries were inconclusive. They could find no evidence that the coachman had purchased arsenic and nothing to connect him with the crime. Wilson was tried and acquitted and disappeared from the neighbourhood. My grandmother was not convinced.

My grandfather, Arthur, had a passion for horses. One of his great pleasures was to ride out early in the morning with my father and spend the day exploring and adventuring in the Simonsberg Mountains. My father had his own pony and, some months after Norman's death when he reached the age of five, he was considered old enough to ride each day to a governess school. The track passed through woods and one afternoon, while riding home alone, my father was once again attacked by the coachman. The terrible death inflicted on Norman had done nothing to heal the man's grievance. He came running out of the trees waving an axe and shouting, 'I'll get you this time!' The pony bolted, my father kept his seat and they galloped home.

When he told his mother of the ambush in the woods she realised that her son would never be safe until the man was convicted of Norman's murder. She hired a private detective from Cape Town called Davis who did his work thoroughly and eventually found the tradesman who had supplied Wilson with arsenic. Armed with the evidence supplied by my grandmother, the police re-arrested Wilson and he was re-tried for murder.* Again he denied all responsibility. He said that he had purchased the arsenic to kill rats.

During cross-examination the prosecutor said, 'You bought more poison than you would need for rats. What did you do with the rest?'

'I threw it on the fire.'

'Was there any reaction when you threw the arsenic into the flames?'

'They flared up.'

'What colour were those flames?'

'Yellow.'

The next prosecution witness established that arsenic burns with a blue flame.

The coachman was convicted of murder, sentenced to death and hanged. My father was able to ride to school again in safety and my grandmother was able to mourn Norman in peace. Or so she thought. Sometime after the trial she travelled to England to visit her cousins. The case had worn her out and she needed a refuge from the anxiety that had overtaken her happy life in Helderfontein. At Southampton Docks she boarded the London train. The porter found her a seat and lifted her case into the luggage rack overhead. The Union Line label read, 'Mrs Arthur Marnham, Stellenbosch'. As the train drew out into the Hampshire countryside and my grandmother began to enjoy the change of scenery and the feeling that she had finally put some distance between herself and the recent nightmare, the woman opposite leaned forward and said, 'Are you related to the lady whose little boy was murdered in the Cape?'

The murder of Uncle Norman had been covered in the press right across the Empire. By the time the story reached the *Auckland Star*,

* Under Roman-Dutch law a person acquitted could be re-tried on the basis of new evidence.

three months after the event, the entire family had been poisoned.*
The crime was a striking illustration of the colonial nightmare: the
feeling that there were scores to be settled and a price to be paid.
A people forcefully dominated would one day take their revenge.
Conrad's *Heart of Darkness* had been published in volume form in
1902.

Nonetheless, the death of Norman seems to have bound my
grandparents to Africa. Although Arthur had originally emigrated
to the Cape to regain his health, and had always wanted to return to
England, both he and his wife spent the remainder of their lives at
Helderfontein. When Arthur died the members of the Methodist
Church in Stellenbosch, which was the church of the Cape Coloured
people, engraved his name on a stone by the door of their chapel,
adding that throughout his time in the Cape he had 'gone about
doing good'. My father left South Africa when he was twenty-one
and never lived there again. He never talked about the fact that,
when he was a small boy, a man whom he had regarded as a friend
had tried to murder him, twice. When he left Helderfontein to study
medicine in England, John X. Merriman, the last prime minister of
the Cape Colony, gave him a farewell present. It was a copy of *On
the Edge of the Primeval Forest* by Albert Schweitzer.

You need a visa for the Congo. The embassy stands in a line of small
nineteenth-century north London terrace houses. It's the only
one with a flagpole. Grey brick on a grey day. There is a grubby blue
and red flag twisted round the pole, drooping in the fumes and the
rain. Many of the houses have become betting shops or fast-food
bars. Rusty aerials wired onto crooked chimneys seem to hold the
stacks in place. For years this was a red-light district. Outside No.
281 Gray's Inn Road, below the flag, there were two CCTV cameras
on the day of my visit, and three unmarked bells. This was a doorstep
in King's Cross but already, after thirty years, there was a sense of

* *Auckland Star*, 9 June 1906, p. 13.

Africa. The unfamiliar flag, the choice of unmarked bells, the feeling
that from somewhere in the trees you were being watched – all said,
'Are you *sure* you want to come in?'

Previously I had been sure I wanted to get out. That was in the
1970s in Haute-Volta, later renamed Burkina Faso. The capital is still
Ouagadougou. There had been trouble over an exit visa. Which did
not exist. In those days, faced with a demand for a document that
did not exist, I refused to pay. I had no money and had spent a
number of years working in Africa. I promised myself that if I ever
got past this uniform without paying for an imaginary visa it would
be the last time.

Now the choice of unmarked bells offered another chance, not
to go back. But I had signed a contract to travel to the Congo and
I needed a Congolese visa, and though none of the bells worked
the embassy door swung open with a light push . . . so the chance
disappeared. Behind me the street door creaked shut. On the floor,
glimmering in the obscurity, lay a mulch of working-girls' business
cards. It is said that the Congolese ambassador to Tokyo once sold
the embassy. His staff probably ended up in the Japanese equivalent
of No. 281. In the gloom, the outer edge of darkness, I could make
out the unpainted wall of the hallway that seemed to have survived
a fire. From the ceiling, a fuse box suspended from a single wire
dangled out of the blackened plaster. On the opposite wall there
was a glass panel and an interior door. Through the glass, what
looked like the counter of a betting shop was just visible. Two barred
windows set above the counter were still in use. One was marked,
'Consular Section – Visas'.

Behind the grille in the downstairs front room of the Congolese
Embassy in Gray's Inn Road, sat a majestically handsome woman
wearing a gorgeous flowing robe. If visitors addressed her in English
she replied severely in French. If you responded in French she switched
back to English. Or vice versa. Question of control. She handed over
a detailed form. The charge for the visa was £40. She assured me
that there would be a lengthy delay, indeed she could not guarantee

any date for delivery. Unless I took the Express Service, 24 hours or less. A further £30 was required, cash, no receipt. There was a second form that required me to confirm my good character. If I took the Express Service I could fill in this second form by myself, certifying that I was unknown to the police. So much for the lesson learnt in Ouagadougou. £70 changed hands. She accepted the offering but did not smile. The visa was ready within 12 hours. The flight left from Brussels.

CHAPTER TWO

The Justice House

In November 1889, Józef Teodor Korzeniowski, a Polish merchant
seaman, was marooned in London and looking for work. Twelve
years earlier, in a black mood in Marseilles, he had shot himself
through the chest. The bullet had missed his heart. Now he held a
deep-sea master's ticket, but could not get a ship. His agent told him
that there were opportunities for riverboat captains in the Congo
Free State, a vast area of the African interior that had been acquired
by King Leopold of the Belgians as his personal fief. Enquiries were
to be made in Brussels. Korzeniowski knew of King Leopold as a
man who spent his life going about the world doing good; he was
notably celebrated for underwriting a civilising mission in Africa.

The African enterprise that seemed to offer a chance to the Polish
sea captain was one of the most extraordinary political arrangements
of its time and had no precedents and no successors. It came about
entirely by the will of one man, the European monarch of a prosperous but uninfluential country, who invented for himself a secondary
function as the despot of a huge area of the unexplored world. Any
armchair fantasist could indulge in similar dreams; Leopold's genius
lay in persuading the leading statesmen of his day to accord his private
empire international recognition. In 1885, by skilful manoeuvring,
he gained control of a region as large as western Europe, which he
proceeded to plunder for as long as he could.

*

Even today the Democratic Republic of the Congo, once the Congo Free State, later the Belgian Congo, still later Zaire, is by far the largest national unit in equatorial Africa. When Leopold first announced his intentions towards the territory he declared, privately, that 'Belgium too must have its share of this magnificent African cake.' At that time his competitors included Great Britain, then the most powerful country in the world; Germany, the principal European power governed by another genius, Bismarck; France, the world's second imperial power; and Portugal, the best-established colonial power in the Congo region. Leopold ran rings around them all. His method was to advance, masked, as a philanthropist. But even a genius needs luck and his great stroke of luck was to acquire the services of the English explorer Henry Morton Stanley at a time when no other European government was prepared to give Stanley the time of day.

In 1874, when Leopold had been on the Belgian throne for nine years, Stanley set out from the island of Zanzibar on the east African shore, leading an expedition that was intended to discover the source of the Nile. He disappeared into the forest for three years. By the time he emerged on the Atlantic coast, Leopold had convened a geographical conference in Brussels. This conference made two significant decisions: it founded the International African Association, whose chairman was King Leopold, and it announced a forthcoming programme of scientific exploration of the Congo basin that would set up a chain of 'missions and research stations' for the benefit of Africa and of mankind. When Stanley returned to Europe he was promptly recruited by the king and together they worked out how best to rule and exploit the Congo.

Until the nineteenth century Africa was protected from European intrusion by formidable defences. There was the surf that made so many beaches too dangerous for landing, the river deltas that drained the continent through sandbanks and rendered the great river mouths invisible, then the river cataracts, the menacing forests with their deadly plants and unfamiliar wildlife, fever, and finally the spears. All this changed when Stanley crossed the continent from east to west and emerged from the trees at Boma in 1877. He had failed to find the source of the Nile, but he had mapped the Congo River and its principal tributaries and so acquired an X-ray of the impenetrable forest that was as exact and fit for purpose as the X-ray of any human skeleton.

Leopold used much of the wealth he gained from plundering the Congo to endow Belgium with a splendid capital, a city that could vie with Berlin or Paris. The king's plans were drawn up on an imperial scale, and in less than twenty years Brussels had been transformed. By April 1890, when Józef Teodor Korzeniowski arrived, palaces, avenues, parks and arcades were already taking shape. Some years later the Polish sea captain, writing as Joseph Conrad, recalled in *Heart of Darkness* his impressions of a city that, as he got to know it better, made him think of 'a whited sepulchre'.

There is a statue of King Leopold II in Brussels that stands at the gates of a public garden just outside the royal palace and it shows a huge man with a long, pointed beard sitting astride a black horse. It has been said that when Belgium was extracted from the wreckage of Napoleon's empire in 1831 it was deliberately designed by technical advisers from Rothschild's bank as a small country that could be dominated by a large bank. Unfortunately the resulting country was so small that it was extremely difficult for the European powers to persuade any suitable candidate to become its king. And then this gigantic man named Leopold arrived, mounted on his gigantic horse.

Today in Belgium there are still some who venerate the memory of the country's most celebrated ruler. In 1960, when violence erupted in the Congo following independence, demonstrators in Brussels even knelt in front of the statue of the long-dead king, invoking his assistance. There are other memorials to the same king both in Brussels and elsewhere, and they are all on the grand scale. The royal palace in the centre of Brussels seems much bigger than Buckingham Palace.

It takes several minutes to walk past it although no giants inhabit it today. When you eventually reach the far end there is a pretty square that predates Leopold, but here too is a statue of a man on a horse. This time the man is dressed in a suit of armour. It turns out to be Godfrey of Bouillon, the founder of the Christian kingdom of Jerusalem. That kingdom, established in 1100 after the First Crusade, lasted for only eighty-nine years before it fell to Saladin. So the royal palace is flanked by two equestrian kings both of whom invented an exotic kingdom to disastrous effect.

Leopold II never visited Africa and never showed more than a nominal concern for the fate of the Africans delivered into his care. But when he acquired what became one of the most lucrative colonies in the world he gave the Belgian people a unifying interest. Brussels and Ostend were endowed with their magnificent structures and parks, the nation was aggrandised by this process and so was its king. When the link was cut, the national fabric began to unravel.

Because Belgium today has a federal structure and a heavily devolved system of regional government the country employs a huge bureaucracy. London and Belgium have approximately the same population. But whereas London has one minister, the mayor, Belgium has seventy. If China had the same ratio of ministers to population, the Chinese government would be composed of 35,000 ministers – and cabinet meetings would have to be held in a football stadium.

And yet a country which is so precisely regulated, and which is at the heart of the movement towards a united Europe, is itself showing signs of national disintegration. In Flanders and Wallonia, the Dutch- and French-speaking regions that divide almost all the national territory, relations between the two communities have become steadily worse. The Flemish generally refuse to speak French and the Walloons still struggle to speak Dutch. A visitor sometimes has the impression that Brussels itself is the only place in Belgium where members of the two communities seem to get along.

Sometime in June 2011, Belgium broke the world record for the time elapsed between the result of a general election and the formation of a new government. For eighteen months, due to communal infighting, the country was without any government at all, though this made little visible difference to national life. In the first months of the interregnum, the fiftieth anniversary of Congolese independence was celebrated, and despite the lack of a prime minister, a foreign minister, a defence minister, a minister for overseas development, or indeed any other minister whose absence from such an event would normally have been unthinkable, Belgium was able to send an imposing official delegation to the Congo, led by King Albert II. The inhabitants of Matongé, the African quarter of Brussels, were so delighted by this situation that they circulated a petition demanding 'the Immediate Re-attachment of Belgium to the Democratic Republic of the Congo'.

The petition was phrased in the pugnacious high-spirited style of Kinshasa, the DRC's capital. It argued that Belgium had always been dependent on the Congo, that the Congo had greatly contributed to the civilisation and prosperity of Belgium, that Belgium should at once be accorded the status of overseas territory of the DRC, that the language problem should be solved by making Lingala the official language throughout Congolese territory – including the outlying province of Belgium – and that all Belgians should henceforward be granted Congolese citizenship. The sting in the joke lay in its underlying truth: Belgium's internal divisions and industrial decline both gathered pace in the years that followed Congolese independence.

One of King Leopold's great advantages as he manoeuvred towards imperial power was that many of his fellow European rulers considered him to be a rather naïve idealist. The Belgian monarch was apparently prepared to risk his considerable private fortune merely to 'do good on a great scale to the wretched people of the earth'. The king himself compared his International African Association (AIA) to the International Red Cross of Africa. And among its stated objectives

was the establishment of the rule of law. There would be justice for
the millions of natives of the Congo, who would henceforth be granted
habeas corpus to protect them from the slave trade.

   In the event, the crimes committed by the agents of King Leopold
in the Congo established his regime, which he called the Congo Free
State, as one of the most ferocious examples of colonial oppression.
Leopold will always be remembered as a brutal tyrant who instituted
a reign of terror and enslaved millions. It will never be known how
many Africans died at the hands of his agents. The majority succumbed
to the consequences of being enslaved: famine, exhaustion and disease
– all of which caused a dramatic decline in the birth rate.*

In view of how things worked out in practice, the most appropriate
monument to Leopold's reign might be the largest construction he
erected, which is still the most prominent in the city, the Palace of
Justice. This stands on the edge of a cliff overlooking the Marolles,
which was at the time the poorest quarter of the town. Built on a
crushing scale, with a dome that is 320 feet high, the court house,
or *Palais de Justice*, exceeds the size of St Peter's in Rome and is
believed to be the largest building raised anywhere in Europe during
the nineteenth century. It dominates the skyline for miles around.

   The Palace has 30 separate entrances and its neo-classical exterior
encloses 350 rooms. These stand above a labyrinth of 5 subterranean
levels housing legal archives and home to a race of blind cats – blind
because they are born and they die in the dark and never see the
light of day. It was inaugurated by Leopold 17 years after work
began. Its most impressive space is the colossal entrance hall, the

---

* The American author Adam Hochschild, in *King Leopold's Ghost* (1998), has
accused Leopold of killing 10 million people in 'a holocaust' of 'genocidal proportions'. But the first real wealth the king acquired from the Congo came from gathering
wild rubber, a labour-intensive activity. If the king's crimes had included genocide
his labour force would have been wiped out and he would have lost his investment.
The Belgian historian Jean Stengers has suggested that the true mortality figure may
have been a fraction of Hochschild's total, although this would be atrocious enough.

salle des pas perdus. The plans for this were authorised by Leopold I but it was actually built during the second Leopold's reign and it was the son who decreed its size. This is beyond impressive; it is overpowering, it brooks no argument, it embodies an arctic authority. Leopold I had been offered the throne of Belgium after the previous ruler, the King of Holland, was overthrown by a popular uprising. The building he and his son constructed stands as a permanent warning against any attempted repetition.

The same inhumanity that marked the king's reign in Africa seeps out from the huge interior space of the entrance chamber, a square formed by four colossal arches linked by stone galleries with staircases and balustrades. Orson Welles wanted to use the *salle des pas perdus* when he was shooting *The Trial*, but was refused permission. Standing in this entrance chamber and looking around, one can readily understand why the architect is said to have gone mad before the palace was finished.

Below the balconies, sixteen oak tables with benches are set against the walls. On my first visit one or two of these tables were occupied by lawyers and clients in consultation; all the clients seemed to be African. Perhaps they were Congolese seeking residential status. As I made notes the brass lamp on my table rattled, like a ship's lamp at sea. On its metal base someone had scratched a message, '*La justice nique*'. Courtroom after courtroom was empty and unused, no one challenged me, there were no security cameras, the walls of one abandoned corridor were lined with photographs of grey-faced men in black robes, long dead.

Eventually I chanced upon a courtroom where two living lawyers were sitting, reading newspapers. A side door opened and three policemen marched in leading a young man in shirtsleeves with his hands cuffed behind his back. The prisoner looked around; neither of the lawyers paid him any attention, then he sat down with his hands still cuffed. The little group waited, three in uniform, two in robes, one in handcuffs, but no more doors opened and no judges came to sit on the distant bench.

At the end of another corridor there was a discreet steel door, with buttons, and hoping to ascend to the dome I entered and pressed button no. 4. But the lift went down, not up, and came to a halt at what proved to be Level 5. There was no heating at this depth. A single light bulb revealed another steel door and a belated notice: INTERDIT AUX PUBLIQUES. The light flickered and seemed to have no switch. A maze of tunnels and wired-in shelves led out into the darkness. The shelves contained the records of evidence and judgements made by the long-dead men in the photographs, a fitting monument to the ultimate futility of sharp-witted lives passed in legal argument. As the lights flickered again I summoned the lift and to my surprise it returned.

Today the Ministry of Justice wants to abandon King Leopold's courthouse which has been overdue for repair for fifty years. Its façade is crumbling, the building is too big to guard and too many prisoners who escape into the underground labyrinth get away. It towers over the city, a mausoleum of human mischance and suffering, one of the last remaining symbols of a united Belgium.

King Leopold's imperial design included several other features that were never completed, among them the *Musée royal de l'Afrique centrale* at Tervuren. This museum, which is housed in a splendid chateau situated in a forest thirteen miles outside Brussels, was opened in 1899 and its initial purpose was to record Leopold's scientific and humanitarian progress through the Congo. The existing structure was originally intended to be merely one part of a much larger palace that was conceived as a museum, not of Central Africa, but of Mankind. But the king died, the Great War came and the imperial project was abandoned.

One has the impression on entering Tervuren today of visiting a petrified zoo. There are displays on African and colonial life and the myths of King Leopold's reign are lavishly illustrated. There are masks, dances, stuffed animals, ceremonies and villages, dugout canoes, idols and drums. A bronze statue shows a group of three, the

African woman prostrate before the Arab slaver, despite the protests of her courageous husband, a reminder to visitors that one of Leopold's stated intentions had been to drive the Arab slave merchants out of the Congo. Another display shows a reconstruction of a twelfth-century Congolese tomb complete with skeleton, copper ornaments and an extensive array of jars and pots. In a curious inversion, the museum's collection, which was so misleading when it was meant to record a non-existent ideal colony, has become a valuable record of the colonial mind. The message, in summary, is that the people of the Congo, naked and illiterate, were savages living in the Stone Age and that the soldiers, engineers and missionaries sent out to them at the king's expense were self-evidently acting to the Africans' advantage. But the evidence undermining this assumption is displayed in the museum. Many of the most beautiful pieces of carving come from the region of Kuba.

For over 250 years the people of Kuba lived under their kings, governed by law and custom, developing a common memory and a culture that was notable for its artistic achievements in weaving and woodcarving. Their territory on the banks of the Kasai River was so deep within the forest that for over 400 years they remained untroubled by the traders and slave-raiders who came from east and west. When in 1885 Leopold II declared dominion over the lands bordering the Congo River he reserved one tenth of that territory, 250,000 square kilometres, half the size of France, as crown property – and this land adjoined the kingdom of Kuba. Leopold had never heard of Kuba, which as far as he was concerned was merely an area of forest that contained many of the finest wild rubber vines remaining in central Africa. But the king of Kuba had heard of the Belgians and he had given orders that anyone assisting these invaders to find their way to his kingdom should be put to death.

However – as Hochschild relates – one Presbyterian missionary, an African-American called the Reverend William Sheppard, penetrated Kuba and reached its capital without losing his head. Although Sheppard was there to preach the gospel, and fulfilled his mission, it is likely that he learned far more from the people of Kuba than they learned from him. Having noted their exceptional beauty he took a young mistress. It was a reverse conversion.

All this happened to Mr Sheppard without any shadow of the 'horror' that surrounded Leopold's emissaries. Then, eight years later, the rubber agents, following in the missionary's track, arrived in Kuba. In 1900, one year after Tervuren was opened, King Leopold's forces reached the capital of the kingdom, sacked it and – in forcing its people to gather rubber – reduced them to the condition of slavery. Shortly afterwards the archaeologists and ethnographers set to work, and shortly after that the first packing cases of cultural treasures left Kuba on their way to Tervuren.

Six months in the Congo marked Conrad for the rest of his life. After spending a few days in Brussels he took the train to Bordeaux, where a Portuguese coaster was waiting to carry him out to Banana at the mouth of the Congo River. His visit to Brussels had been a success. He had been hired as a steamboat captain and had signed a three-year contract with the *Société anonyme Belge pour le commerce du Haut-Congo*.

In *Heart of Darkness* Conrad recalled the city he had left. He described the streets lined with tall, narrow houses 'as still and decorous as a well-kept alley in a cemetery'. He remembered the 'deserted street in deep shadow' where he had been interviewed; the woman knitting in the antechamber, 'guarding the door of Darkness . . . full of desolation and sympathy . . . Not many of those she looked at ever saw her again.' The mortality rate among the men sent out to Matadi and the trading stations upriver, in the forest, was high. Conrad's own health was to be ruined by his brief period in the Congo, and the skipper he was hired to replace had been murdered by Africans.

CHAPTER THREE

The Merry Dance of Death and Trade

Conrad's first impression of Africa came on his voyage out: an encounter with a French warship anchored off the tropical coast, lobbing shells into a silent forest. He described the moment in *Heart of Darkness*. 'In the empty immensity of earth, sky, and water, there she was, incomprehensible, firing into a continent . . . There was a touch of insanity in the proceeding . . .'

His Portuguese coaster out of Bordeaux called at a string of trading posts as it passed down the western shores of Africa. It did not enter harbour very often because there were few harbours to enter, and many of the river mouths were unsuitable for navigation. The west coast of Africa is a lee shore, not as dangerous by 1890 as it had been in the time of sail but still potentially fatal to a steamship with engine trouble. This had been another geographical detail that helped to explain the historical isolation of the entire continent. The slave trade had been abolished fifty years earlier, and by now the original explorers in quest of knowledge had given way to settlers seeking wealth. The French warship observed by Conrad was stationed off the coast of Dahomey, until then the most notorious and feared of the west African kingdoms. The ship was not firing entirely without purpose. It was firing the opening shots in a war that would last for three years and result in the French overcoming the kingdom of Dahomey and establishing the foundations of the Soudan, a vast colonial empire that was later broken up into a dozen sovereign states.

Four hundred years earlier the first Portuguese explorers, having crossed the equator, continued south along the forest coast and sailed into a patch of ocean that was dark red and so realised that they were passing through a river current. It was at this point that the Portuguese explorers - and Conrad's ship - turned in to the shore once again and anchored off Banana, in the broad estuary of the Congo River. This is, with the exception of the Amazon, the greatest outflow of fresh water into the sea anywhere in the world. Here Conrad was able at last to stop 'watching the coast', of which he had seen more than enough; that coast, 'smiling, frowning . . . insipid, or savage, and always mute with an air of whispering, "Come and find out".' At the river mouth Conrad changed ships and was carried upstream to the first of the rapids that had guarded this highway into the interior until the day thirteen years earlier when they were finally unlocked. Then he continued on foot, walking up a road that was littered with the corpses of men who had been chained together and forced to build a railway. For 230 miles he picked his way along the periphery of a war zone. From the moment of his arrival, Conrad was introduced to the horror and brutality of King Leopold's Free State.

Joseph Conrad's time in the Congo very nearly killed him. He contracted malaria and dysentery and one night while trying to nego-tiate a river bend in a canoe he almost drowned. His ship had reached Banana in June 1890. By December, he was on his way home, inva-lided back to Europe. During his six months in the Congo, Conrad made one long voyage upriver to Stanleyville, now called Kisangani, which was the 'Inner Station' of the Belgian trading company that employed him. Shortly after his final departure for Europe some of the company's agents were captured by hostile natives, tortured and put to death; in the words of *The Times*, 'their heads stuck on poles and their bodies eaten'. It was a local custom. But Conrad escaped this nightmare fate. He survived and ten years later he produced *Heart of Darkness*, which must rank among the most complex and richly allusive texts in English literature.

Heart of Darkness opens with an unnamed narrator sitting in a boat anchored on the Thames, downstream from London, at night, waiting for the tide to turn so that the little craft's seaward voyage can continue. He is listening to a story told by another member of the crew, a seaman called Charlie Marlow. Marlow recalls how he was once engaged to work as a riverboat captain in an imaginary African colony, clearly based on Leopold II's Congo Free State, for a company whose agents were colonising the interior and collecting ivory. The company's general manager instructs Marlow to sail upriver into the interior and check on the wellbeing of an agent called Mr Kurtz, a brilliant and solitary figure who is the chief of the Inner Station, 'an emissary of pity, and science, and progress . . .' Whereas the company's secret policy was to 'tear treasure out of the bowels of the land, with no more moral purpose at the back of it than there is in burglars breaking into a safe', Mr Kurtz believed that 'each station should be like a beacon on the road towards better things, a centre for trade of course, but also for humanizing, improving, instructing'. In other words the disagreement between the general manager and Mr Kurtz reflected the conflict between the true and the stated intentions of King Leopold's African enterprise in the Congo.

Marlow's appalled description of his river voyage is couched in the terms of the period; he sees Africa with the eyes of an English seaman turned colonial servant. But *Heart of Darkness* is written on several levels simultaneously; as F. R. Leavis noted in *The Great Tradition*, Marlow is an invention 'for whom Conrad had more than one kind of use, and who is both more and less than a character and always something other than just a master-mariner'. In this case he is a man trapped in a land-locked nightmare. Marlow describes the hazardous journey upriver – the stream is full of whirlpools and hidden rocks, and the people living on its banks are in a state of insurrection. He describes his meeting with Mr Kurtz, the outcome of that meeting and his eventual arrival back in Brussels.

Objecting to the suggestion that Conrad's novel was intended as a charge sheet against Leopold's regime, the historian Jean

Stengers noted that most of the crimes committed by the government of the Congo Free State were due to the way in which rubber was exploited, and that this exploitation did not begin until a year or two after Conrad had left the Congo. That is perfectly true, but Conrad's main point was not to criticise the behaviour of certain rubber-gatherers. It was to question the very nature of the colonial relationship and to highlight a problem that went far deeper than any atrocities associated with the collection of one commodity. The violence that Conrad observed with his own eyes was not a consequence of the rubber trade; it was part and parcel of the penetration of Africa, a response to resistance by local rulers and their forces. It was also a consequence of the ivory trade, which had formerly been in African hands but which, under Leopold, had been monopolised by the administrators of his Free State. Conrad's letters and diary show that this menacing atmosphere was everywhere; as his character Marlow recalls, the men who lived 'in that dark immensity inhabited a vast, secret, hidden world, which knew nothing of ours'. There was horror enough in the colonial penetration of the Congo long before rubber became a prize.

Conrad's title never referred simply to the Congo or to Africa. Though the story is set in the Congo, the darkness is not of 'darkest Africa', and though the Congo is at the heart of the continent, the heart of the title is not African at all; it is the colonial heart, and its darkness – which is 'impenetrable' – is the colonial future or conse-quence, the world we live in today. This deeper meaning unfolds gradually as the voyage proceeds.

Waiting in the departure lounge at Brussels airport with the film director Manu Riche, I bought a copy of *Le Soir*. There was news of an air crash at Goma in the eastern Congo, with photos, twenty-one dead. A DC-9 had crashed on take-off. A local airline, Hewa Bora. But we had tickets on Brussels Air, so it was nothing to do with us. Then I asked Manu if he had ever heard of Hewa Bora and he said that he thought that we were booked with them for our next two flights.

The night before I had an unusually vivid dream. It was about an old lady, and a dog that wept. It was one of those dreams you cannot entirely leave; bits of it kept coming back as we flew over the Sahara. Conrad wrote, 'No relation of a dream can convey the dream-sensation . . . that notion of being captured by the incredible which is of the very essence of dreams.' This is a widely held view; I re-read it during the flight. Then we landed and walked into a different dream; the dream of Africa.

Immigration at Kinshasa airport and after 30 years everything seems reasonably familiar. It is evening, the early dusk of the tropics, and passengers are queuing up on the tarmac because they cannot get into the building. Some people are being filtered through the crowd, the African passengers. The whites remain outside. Smartly dressed policemen with sticks are marshalling us into two lines, shouting, '*Blancs à gauche, sauf Belges*', 'Whites to the left, unless they hold Belgian passports'. Soon there is no one remaining on the tarmac except for a small group of white passengers who do not hold Belgian nationality. 'Whites to the left'? It is just like the old days in Leopoldville, except then it was the blacks who had to put up with these minor inconveniences. Our passports are collected and taken into an office marked 'Head of Immigration'. We are called in one by one for a personal interview with this senior official. Judging by his manner this is a confidential affair. When my turn comes he is the soul of courtesy. Have you been here before? Business or tourism? Where is your letter of introduction? As a matter of fact it is already in the baggage hall in the pocket of a Belgian *cinéaste*. This is regrettable, it is not normal, but for the Head of Immigration there remains one essential question: '*Vous avez les moyens?*' Yes. 'How much?' What? '*Combien, combien . . . ?*' The Democratic Republic of the Congo has a limited social-security system and it is hard to imagine that many European down-and-outs are flying into Kinshasa hoping to live off the state, but he wants to have a peek in my wallet. We look in it together. Apparently there is enough there. I am free to go. With renewed courtesy he waves me out of his office and into another queue: passport control. Here another officer, junior but older and angrier, is holding my passport. And he, of course, has been informed about the amount of money in my wallet and the missing letter of introduction. No letter, no entry. The passport remains with him. At this moment a furious row breaks out at the neighbouring *guichet* where the only African passenger still in the immigration net is attempting to enter the country without her yellow-fever vaccination certificate. She is not of the DRC, she is from Gabon, she is very well dressed and she is accustomed to being obeyed. But so is the Yellow Fever Inspector, also female, who is not from Gabon and who is, in addition, wearing a white hospital coat. The battle sways back and forth across the hall, the mood becomes near hysterical, the crowd of participants on both sides grows. Finally the whole struggling mob bursts out onto the tarmac and disappears into the night. Perhaps it is time to wake up? But no . . . the dream continues.

'*Qu'est-ce que vous avez prévu pour payer ce monsieur?*' A small and rather diffident man in khaki porter's uniform is standing at my elbow and murmuring. He has a kind smile and would like to help. What have I put aside to pay the passport-control officer? 'Nothing.' Such delicacy in the question: my new friend suggests that twenty euros should cover the omission of a letter of introduction. Surrounded by a growing number of porters, taxi drivers, police officers and phoney police officers – and by a newcomer called 'Thomas' who claims to be my 'protocol' – I crack and hand over the first price. The crisp blue note is snatched by a uniform and carried into passport control where two officers examine it closely. Genuine. My passport, held out over my tormentor's shoulder without a backward glance, is returned. I am through the surf and onto the beach. The dream is over. All that fuss for twenty euros. Thomas seizes my luggage and leads me to a private taxi. He, it turns out, is real – and a friend of the director.

*

'Papa' Thomas was older. He carried the honorary title of 'Papa' because of his great age, about fifty-five. He was our driver. He was *costaud*, he looked as though he could handle a paddle were he to find himself in a dugout canoe. He was a survivor, he improvised. He did not seem that old, but he said that there were not many people in the DRC as old as he was. He drove fast, but in a reassuring way. His car broke down once and, looking under the bonnet, I discovered that the accelerator wire was held together by a piece of string. Why? 'No spare parts.' Thomas lived with his wife or wives in some distant suburb and rose very early in order to meet us after our breakfast. I asked him about the political situation. He weighed his words. 'Things are getting better,' he said, 'slowly.' And the president? 'He's a young chap. He's not an exhausted old man. He's better than his predecessor. But we need to go faster. We are not yet at cruising speed. We are not yet up to the standards of colonial times. We are still in first gear.' He saw politics in terms of his car.

Driving in from the airport, along a highway packed with pedestrians, we passed a partially built overhead walkway, its concrete stairs poking into the sky on either side of the four-lane highway that leads to the seat of government. The bridge steps were in place but there was no ramp joining them, just the pedestrians in exactly the same position as before, all over the road, while the lorries and cars weaved at high speed between.

Papa's 4x4 rattled along, threading its way through the abandoned mechanical detritus of the Western world. We passed a huge billboard advertising the presence of the Police Battalion for Criminal Investigation. At intersections the traffic police in yellow shirts stood on their podiums waving their arms and sometimes blowing a baffling series of notes through their whistles. Most of the time they just stood there without waving, gazing down through mirror sunglasses at the chaos below. Without their intervention the situation did not sort itself out, but neither did it get worse.

On a pavement in the centre of the city a man was sitting by a fruit-juice stall, listening to the radio news. We started to talk and he said that he was a teacher but that he was on strike as he had not been paid for some time. He was supposed to earn £75 a week, plus salary increases, but the money had stopped coming through. 'They say that we are paying $50m a day to repay the IMF for all the money Mobutu stole. That's why the Ministry of Culture has no budget, and that's why I don't get paid.' Meanwhile the DRC's elected deputies were paid ten times as much as he was, regularly, and were each given a complimentary 4x4.

As we talked a small boy passed by holding a piece of string. Attached to the other end of the string was an empty orange-juice carton with two sticks pushed through it and four little wheels revolving as he walked. He seemed delighted with it. There are thousands of street children in Kinshasa, some of them third generation, descended from *grandpères de la rue*. They are expelled from home as infants, accused of sorcery, which generally means that their mothers have no money to raise them. If they survive they work as pickpockets or cleaners.

The teacher noticed my interest in the toy. 'Nobody here sits around wringing their hands about problems,' he said. 'They have a problem, they work out how to get round it.'

Conrad in 1890 described the embryo settlement, the Central Station that was to become Stanley Falls, then Leopoldville and then Kinshasa, as 'this scene of inhabited devastation'. Twenty years later, when the Belgian colony succeeded the personal rule of the king, the city of Leopoldville became one of the showpieces of colonial Africa. It had shady boulevards, modern hotels and by the 1960s steel and glass office blocks, a university and a zoo. Then, under Mobutu, things went seriously wrong. Today Kinshasa, after two civil wars, is once again 'a scene of inhabited devastation', but on a much larger scale. It resembles a city that has been submerged by a tsunami that has risen from some filthy, subterranean, sewage-littered sea. But this tidal wave attracts no relief fund, it just rises and rises and gets worse and worse. This seems to be the fruit of King Leopold's experiment, one hundred years on.

That first evening we dined in Le Blok de Bandal, an open-air restaurant in a street market. There was no street lighting – 'power cuts' – but the restaurant provided strings of light bulbs that were powered from a generator behind the kitchen. The beer was cold, the food mysterious; the music was exuberant and heavily amplified. A boy carrying a tray of nuts and cigarettes circulated between the tables. Behind him a trail of younger children stretched out their hands for the scraps on the edges of our plates. When we drove away they ran beside the car, hoping for money or more crumbs. They had already eaten half the food on the table. The traffic cleared and we drove off and left them hopping around in the dark, silently, like huge moths, trying to avoid the blows that the larger boys were handing out. The smaller boys danced in this way, almost absent-mindedly, sensing the invisible blows in the dark.

Our hotel was a cheap one, out near the airport road. It was down an alleyway with a uniformed guard dozing in an armchair by the main gate. My room was clean, although there was a hole in the wall by the shower large enough to admit a rat, and whatever happened to be chasing it. Before falling asleep I remembered the first night I had ever spent in Kinshasa. It had been in 1975 during the Mobutu years when the city was renowned for its extravagance and expense. I had dined in a restaurant surrounded by European expats who were eating *moules* that had been flown in from Brussels, and getting drunk on good French Muscadet – items that I could not afford. I had not intended to spend the night in the country at all and by the time I reached the centre of town all the hotels were full. Eventually I had found a bed for the night in some sort of lodging house. The room was full of cockroaches, quite large, like small birds. When I extinguished the light they started to socialise. You could hear them flapping through the air and then crash-landing beside the water glass. Or sometimes on the pillow. If I turned on the light they froze where they were, glistening and stout. It was one of those unforgettable nights when one wondered why the hell one had not stayed in Europe. Kinshasa at night was supposed to be dangerous in 1975, although the worst thing that happened to me was when a soldier with a rifle climbed into my taxi and announced that we were making a diversion, via his house. When he eventually got out he tried to remove my Olivetti Lettera 22, a state-of-the-art portable typewriter. The taxi driver paid him to leave it on the seat, a very small amount of money.

Papa Thomas was up early and waiting to take us to the zoo. The radio was playing in his car so I asked him once again about politics. He had no irons in the fire and, unlike better-educated men, was prepared to discuss public affairs quite openly.

'What happened to the last president, Thomas, the one who was old and tired, like us?'

'Heh, heh, heh.' After a while he stopped chuckling. 'The last president was assassinated in his palace, here in Kinshasa. We in Kinshasa did not vote for this man.'

'Who killed him?'

'We do not know. It is said that he was killed by his most trusted bodyguards.'

'But I thought he had child bodyguards?'

'Yes, that is right. They say that his most trusted child asked him for some more money and then, when the president refused, the child shot him.'

We thought about this in silence. A man comes out of the forest, from the east. No one from that region has ever ruled in Kinshasa. Everywhere his soldiers go, they wreck. Rape, looting, random killing, they help themselves to whatever they can find. When they get to Kinshasa they wreck that too. Mobutu has fled. His men have ripped off their uniforms and thrown away their guns. Many of them have taken the ferry across the river to Brazzaville, capital of another country, the (once French) People's Republic of the Congo. And so Kabila, the bandit from the east, becomes the president. He has the backing of neighbouring African states, whose armies have pillaged half the country; he has the support of the international community because he is not the great tyrant Mobutu, who has become a notorious embarrassment. He promises to call elections and to restore democracy and everything will be different. And he moves into the palace. Where he is shot by one of the boy-soldiers whom he has forced to fight for him.

'What happened to the boy who killed the president?'

'He too was shot. There are no child bodyguards in the palace today,' said Thomas. 'The new president got rid of them.'

We had arrived at the zoo.

To enter the zoo in Kinshasa you have to cross a muddy wasteland that may once have been a park. Then you reach the sign by the turnstiles: 'The largest zoo in Central Africa. Entrance – Adults 500F, Foreigners ["*Expatriés*"] 700F.' The man who sells the tickets murmurs, 'There's not much left to see. We're broke.'

Before leaving Belgium I had visited the zoo in Antwerp, a model of its kind, conveniently close to the railway station. There was one huge cage that was inhabited by a clan of chimpanzees. One of them looked rather down in the mouth, and to reassure the public the authorities had posted a notice by the glass wall of the enclosure saying that visitors need not worry about the sad chimpanzee as he was being kept under observation by psychologists.

But that was Antwerp. Kinshasa would be different. Past the gates the first impression was of a rather strong smell. Most of the cages had been knocked down or abandoned, but those remaining had not recently been cleaned. Nonetheless, the cages were still correctly marked: 'Scientific name: Pan Troglodytes. Common name: Chimpanzee. Vernacular name: Soko Mutu. Origin: Democratic Republic of the Congo. Diet: Omnivore. Lifespan: Over 40 years.' The creature inside seemed unlikely to last that long. It paced round its wire enclosure – which was about the size of a small hotel lift – making eye contact with anyone in range. The wire looked flimsy and there was a hole in the floor, which was littered with rubbish: carrots, turds, bread crusts and an empty sardine can. Soko Mutu had pushed most of this stuff into one corner, possibly hoping that someone would come and remove it. It had also acquired a plastic bag which had been stuffed into the hole in the floor. A nearby cage appeared to be derelict and empty. A closer look revealed that the roof had collapsed onto its occupant, a dwarf alligator.

The only animal that looked properly nourished was a leopard called 'Maréchal', after its former owner. Mobutu used to keep a menagerie of heraldic beasts running free in the grounds of his palace. When Mobutu left, the survivors were moved to the zoo. Maréchal looked big, strong, fast and ready to eat the human idler who spent part of the day teasing him.

Two school buses on an educational outing drove into the gardens and a gentle rain began to fall. The schoolchildren were neatly dressed, lively, polite and curious. The buses looked as though they were on the point of exploding, like the buses driven into a circus ring by the clowns. As they banged past, smoke poured out from unexpected corners, exhaust systems sparked against the stones. A keeper emerged from the ticket booth and started to rearrange the litter round the chimpanzee's cage with a twig he had found on the ground. A group of young handicapped men dozed in their wheelchairs. The keeper said that they were allowed in free of charge to get a bit of air.

The director, who had been filming, was approached by two men in ragged suits who claimed to be plain-clothes police officers and demanded to see his permit. When they were asked for ID they pulled out torn and greasy police cards that looked as though they had been found on a corpse – which was entirely possible. The director started to film their cards and they retreated. The schoolchildren reached the cage containing a rather small gorilla and rebuked another idler who was teasing it and teaching it to clap and beg. A line of half-Arab horses ridden by soldiers trotted out of the cavalry barracks that adjoins the zoo and started to exercise among the cages. An albino man on crutches who had joined the men in wheelchairs, his head bound in a green cloth, started away impatiently when he saw the camera. I asked the keeper why there were so few animals and he said that after Mobutu left, the *Patrons* stopped paying for food for the animals and failed to pay the staff wages, so the keepers had been obliged to eat a number of their charges. The rain settled in, the children climbed back onto their bus which drew away slowly in a cloud of blue smoke, the crook and the lame took shelter under a tree, and the turnstiles closed for lunch. Monkey meat is a delicacy in West Africa. Small wonder that Soko Mutu was looking anxious.

We planned to have lunch with an official in the Belgian Embassy, and dropped by his office to pick him up. The embassy is a remarkable sight. It looks like the Iraqi Ministry of Defence before the first US missiles hit Baghdad. It is in the centre of the city, chipped out of ferroconcrete, surrounded by a wire security fence five metres high and guarded by helmeted men carrying machine guns. The Belgian diplomats did not seem to be taking the sanguine view. The steel gates of the embassy swung open and a convoy of armoured limousines came through at speed. Clearly lunchtime. Our man was busy but kept the appointment. He was assisting a military delegation from Brussels. 'Selling arms?' 'We call it military co-operation.' Then there was another item in his in-tray – yesterday's air crash at Goma. 'All four Belgians have survived. Will you be flying around?' 'Yes. Same airline.' 'Ah, *bon?* Let's hope it's not the same pilot.'

I wanted to ask the Belgian diplomat how the Belgian foreign minister's official visit was going; I already knew that the minister had been kept waiting for seven hours by President Kabila on the previous day. The diplomat turned the conversation to his preferred topic, which was the history of the Congo. He said that when Stanley first met King Leopold he told the king that the Congo was worth nothing without a railway. The river was the key to the vast interior, but you could not reach the river from the sea because of the impassable cataracts between Kinshasa and the coast; what was needed was a modern railway. The diplomat regarded the building of the railway at that time and in those conditions as 'heroic'. He said that between 1921 and 1931, under the colonial administration, the railway was

rebuilt and a Belgian historian, Jules Marchal, has recently estimated
the number of forced labourers who died on that job at 7,000. It is
these men who are commemorated in a superb bronze sculpture that
stands by the bridge at Matadi Expo. It shows three African porters
resting after their labours. The inscription reads, 'This railway freed
the porters from their burdens.' The diplomat regretted that the
inscription had recently been defaced.

When 'Zaire' died at the end of the Cold War, Washington withdrew
its backing. In Katanga, big American mining companies closed down
overnight, locked up and went home. Mobutu's house of cards started
to collapse. The army, which was frequently unpaid, began to steal
from unarmed civilians. State governors and ministers lost their fear
of a president who could no longer pay his soldiers and started stealing
more on their own account. The head of the air force flew Zaire's
entire fleet of Mirage fighter-bombers to France for routine attention,
and then sold them. Mobutu took to the river in 1990 and spent most
of his time on his luxury yacht, the *Kamanyola*, where he lived with
his identical-twin wives, Bobi and Cosia. The vessel had 60 cabins,
2 state apartments, a banqueting hall for 100 guests, a helicopter
landing pad and a crew of 300. Then in 1997, Mobutu took fright
and fled the capital for his marble palace in the forest at Gbadolite
in the extreme north of the country. This had an airfield with a
runway long enough for the presidential 747, and was within sight
of the river border with the neighbouring Central African Republic.
Mobutu, dying of cancer, left the country for good in 1997, three
months after the raggle-taggle army had limped out of the forest and
into Kinshasa. By then, towns all over the Congo had been totally
wrecked. The United Nations has been trying to sort out the mess
ever since.

The UN military force in the Democratic Republic is known as
MONUC and numbers 17,000, the largest UN force anywhere in
the world. Seventeen thousand troops sounds a lot, but they are
attempting to police a country the size of western Europe that is

populated by 'over 200' or 430 different tribes, depending on whether you accept the official figures or a well-informed estimate. Its supporters argue that the presence of MONUC may be of limited practical value, but it has maintained a weak president in power, limited human suffering on occasion and enabled the DRC to maintain the appearance of a viable sovereign state. Most of the troops are either Indian or Pakistani. In Kinshasa some speak of these armed peacekeepers as just another band of uniformed brigands. Allegations of child-rape and abduction are frequent. In Kivu, MONUC officers are said to be running a gold-smuggling operation. The Belgian diplomat did not dispute this but pointed out that without the presence of MONUC in the DRC it would have been impossible to hold the presidential elections. Organising the elections had been another of his headaches. The electoral register had not been updated since 1981. During the civil war in 1993 the records supporting the electoral rolls were destroyed. Since the country has no roads it had been impossible to distribute voters' cards. MONUC had 100 planes in the DRC, by far the largest fleet in the country. 'What would have happened without MONUC?' he asked. 'What happens with them?' Thomas replied gloomily.

It was time for the diplomat to return to the embassy; the military delegation from Brussels needed him. He urged us to visit the National Museum.

The National Museum of the Democratic Republic of the Congo stands on a hill inside the grounds of Mobutu's palace; it overlooks Stanley Pool and the eddies that warn of the beginning of the Congo River cataracts. On a clear day you can see right across the grey, brown water to Brazzaville, capital of the People's Republic of the Congo. The museum was damaged during the civil war and is still closed. Professor Joseph Ibongo, Director-General of the National Collection, agreed to see us in his office. The clock in the waiting room had stopped at three minutes to three, but for form's sake there was a brief delay before we were admitted.

The professor said that the national collection consisted of some 60,000 objects and that his predecessor had been shot dead just outside the window of his office. He was a quiet-mannered man who obviously cared deeply about his collection and was discouraged that it was in such a bad state. The museum had once been a dependency of the Royal Museum of Tervuren and he himself had studied at the University of Louvain many years before, but the relationship was no longer close. He mentioned that nowadays when he wrote to his *confrères* at Tervuren they seldom took the trouble to reply. The professor spoke with great eloquence about the DRC's cultural identity and the museum's fundamental role in establishing this. He wanted his fellow citizens to realise that they had a national heritage, to be familiar with it and to be proud of it, but added that at present the entire collection was packed up in a warehouse and he had nowhere suitable to display it. He estimated that 1.3 million euros were needed to place the collection on a secure scientific footing; meanwhile it was deteriorating in storage that was primitive and unsuitable. Naturally, in these circumstances he had been unable to increase the collection, but he had acquired one object of great historical value and he wondered whether we would like to see it.

Lying on the ground outside the professor's office, exposed to the heat and the dust and the rain, was the rusting iron hull of a small riverboat that had been found in a junk yard behind the Ministry of Public Works. Professor Ibongo said this was Stanley's boat, the boat he had used on his return to the Congo travelling *incognito* as 'Monsieur Henri' to work for Leopold II. The boat was much smaller than the nineteenth-century steamboats that had been in use after the railway line from Matadi was opened, and forged on its bow were the letters 'AIA' (*Association internationale africaine*). This was the body originally set up by Leopold in 1876 which employed Stanley on his return in 1879 and which became defunct in 1882, when the king renamed it the AIC (Association internationale du Congo). This rusting hulk was the original instrument by which the people of the forest had been enslaved.

The rest of the national collection was to be found inside the adjoining sheds. Here there were rows and rows of metal shelves holding carvings in wood and stone, artefacts, vessels, weapons, masks, stools, ornaments and amulets. On the floor were drums – both war drums and talking drums – the size of boats, great hollowed-out trunks of wood shaped to respond to the beating of wooden mallets. 'Hold back your tears when you view the national collection,' the professor had said. In the dusty corridors between the lines of shelving, the objects could just be made out in the midday gloom. Here was 'the appalling face of a glimpsed truth . . . the vision, the gloom . . . the beat of a drum like the beating of a heart' – all the trappings of the dance as an instrument of war. Here were the horned heads, the dried gourd, the black feathers with pendant tail . . . The world of the trees from the time when trees were king, the vast secret, hidden world that was impenetrable to thought, the heart of a conquering darkness. There were wooden figures so beautiful that you wanted to reach out and honour them, beside fetishes, twisted, clotted and black, which you would rather not see at all. As we walked between the racks trying not to push over an earthenware jar or be nicked by the tip of a rusting spear we were accompanied by a growing party of assistant curators who looked on eagerly, watching our faces, as if curious to see what psychological power these once-terrible objects retained.

We passed from shed to shed. Outside, huge copper statues of Leopold II and his son Albert I had been stretched out on the grass. Stanley lay on his back, snapped off at the ankles, with his empty iron boots beside him. In a shady corner of a terrace overlooking the Congo River the king sat on his horse, uniformed, hatless and thoughtful, perhaps wondering where it all went wrong. In the last shed the national collection terminated unexpectedly with an array of Toby jugs and Staffordshire pottery. Had these been abandoned by the settlers who fled for their lives when independence came in 1960, leaving behind them their fetishes – cow creamers and King Charles spaniels and gentlemen in kilts standing ten inches high? Or were they once owned by the *Evolués*, the officially 'civilised' natives of the colony who were permitted to live side by side with their white masters?

The very last exhibits were the fruits of a later defeat. The empty gilded frame that held Marshal Mobutu's official portrait, ten feet high and five feet wide, was propped against a wall. The portrait itself has not been recovered. Perhaps everyone had seen enough of it. In the days of Mobutu's power, his portrait had been the only one allowed on public display. Beyond it in a lumber room were two presidential thrones, one gilded with Napoleonic pomp, the other of teak and leather and draped in leopard skin. Thomas, with a broad smile, lowered himself onto the leopard skin and posed for a picture before he was sharply ordered by an assistant curator to stand up. The throne was empty but it had not lost its symbolic power.

We said goodbye to the director-general and walked up the hill behind the museum towards the presidential palace and the remains of another of Mobutu's extravaganzas, the open-air theatre. The audiences who had once thronged here to listen to Miriam Makeba and Stokely Carmichael had been confident that this splendour was the future of Africa. The approach road led between the enclosures where Mobutu kept his wild animals; the theatre stage and the auditorium were decorated with onyx and marble. Today the theatre is derelict, most of the marble has been stolen, lichens are growing through the stage and the forest is closing in. Looking around, our guide, the assistant curator, said, 'In this country history repeats itself.' He seemed to be one of a small band of survivors, the competent men and women who are still playing by the rules, steadfast at their posts, while the great idea that they have trusted for so long, disintegrates around them. You cannot direct a museum if no one answers your letters, you cannot run a filing system without electricity to light your desk. Yet against all the odds these men and women still hold out a glimmer of hope that they will one day be reconnected to the rational world.

*

In 1959, one year before the Belgian government, in a fit of panic and responding to strong pressure from Washington, resolved to give the Congo its independence, a nuclear reactor was constructed at the university in Leopoldville. The reactor was 'a gift of the people of the United States', offered in return for the uranium that the Congo had supplied during the war for the development of the atomic bomb. A plaque recording these acts of mutual generosity was placed at the entrance to the compound surrounding the reactor.

In 1974, fourteen years after independence, by which time Marshal Mobutu was already notorious as one of the most corrupt and incompetent rulers in Africa, the Belgian government decided to upgrade Kinshasa's nuclear reactor and replace it with a new one. The stated purpose of this gift was to enable Zaire to generate its own nuclear energy. By this time Zaire was planning one of the world's largest hydroelectric power stations to harness the energy of the impassable Congo River cataracts near Inga. But as Mobutu launched his programme of 'authenticity' – changing his name from Joseph-Desiré Mobutu to Mobutu Sese Seko, abolishing all Christian names in the country, instructing his people to address each other as *citoyen* and forbidding them to wear neckties – Belgian engineers and nuclear physicists struggled to start up this reactor, designed to generate the daily output of the hydroelectric scheme in less than a second.

Since then, the DRC's nuclear reactor has become notorious in international atomic-energy circles. The building is in the same state as the rest of the city. It is a squat concrete block that at first glance resembles a barracks or a prison. But white paint is peeling off the concrete and weeds are sprouting from its walls and some of the window glass is missing or cracked. Since it contains a reactor, the Kinshasa Regional Centre for Nuclear Studies (CREN-K) is supposed to be a high-security site. In fact, the wire fence that surrounds it can be pushed over with one hand. There is a sign at the main gate, 'Entry Forbidden', but the 24-hour security guards are rarely in place and the security lighting system is out of order. The buildings' walls are one metre thick and the reactor is protected by three separate

locks, the keys being held by three different people. Or possibly more.
In an absent-minded moment some years ago the director of the
DRC's Atomic Energy Commission handed over a complete set of
keys to a stranger who has not been seen since. And there is another
problem. The nuclear centre was constructed on marshy ground and
the structure is now subsiding. The largest crater, close to the building,
is fifteen metres deep.

The United States government cut off supplies of spare parts for
the reactor in the 1980s and there have been repeated calls for it to
be closed. But no government of the DRC would willingly agree to
lose Africa's first nuclear reactor. For the Congolese this decrepit and
potentially lethal installation is a proud symbol of sovereign status.
Shortly after the director lost his spare set of keys, two of the enriched
uranium rods went missing. One was subsequently recovered by
Italian police in Sicily, apparently on its way to a Middle Eastern
customer. The other has never been traced. In 1999, a steel splinter,
possibly shrapnel, buried itself in one of the concrete walls and the
reactor was shut down. In 2004 the reactor was inspected and found
to be in such a dangerous state that it was strongly recommended it
should be dismantled. Instead, the Congolese Atomic Energy
Commission has announced plans to fire it up again.

Although the Kinshasa reactor has so far missed every safety target
it has been set, the anti-radiation protection for its 200 staff is inadequate or non-existent and there is a danger that it could contaminate
the city's water supply, an agreement was nonetheless signed in 2005
with a British mining firm, Brinkley Africa. In return for repairing
the reactor and using it for medical research, Brinkley Africa were
authorised to prospect for uranium in Katanga and to reopen the
world's largest known uranium field at Shinkolobwe. Then, in March
2007, Congo's Minister for Scientific Research, Sylvanus Mushi,
arrested the director of the Atomic Energy Commission, Dr Fortunat
Lumu, who had signed the agreement with Brinkley, and threw him
into prison. Dr Lumu was charged with 'stealing a large quantity of
uranium'. He was released after a week when charges were dropped.

But it was the end of the agreement with Brinkley Africa. Dr Lumu was not alone in his 'seditious project', according to Sylvanus Mushi. Equally guilty was his own predecessor Gérard Kamanda wa Kamanda, who was accused of plotting to use the profits from exporting uranium to fund his own re-election campaign. Kamanda wa Kamanda denied any such intention. He said that the object of the Brinkley contract was to put an end to the dangerous and illegal export of stolen uranium. He pointed out that whereas he himself was a former protégé of President Mobutu, his successor Mushi was a man of no science and little credibility. Mushi, he added, was merely a former commander in the Mai-Mai tribal militia, notorious for teaching its boy-soldiers that *ju-ju* charms would ward off bullets. The dispute slowly resolved itself into a classic conflict of interest between two influential men, both anxious to exploit the Congo's mineral wealth for their personal advantage. Ten years after the departure of Mobutu, the nation's treasure chest was still being plundered by the nation's leaders.

Kinshasa's nuclear reactor has never produced a single volt of useful energy, and today it stands on the edge of the university campus in a state of advanced decomposition. The reactor is encased in a tank of water that is charged with graphite, which is degenerating. When started up the reaction is driven by uranium rods, although the two which are missing have never been replaced. The CIA has confirmed that if a rod were to be removed and wrapped in sticks of dynamite, it would make an effective dirty bomb and it would be 'Adieu, Kinshasa'.

To retrieve and inspect the rods there is a bridge that leads from the control room out over the centre of the reactor. A fishing rod complete with reel stands beside the entrance to the bridge; this is the method used for the delicate operation of retrieving the uranium rods. The central feature of the control room is the control panel which was installed in the 1980s and is totally out of date. On the desk in front of the control panel is a large yellow button which, if pushed, will fire up the reactor. To prevent engineers from touching this button by mistake, a transparent, plastic, ice-cream container has been placed over the button. The ice-cream container, like the walls of the reactor, is cracked.

The former director of the Kinshasa Centre for Nuclear Research did not allow these practical problems to distract him. Before taking up his post in Kinshasa he spent some years at the University of California at Berkeley. On his return he published a paper on the future of African science, which is, in his view after forty years of independence, 'lacked creative energy'. He considered that this was not just because of a lack of money or training, but a consequence of the 'African psychological character'. The growth of knowledge, he said, had never been an imperative for man in Africa and the oral tradition that dominated south of the Sahara did not energise the mind. But African scientists should attempt more than a poor imitation of colonial science, which was nearing a dead end with chaos theory. In the future, he suggested, the African specific psychology with its strong creative imagination would have the advantage.

Meanwhile the nuclear reactor, like Stanley's boat, like the brass cannons in the unlit sheds of the National Museum, like the boiler beside the track walked by Marlow 'wallowing in the grass', takes its place among the captured totems of colonial rule. Kinshasa is not the capital of a sovereign state so much as the abandoned control panel of a long-dead empire. Beyond the surf, beyond the cataracts and the humidity, the keys disappear and the trees are once more king.

The drive to the airport conducted at Papa Thomas's usual confident pace took us down a new route. We passed the *Institut Georges Simenon*, named for the Belgian novelist who wrote several books about the *colons* of the Belgian Congo, none of them complimentary, and then the *Institut enseignement médiatique*, a journalism school that must have closed down since it seemed to be totally burnt out, possibly by shellfire. Whenever the car slowed down we were plunged back into the smell of urban Africa, rotting vegetation, mulched-up rubbish and sewage, stewed up by the humidity into a choking, half-breathable soup.

Papa's mobile telephone warbled and so, with a flight to catch, we pulled over while he conducted a lengthy conversation with some dear, long-lost friend. By the side of the road an artisan standing on a stool was hand-painting a billboard with publicity for an internet training course, '*Formation Bureautique*', with photocopying thrown in. The schoolchildren picked their way over the fallen trees and tropical puddles, in their impossibly white shirts and pressed short trousers, between the tumbledown little shacks with their hand-painted and wonderfully optimistic identities: 'Maison la Gloire', 'Chez Mère Pierrette', 'Faculté de la Sade', and then the 'Maison Don de Dieu', where you can buy or sell plumbing materials and sanitary supplies. Papa Thomas finished his conversation and we were waved back onto the highway by a huge yellow-shirted policewoman, who, job done, moved on through the crowds, which she parted like a bow wave, towards her destination, the Laboratoire de l'Elégance.

The wittiest sign was over a barber's shop – 'Espace Schengen'. The Schengen Agreement is the European Union treaty that abolished internal European frontiers and border controls. Since then a short sea passage from the Saharan shore to the Canary Islands (Spanish) or from Libya to the Mediterranean island of Lampedusa (Italian) opens the highway to Brussels and the Palace of Justice.

It took Conrad most of ten years to distil his experience of Africa into a novel that is barely 100 pages long. His dense, multi-dimensional text, that repays re-reading again and again, established the evil and insanity at work in the Congo Free State, the overpowering presence of the forest, the criminal intelligence masked as lawful force that was directing operations, the enslavement, the fear of the unknown, the ferocity of the African counter-attack, the deadly climate, the stripping of the land. At one level the darkness of the title describes a child's idea of the distant unknown and the literal, stifling gloom of the high forest. But darkness quickly becomes a metaphor for the death that awaited so many of the company's agents, for the wicked intentions of their directors, the secrecy surrounding their enterprise, the fear inspired by their defiant victims, and the effect all this had on the mind of the central character, Mr Kurtz.

And while Conrad was writing, the British Army, in the Transvaal in search of gold, attacked the Boer Republics and herded civilians into concentration camps where thousands of women and children died of disease and starvation. Meanwhile in Europe the nations that were set on civilising Africa advanced both their open and their secret preparations for a general war.

As the European empires – Great Britain, France, Germany, Austria-Hungary and Russia – moved closer and closer to their own destruction, the peace conferences and congresses and conventions multiplied. The 1899 Hague Conference set up commissions on arms and the laws of war. A leading figure at this conference, and at the Second Hague Conference in 1907, was Auguste Beernaert, who had been one of those Belgian politicians most supportive of King Leopold's African adventure. Leopold appreciated his former prime minister so much that he once paid Beernaert his highest compliment; the king described him as 'the greatest cynic in the Kingdom'. Beernaert went some way to confirming the king's opinion in 1909 when he accepted the Nobel Peace Prize.

At the 1899 conference the United States delegate, Captain Alfred Mahan, a naval officer and military theorist, objected to a proposed ban on 'asphyxiating gas' on the grounds that he had no wish 'to restrict the inventive genius of US citizens'. The British delegate on the other hand objected to the banning of dumdum bullets, a British invention, because they were the only effective means of stopping savages from continuing their charge after they had been wounded. Both restrictions on the future freedom of military behaviour were nonetheless adopted. It was as though some martial Olympic committee was writing the rules of sport shortly before the opening of the Games.

On 4 August 1914 the Great Powers declared those Games to be open, and on 15 August of the same year the United States, a nation still at peace, celebrated the formal opening of the Panama Canal. And so, on both sides of the Atlantic, the tranquil waterway described by Marlow flowed on. And in 1915, in the forest south of Kuba, an English geologist employed to prospect for copper by the Union Minière du Haut Katanga ascended a low hill called Shinkolobwe, and realised that he was standing on a very large deposit of uranium.

PART II

JOURNEY THROUGH A FALLEN EMPIRE

PART II

JOURNEY THROUGH A FALLEN EMPIRE

CHAPTER FOUR

The Land of Too Much Food

'The word "democracy" as in "bringing democracy to . . ." generally means "pipeline".'

Observation of former member of the
United States Coastguard (2013)

'Welcome to the land of too much food. That's our national motto. Get fat if you can!' The waiter in the hotel breakfast room has noticed our dismay as we gaze down at the overloaded plates. 'Cream and sugar right on the table, sir.' This is not exactly cream. The thin milk seems to slip down into the depths of the coffee, reluctantly, as though it is drowning. It does not resurface. One has to keep adding more to persuade the coffee to change colour. Or color, for this is New Mexico. The film-maker's recce has moved on.

Behind us, beyond the glass wall of the breakfast room, in the gloom of the hotel lobby, North Americans are moving across the carpet. They seem larger than other races. But large to little purpose. Large does not always equal powerful. Behind the glass they resemble creatures trapped in an aquarium. In this hotel they come in couples. Faithful, awkward, elderly – anxious not to offend – they move slowly, as though under water, across the carpet. This is Albuquerque, early in May, start of the property-buying season. And this is 2008. The term 'sub-prime' has become a national catchphrase and is spreading around the world. This is retirement country. The city airport is called not 'Airport' but 'Sunport'. It isn't an airport anyway, it is a small corner of the gigantic military facility known as Kirtland Air Force Base. It was from here, in 1945, that the B-29s departing for Tinian, and then Hiroshima and Nagasaki, took off. Today, on Wall Street, traders are being summoned into conference rooms and fired, in groups of 100. And the old guys in baseball caps and jeans continue to move across the lobby. They are heading for the elevator. They hope not to share it with you. But if this happens they will make eye contact and smile. Don't hit me, they smile, don't hit me.

The Sunport has a superb car-hire facility. You do the paperwork and then pass through a door to a shady area where there is a fleet of several hundred good-as-new cars waiting, with the keys in the ignition, arranged in groups by size. You locate your price group, 'Nos 72 to 90. Take any car.' Take any car? There are red ones, white ones, gunmetal ones, all the doors are open, all the keys are in. It's like being a child in a toy shop – which one do I want? Before long you feel like lying on the ground and bawling and drumming your heels against the concrete. The director of films climbs into a green one, and switches on the radio. 'Biiig 98.5 with Barbara!' It's a man's voice. 'Yeess, it's Barbara next. Get your radio specs on . . . Biiiig 98.5 plays classics all day long with Beatles on the hour, every hour.' All this and the sun and the desert and the sky, and we had not yet left the Rental Center. Welcome to the land of too much choice. Welcome to the land of too much.

There were balloons over Albuquerque that morning; it was a festival of balloons. Everywhere one looked these large, brightly coloured, inoffensive objects were rising from the ground and bobbing gently around the sky, celebrating another fine, gentle day at the International Sunport. As they floated slowly through each other's space and wandered around to no visible purpose, they recalled Swift's Laputans who lived on a sphere suspended in the sky, thinking deeply and losing themselves in obscure calculations. The city guide listed twenty-six museums and parks, and I was tempted by the Museum of the Computer Chip and the International Rattlesnake Museum. But instead I drove out on Interstate 25 to see a collection that was more exotic than either, the National Atomic Museum which is housed on the boundary of the Kirtland Air Force Base.

I remembered the National Atomic Museum from a previous visit. There used to be a rather ramshackle B-29 Superfortress parked outside, the plane that dropped the Bomb. There were information plaques dotted around the site. The B-29 was a 'Hemisphere Defense Weapon' ordered by the War Department in February 1940. It was a wonder of the aerial world, and could carry 16,000 pounds of bombs at 400mph over 2,700 miles. Its specification was based on the latest information gathered from 'the bitter air war going on over Britain and Europe'. B-29 No. 1 took off from Boeing Field, Seattle, on 21 September 1942. Five months later, the chief test pilot and his ten-man crew were killed testing B-29 No. 2. 'The tragic accident was caused by an engine fire, a problem that would haunt the B-29 throughout its career.' I was struck by the use of the verb 'haunt'. These planes killed many hundreds of thousands of people, mostly civilians. And the crews were 'haunted' by fear of an engine fire. As I read this, a dove that had been sitting on the plane's black nose-glass fluttered over to the propeller shaft of No. 3 engine and then hopped inside the engine assembly. The plane's bomb doors were open and one could look up into the bomb bay from which 'the gimmick' had been released over Nagasaki.

What is striking about the National Atomic Museum is its exuberance. The B-29 has become part of the American nation's heroic myth. When Senator Joe McCarthy wanted to gain a little military credibility he would mention that he was an ex-tail gunner in a B-29, in sole charge of a single 20mm cannon. This is the plane that flew in raids over 460 strong – in one of which 80,000 people were killed by high explosives in a single night. The museum takes its tone from one of the exhibits, a front-page report in the *New York Daily News* of 7 August 1945: 'ATOM BOMB ROCKS JAPS – Packs the wallop of 2000 fully-loaded B-29s: "More on Way" Truman warns.' In the visitors' book someone has written, 'Bombs are fun. Let's drop more.' A section of the museum is devoted to the rise and fall of Communism, another larger section is headed, 'Justification for the Bomb'. 'In 1940 the Germans were ready to build their first sub-critical uranium pile . . . By 1941 they were winning the race for the atom bomb. They had a heavy-water plant, high-grade uranium . . . and the greatest chemical engineering industry in the world.' There are lots of bombs on show, including the casings of Little Boy and Fat Man, the bombs dropped on Hiroshima and Nagasaki. Younger visitors, about the same age as Dr Strangelove's grandson, sometimes attempt to climb up onto the bombs.

On one visit I was shown round by a laid-back air-force vet who had been stationed in Germany during the Cuban Missile Crisis in 1962. At the end of the tour he risked an unexpected confidence. 'I was in the missile control room at the time of Cuba so I know that at one point we were two seconds from launch. I was ready to go ahead then. But knowing what I do today, I'd probably kick the shit out of the console.' In the gift shop a very helpful lady thanked me for supporting the museum and explained that the silver earrings that were scale models of Little Boy and Fat Man were still on sale but kept behind the counter, following complaints from Japanese visitors. She assured me that these little bombs were the work of Native American Navajo silversmiths. As I left I noticed another section with the thoughtful title 'The Challenge of Nuclear Stewardship'.

Today the B-29 has been joined on the tarmac outside the museum by an array of even more terrible machines. They stand neatly parked in chronological order, each more fearsome than its fearsome predecessor, each name – Matador, Mace, Titan, Thor – more threatening than the last. Lined up on the edge of the airfield, they look like a giant's box of broken toys. A fellow visitor identified himself as a retired critical-mass physicist. He was a large man with a friendly manner and we began to talk. He said that he was a committed

Christian who had spent his entire career working on nuclear weapons. 'I truly believe they were given to us by God,' he said. 'That was the only thing the Russians were scared of. That's why we won the Cold War.' Somewhere beneath us, buried deep in the ground, the United States government has situated its storage chambers for the national collection of derelict nuclear warheads. About a week after my conversation with the Christian bomb-scientist, I read a report in the *Albuquerque Journal* about the incidence of drunken behaviour among US nuclear-weapons couriers who work out of Kirtland Air Force Base. These men are trained by the Office of Secure Transportation. They are heavily armed and they are employed to drive nuclear weapons, warheads and plutonium around the country in high-security trucks. According to the report there had been sixteen alcohol-related incidents among the nuclear-guard force during the previous three years. It seemed that there was a tendency for the guards to park their loaded trucks overnight, go to a bar, have a hell of a good time, get drunk and start a fight. But not to worry, next morning they and their warheads were back on the road.

The message of the National Atomic Museum is that the wartime atomic bomb was good news and remains a continuing source of national pride; it is the museum of the military justification of the use of the bomb. As such it bears some resemblance to the Musée royal de l'Afrique centrale at Tervuren. They have become museums of outdated myths. Together they contain the nucleus of a Black Museum of Mankind. The headline reproduced from the *New York Daily News* was certainly prophetic. Every word the wartime press carried about military operations was authorised by censors. And yet the morning after Hiroshima – a city destroyed in fractions of a second, ostensibly to persuade the Japanese to surrender – President Truman, who later claimed that the atomic bombing missions were 'an operational choice left to area commanders', was warning that there were 'More on the Way'.

*

The road from Albuquerque to Santa Fe runs north beside the Rio Grande, on Interstate 25. This was the trail into New Mexico, 'the Siberia of New Spain', that was followed by many of the original Spanish colonisers in the seventeenth century. Leaving Albuquerque, the road passes below the heights to the east. There is a 1,000-foot cliff, lime on granite, and you can make out the spires and shields of a radio transmission station grouped among the crags of the summit. The light of the evening sun picks out every detail of the fractured rock face and the radio masts glint like the spears and banners of a phantom army against a stormy sky. This landscape was the scene of the first contact between North America and Europe, following Columbus's voyage across the Atlantic in 1492. Columbus's followers settled in Cuba, and in 1519 one of those adventurers, Hernán Cortés, acting without orders and in quest of gold, sailed to the American mainland, overthrew the Aztec Empire and renamed it New Spain.

From the city of Mexico, the Aztec capital, Cortés ordered his captains to spread out, conquer and convert. This was a long, drawn-out process but by 1540 a Spanish general named Coronado had crossed the terrible north Mexican desert and entered what is now known as New Mexico. He had been ordered by the viceroy of New Spain to subdue the Indians but to treat them justly. In defiance of these instructions, Coronado stormed the first three Indian settlements he came upon. His violence was partly the consequence of frustration, since he had been led to believe that the Rio Grande valley contained cities full of gold and silver. Instead he found villages built of mud and rock. But the fourth settlement he reached, now known as San Felipe, was well situated beside the river and shaded by willows and cottonwood trees. This was where he decided to take up winter quarters. The inhabitants were driven out and took refuge in the Sandia Mountains which rise to 10,000 feet and were known to be the home of the twin war gods, of Wind Woman, and of their supreme protector, Spider Woman.

Coronado spent three more years trekking between the buffalo plains and the Grand Canyon, and mapping a vast area. He came upon a desert gulch just south of his first winter quarters and named it the *Jornada del Muerto* ('the Trail of Death'). But he failed to find gold and so he withdrew from this hostile terrain and, on his return to Mexico City, was arrested and charged with brutality towards the Pueblo Indians. It was to be fifty-five years before another Spanish expedition – soldiers accompanied by Franciscan friars and led by a man named Juan de Oñate – returned to New Mexico and set up a fortified mission which they called Santa Fe, City of the Holy Faith. With their arrival in 1595 – twenty-five years before the Pilgrim Fathers reached New England – the great days of the Pueblo Indian civilisation came to an end.

In New Mexico, the Spanish colonisers converted the Indians, forcibly where necessary, married some and enslaved others. In 1680, the Indians rose and drove the Spanish out of Mexico. A Spanish general named Don Diego de Vargas reconquered the territory in 1692, and it remained part of Spain's American Empire until 1821, when Mexico declared its independence from Spain. At that time Mexican territory comprised modern Mexico with the addition of the lands now known as Texas, New Mexico, Arizona, Colorado, Utah, Nevada and California.

Today this historical succession of peoples and power can be traced in national communities that are separated like historical strata. The original 'Americans', the Native Indians, are still living on their ancestral lands or in nineteen pueblos, autonomous societies scattered throughout the state. Native American historians have divided the pueblos into three regional groups and three language groups, and one of the languages is divided into three dialects. Because they are still settled in the places where they were living when the first Europeans arrived, the Pueblo Indians have been able to retain much of their original cultural identity. They were also relatively fortunate in being conquered by Spanish Catholics who, in the seventeenth century, lacked the power to destroy this alien culture. In consequence, according to the historian Joe S. Sando, the Pueblo Indians of New Mexico have developed 'a unique mixture of European governing structure, Christian formalities and beliefs and legal forms imposed upon the people by governmental requirements'. Responding to 'the bombardments' of three successive forms of foreign domination, they have somehow survived.

The second historical stratum is that of the descendants of the Spanish colonisers who intermarried with the Indians and who became the first Mexicans. They are Spanish-speaking, the people Octavio Paz described when he wrote,

> The Mexican, whether young or old, *criollo* or *mestizo* [of Spanish blood or of Spanish and Indian blood], general or labourer or lawyer, seems to me to be a person who shuts himself away to protect himself: his face is a mask and so is his smile. In his harsh solitude, which is both barbed and courteous, everything serves him as a defence . . . He passes through life like a man who has been flayed.

It is the Mexican who inspired Paz's prose masterpiece, *The Labyrinth of Solitude*. In New Mexico, citizens of Mexican descent are known as 'Hispanics'. They form a political constituency; they are not always members of the dominant class. They are sometimes identified by their appearance and accused by state police officers of being illegal immigrants, or of 'DWM' (Driving While Mexican).

Just as the Native Americans resent the history that has deprived them of their lands, so the Hispanics resent the presence of the Anglos, the dominant entitled class of New Mexico, the settlers from the East who arrived last, conquered everything in sight and were of generally Protestant obedience. The particular historical resentment of the Hispanic is founded on the Treaty of Guadalupe Hidalgo. In 1848 this treaty ended the Mexican–North American War and ceded half of the land of Mexico, including the territory of New Mexico, to Washington. New Mexicans had been ruled by Mexico for only twenty-five years and their strongest cultural link was with Spain. They continued to speak Spanish, to practise Catholicism and to call themselves Hispanics. But in Washington they were known as 'coloured races' who did not deserve equal treatment. Weaker people were less worthy in the eyes of the Lord and would have to adapt or die. For the Hispanics of New Mexico, the day in 1821 when Mexico declared its independence from Spain was a black day.

Heading north along Interstate 25, one soon reaches the pueblo of San Felipe. The Spaniards called this road the 'Camino Real' – the Royal Road – because it was the most direct path back to the Kingdom of Spain. The first sign of San Felipe today is a concrete tower and a flashing neon sign. 'Welcome to the San Felipe Pueblo,' it says; 'Free Games – Mega Casino – Come and Play.' The San Felipe Nation, like other Pueblo Indians, now has the right to operate casinos. The casinos are run by professionals from New Jersey, the gamblers are supplied by the retired classes of New Mexico. And the San Felipe Nation sits back and enjoys the profits. The casino car park is full of very large cars and inside the building the people who drive them reappear – no longer in couples, now moving alone, slowly, but with some dignity, towards the favoured machine. Once arrived at their destination they clamber up onto the stools, gaze at the twinkling lights, feed in the coins and start to pull the levers. In the real world the sunlight blazes down. In the casino there is no daylight at all. The entrance doors are made of smoked glass. Here it is always some glamorous imaginary hour, like three o'clock in the morning. In fact, it's half an hour after breakfast and the gambling has begun. Separated as they are by the precise distance between each machine, with no social interaction, no chance of catching a friendly eye, the gamblers gaze into the spinning interior, feeding in the coins. As the slot machines swallow their savings the ladies narrow their eyes, meaning, 'Come on. I'm not cleaned out yet.' Their husbands lean forward, shoulders hunched, as though committed to some mad cavalry charge that is bound to overrun the line of destitution.

At regular intervals there is a crash and one of the machines gives in, excreting a pile of very low value silver pieces. But zombies do not blink. CRASH! Out come the coins and absolutely no reaction. It's like the set of a horror movie. The San Felipe Nation is running a day-care centre for fleecing elderly Anglos. The proportion of male fun-lovers is low, the average age appears to be about eighty. Some of them are so frail that they seem to be hanging off their levers rather than pulling them. 'Come and Play! Don't Look UP.' Welcome to the International Sunport, where paranoia stalks the land.

The pueblo of the San Felipe Nation is out of sight of the Mega Casino, on the opposite side of Interstate 25. It has not moved a yard in the last thousand years. The Rio Grande still runs through the centre, there are still cottonwoods and willows on the river bank and vegetable plots have been scraped out of the earth between the houses. The church is locked, and the sacred *kiva*, the ceremonial underground chamber at the heart of the pueblo, is of course unapproachable, but a door opens and Wilbert emerges to greet us. San Felipe is one of the historic pueblos of Sandoval County. Its people speak Keresan. But Wilbert speaks English. He confirms that this is the historical San Felipe Pueblo and introduces himself as an artist in acrylic. He happens to have a couple of his paintings under his arm. We examine these politely, and decline. He explains that he lives with his mother. In fact it was his mother who sent him out with the acrylics. He gives us her telephone number in case we change our minds. He adds that this would be quite a good time to leave the village as there is no one around at this time of day.

On the way out, just before we cross the tracks of the main line south to Albuquerque, we pass a little diner with a store attached. Good place for a coffee. The diner is neat as a pin, but it is closed. The store is open. The lady running it explains that there is a feud in the pueblo. She is on the way to closing down. She used to do good business, but her only remaining customers are the San Felipe children. Her shelves are nearly empty. She says that the adults all use the big drugstore that has been erected beside the casino gas pump. The casino has ruined her.

*

The first time I went to Santa Fe in 1999 I flew there from Denver in a light aircraft that just about cleared the Sangre de Cristo mountain range. The plane bucketed around over what seemed to be empty forest and grazing land, land that has been bitterly disputed since the Spanish conquest. The approach to Santa Fe by road, along the banks of the Rio Grande, was less dramatic. On the verge of Interstate 25 the police had erected signs offering rewards to public-spirited citizens who called toll-free on their cell phones to denounce each other's delinquent driving. The river at this point seems to shrink, supplies are interrupted by the needs of the town, with its swimming pools, golf course and numerous lawns, one of the largest of which lies within the walls of a huge military cemetery.

Santa Fe is one of the towns whose name spells out the history of the west, like Tombstone or Dodge City. And today it has certainly succeeded in preserving a sense of its past. According to the state's Historic Preservation Division it contains about 10,000 historically significant buildings. At first glance it looks like a place where eccentric Americans from the East and West Coasts meet to lead the simple life in conditions of considerable luxury. But the authentic complexity of New Mexico keeps seeping through. The official guide announces baldly that 'Siesta was practised until World War II.' The Hispanic influence recedes slowly, and even today one finds oneself ambling along the sidewalk, through the dry heat of the region, at the local, deliberate, step-by-step pace. Staying with friends I saw a lizard in their garden, as well as a chipmunk and a two-foot snake. The local plant nursery advertised Bluegrass sod rolls and gopher traps, and my bedroom was haunted by the ghost of a very disturbed Chinese woman – a presence that was visible to Toby, the resident pug, even in daylight.

Santa Fe has a Romanesque cathedral dedicated to San Francisco and constructed by the *Auvergnat* Archbishop Lamy, who ruled this mission diocese for thirty-four years and inspired Willa Cather's masterpiece, *Death Comes for the Archbishop*. At 7,000 feet, it is one of the highest settlements in the state. The town is spread out among low sandy hills and dominated to the north-east by the Sangre de Cristos, an outcrop of the Rocky Mountains. The settlement attracts creative people. At dinner one evening my conversation with a guitar-maker, who was trying to explain the acoustic applications of Heisenberg's uncertainty principle, was interrupted by a physicist working at the nuclear-weapons facility at Los Alamos eager to share the news that it was necessary to bury a bluebird facing east after you have plucked its tail feathers to present to your Zuni rain doctor. Even today water and rain remain central preoccupations. When the first Spanish explorers described New Mexico to the viceroy of New Spain, they said that it was 'big, dry and hot', and little has changed. People in New Mexico still fight over water, and sometimes they still kill for it.

In Santa Fe there are 67,000 people and 61 gourmet restaurants. I have patronised two of its vintage wine shops and can confirm that they offer some of the finest and most expensive wines available. The open-air Opera is celebrated. Santa Fe may be an oddity among American towns, but America lies all around. We passed a roadside advertisement for a builder who was looking for work from Santa Fe's hundreds of resident artists. The sign read 'Your art might suck. Your studio doesn't have to.'

The heart of the town is the Plaza, which dates back to the original Spanish foundation. In the nineteenth century it marked the final destination of the covered wagons that had lurched out of the East along the entire 900 miles of the Santa Fe Trail. The cathedral stands to one side, the governor's palace to another; like all the plazas of the Spanish Empire it was laid out to the plans of Philip II of Spain. In the centre of the square there is a pink granite obelisk with a memorial plaque to the soldiers of the Union Army who died in the Battle of Valverde in 1862. Their Confederate opponents are merely referred to as 'the rebels'.

On the opposite side of this obelisk another plaque commemorates in bronze letters, 'the Heroes who fell in various battles with savage

Indians'. The savages in question were the Plains Indians who once attacked Santa Fe 17,000 strong, and drove the Spanish settlers out. In 1974 the word 'savage' was neatly chipped out of the marble, but the letters can still be read in the shadows on the stone.

CHAPTER FIVE

The Solitary Passenger

Bandelier - haven of the Ancient Ones, the Anasazi, 'the People who are Not Us'.

On a seasonal and extremely cold day in November 1895, a solitary passenger descended onto the platform at Lamy, arriving from Denver by the Atchison, Topeka and Santa Fe Railroad. Lamy was, and still is, the station for Santa Fe. The man travelling alone was a short, slight figure dressed like an Easterner in a formal, dark suit with waistcoat and watch chain, though he had taken the precaution of adding a knotted kerchief round his throat and a cowboy hat. He had dark brown eyes that glowed and the sort of handlebar moustache habitually worn by strongmen in the circus. He was fond of practical jokes and despite his mild appearance was noted for his filthy temper; ever since childhood he had suffered from fits of depression. His name was Aby Warburg and he carried a special pass from the Ministry of the Interior and the Ministry of War in Washington authorising him to travel through Indian country.

Now as he stood by the horses and waited for his bags to be loaded onto the carriage that would carry him up to the Palace Hotel, and as he looked up at the peaks of the Sangre de Cristo Mountains, he was excited to be nearing the end of a journey over thousands of miles, but also back through two thousand years into a world that obsessed him. Warburg's life's work was the study of the significance of antiquity for modern civilisation. When he stepped off the train at Lamy in 1895 he entered Greece in the classical era.

Aby Warburg was the oldest son of a banking family settled in Hamburg who had turned his back on a senior partnership in the bank and chosen to become an art historian. In an age when German scholarship in both science and the classics was pre-eminent, Warburg was to become one of the most influential members of his discipline. In 1895 he lived in Florence and conducted most of his research in the city and state archives, where his doctoral thesis had been devoted to Botticelli. He had interrupted his studies for family reasons. His younger brother Paul was to be married in New York. Another brother had been married in New York earlier the same year and Aby Warburg had failed to attend that wedding, so there was no question of avoiding the second. Both brothers were marrying into the same New York Jewish banking dynasty, the Kuhn-Loebs. Before they founded their bank, the Kuhns and the Loebs had lived in Cincinnati where they had made a fortune during the Civil War supplying uniforms for the Union Army. The subsequent bank prospered on Wall Street by breaking into the railroad speculation market, with such success that by the time of the Warburg alliance it was second only to J. Pierpont Morgan, and the Kuhn-Loeb family home was a mansion on Fifth Avenue.

Although Aby Warburg was devoted to his family, New York did not please him; he described the city as 'the largest department store in the world'. In the previous months he had been pursuing a line of research into connections between classical pagan imagery and Christian art. In the archives in Florence he had discovered designs by Bernardo Buontalenti for an *intermedio*, a musical and theatrical performance that took place during the wedding of Grand Duke Ferdinand dei Medici in 1589. The *intermedio* showed Apollo doing battle with the serpent Python. According to legend, Apollo defeated the monster and freed the land from a reign of terror; harmony was

restored to the kingdom. The duke, by association, was properly flat-
tered. This intrusion of a dramatic and violent pagan myth into a
joyful Christian religious ceremony was exactly in Warburg's line of
research.

Warburg was an opponent of 'the connoisseur school' of art
history* and was drawn towards the psychological understanding of
civilisation. He was well aware that his raw material in the form of
primitive cultures was fast disappearing. Whether or not he initially
intended to visit New Mexico during his time in America is uncertain,
but on the boat to New York he met a fellow passenger who was on
the staff of the Smithsonian Institution in Washington D.C., which
had recently published research into Dakota Indian wall paintings
and Indian religions. After the wedding, Warburg took the train to
Washington and was welcomed at the Smithsonian, which he later
described as 'the brain and the scientific conscience of the Eastern
States'. Here he discovered not just wall paintings but Indian ceramics
and descriptions of rituals such as the Hopi Indians' Snake Dance.

The scholars Warburg met in Washington provided him with
detailed information about the world of the Hopi Indians and the
cliff dwellings of their remote ancestors which had been discovered
seven years earlier on the Mesa Verde in Colorado by a rancher who
was also an amateur archaeologist. This region – bounded by the
Colorado and Rio Grande rivers and now known as the Four Corners
because it marks the meeting point of Arizona, Utah, Colorado and
New Mexico – contains abundant archaeological remains of complex
Indian settlements dating back 1,400 years. In Washington, Warburg
also met James Mooney, who was attached to the Bureau of
Ethnology, and who had recently published a paper on 'The Ghost
Dance Religion and the Sioux Outbreak of 1890'. In this, the last
significant demonstration of Indian resistance, the Sioux tribe of
Plains Indians, inspired by their Ghost Dance religion, had talked

---

* He once described the professional attributer Bernard Berenson as 'one of a
snuffling riff-raff'.

of regaining their land. This ambition had culminated in the Massacre of Wounded Knee, when over 300 Sioux, including women and children, were butchered by the US 7th Cavalry. What interested Warburg was Mooney's argument that the Ghost Dance could be recognised in the context of familiar Hindu, Hebrew and Christian doctrines. It was this promise of traceable cultural evolution that drew Warburg to the Native American Southwest. He had no immediate commitments in Florence or Hamburg; he had the time, the connections and the money. He could travel at his own expense, but it was the Kuhn-Loebs who provided him with a free pass for the Atchison, Topeka and Santa Fe Railroad.

Warburg had come to the Southwest at just the right time. The struggle between Indian and settler in New Mexico had ended ten years earlier, and the Swiss-born anthropologist, Adolph Bandelier, had begun to study the traces of prehistoric life in the surrounding landscape. The highlands between the Colorado River and the Rio Grande had been inhabited for over 11,000 years, since the end of the Ice Age, by people who were possibly the direct ancestors of the surviving Pueblo Indians. In the Southwest, Warburg could travel with a guide by pony-trap, or through the remoter regions on horseback, since - unlike many historians of the Quattrocento - he was a competent horseman, having discharged his military service in the Prussian mounted artillery. During his stay in Santa Fe, Warburg made the Palace Hotel his base, whence he would venture out into the prehistoric land.

The geology of the Rio Grande valley which now surrounded him is impressive, not to say terrifying. The fertile plains are ringed and slashed by plateaux (known as *mesas*), canyons and gorges that were formed 30 million years ago by volcanic eruptions. One feature of the land, a rift that is over 600 feet deep, known as the Rio Grande Rift, dominates human and animal life over thousands of square miles, ensuring an abundant water supply and fertile grazing. As Warburg travelled between the Mesa Verde and the Rio Grande he would have ascended the staircase of *mesas* that provide a natural viewing platform over the centre of the territory. To the east there is a line of cratered peaks. The highest rise to over 13,000 feet and have names such as Angel Fire, Hermit Elk and Agua Fria. The people in the valley looking east towards these mountains at sunset would have seen the snow-capped peaks turn red in the last light, which is how they acquired their Spanish name, Sangre de Cristo – the Blood of Christ.

One of the western *mesas* that Warburg passed was called Los Alamos. There was nothing on it at the time except a small ranch established a few years earlier by homesteaders from the East. Below Los Alamos to the south is a long, sloping plateau called Pajarito which is formed from soft pumice stone, or tuff. This was originally volcanic ash. It stands in contrast to the black basalt layers, the aftermath of an earlier explosion, which form a much harder rock that contains deposits of obsidian, a volcanic glass. The highlands between the Colorado and Rio Grande rivers are a laboratory of human evolution and of the geological conditions that made it possible. Warburg had entered a region that was in fact far older in terms of human settlement than classical Greece.

The ancestors of the American Indians may have come from China, or even Japan. As the ice receded they moved north through Asia, crossed the Bering Straits and then turned south into an uninhabited continent. These people moved in hunting bands, slowly and steadily, following the migratory patterns of the herds that sustained them. They used spears and arrows to kill, they may have ridden horses, and they certainly used dogs. Warburg in 1895 was looking at the same landscape those wanderers saw when they first reached the 37th parallel and moved into New Mexico. Only thirty years before Warburg's arrival their descendants, the Plains Indians, were using the same weapons to hunt bison, the animals whose bodies provided them with food, clothing, shelter and, sometimes, fuel. The bison and deer were all that was left of the prehistoric herds. Originally the hunters' quarry had included many species since extinct: giant bison with horns spreading over six feet, huge beavers, camels, giant moose and musk-oxen and the woolly mammoth. Most of these species were hunted out of existence and in response human numbers also declined.

The exact process by which some of the hunting tribes settled into communities sustained by agriculture is not understood, but wherever there was a water supply, tuff and fertile soil, favourable conditions existed. And the Pajarito Plateau terminates at a rock face called the Frijoles Canyon, which offered all three conditions and the further advantage of a defensible situation. The obsidian deposits provided valuable tools that could be traded or used to cut cave dwellings out of the soft pumice-stone cliff-face. In the canyon there is good soil and a creek that drains the high plateau. This runs all year round and grows in strength until it eventually plunges into the Rio Grande through a spectacular series of falls. It was here that Adolph Bandelier made his discovery – fifteen years before Warburg's arrival – of a settlement that had once numbered more than 2,400 habitations. Today's Pueblo Indians call the people who lived here the 'Anasazi', which means 'the Ancient Ones' or 'the People who are Not Us'. They are known to have cultivated beans, maize and squash. They used irrigation in the winter to increase the size of their plots, but the average annual rainfall was only fifteen inches, and they knew they could not survive without the summer rains. They knew about rain. The lightning that cleared the forest by starting fires also brought storms and water. The lightning that could kill also brought life. Without the lightning they would die.

The Anasazi were themselves descended from communities established at the centre of the Four Corners region near the Mesa Verde. They had reached Frijoles Canyon by moving south-east through the mountain passes. The dwellings they constructed in the canyon were fortified; the largest contained over 1,000 separate rooms. The layout of the Frijoles complex, now named Bandelier, suggests a haven to which people could fall back in time of danger, perhaps in winter when food was scarce and nomadic hunters might attack and plunder their stocks. At the centre of each group of dwellings there were *kivas*. The exact purpose of the Anasazi's underground ceremonial chambers is unknown, but it is clear that they were the site of complex religious rituals. This religion not only governed their behaviour; it enabled them to organise and co-operate and eventually to develop a society that prospered for hundreds of years.

On the wall of one of the *kivas* at Bandelier there is a painting, a black zigzag design that is found throughout the Southwest as well as in the Aztec and Mayan remains of Mexico and Guatemala. This zigzag is the Plumed Serpent, the snake god that moves like lightning and is drawn in the shape of lightning, the snake that brings life because it represents water.

The Anasazi lived in Frijoles Canyon until about 1600, which is when the Spanish conquistadors reached what is now the state of New Mexico. For the next 300 years, following the arrival of the Spanish, New Mexico was to be the setting for a violent, four-handed struggle between men living in the post-Stone Age: the nomadic Plains Indians; the descendants of the Anasazi, the Pueblo Indians; the Spanish colonisers; and finally the North American Anglos. So runs the story that this violent geology framed, and Warburg arrived just after the struggle had finally been settled.

The means used by Warburg to reach Santa Fe was also the means by which the struggle was decided since it was the railroad that terminated a nomadic way of life that had lasted for 10,000 years. The process was inexorable but it was not swift. The Santa Fe trail that linked the Spanish mission station to Missouri 900 miles to the east was opened in 1821 but it was 1886 before the last bounty payment was paid out for an Apache scalp.* Only nine years before the arrival of the art historian from Florence, land-owners were still honouring the going rate of $100 for a male scalp and $50 for a woman's. These payments were illegal in the state

---

* At the time of Warburg's visit the office of the Governor, in his Palace in the Plaza of Santa Fe, was festooned with Indian ears and scalps.

of Colorado but continued to be made in New Mexico, which was not yet a state but a 'territory'. Even in 1895 settlers living in Texas and New Mexico were still very frightened of the Plains Indians. Searching for links between antiquity and the modern world, Warburg could hardly have entered a more dramatic laboratory.

CHAPTER SIX

The Empire of the Interior

*'The men in blue destroyed everything which the most infernal Yankee
ingenuity could devise means to destroy; hands, hearts, fire, gunpowder
were the agencies which they used, and behind everything the spirit of hell.'*
A Confederate veteran of 1865

The epic myth of the United States is the myth of the frontier,
the Wild West and heroic settlement. It is a story of progress
and conquest – a steady movement of pioneers from the eastern
seaboard out to the Pacific coast along fabled paths: the Oregon
Trail, the Pony Express, the Overland Stage and the Santa Fe Trail.
The settlements these heroes established have evocative names:
Flagstaff, Fort Defiance, Paradise, Rising Star, Fort Bliss. The tale
is often told in terms of the desperate 'last stand'. The narrative
is a story of one last stand after another until, after 100 years of
them, the gallant band of 90 million survivors ran out of savages
to be scalped by. But what is singular about New Mexico among
the fifty states of the United States is the abundant evidence of a
far older pattern of struggle and migration. This land was not
conquered from the east, but from the south, and the difference
is visible today.

When the Pilgrim Fathers disembarked from the *Mayflower* in
1620 a century had already passed since Cortés had sailed from Cuba
to the American mainland and defeated the Aztecs. The Aztecs of

Mexico and the Mayans of southern Mexico and Guatemala were among the most sophisticated Indian societies that can be traced, with the most complex and scientific religious beliefs. The Mexican poet Octavio Paz, trying to explain why the Indian empires were overthrown by a handful of men in armour carrying swords and lances, suggested that it was due to a loss of faith and amounted to a form of collective suicide. He quoted a Mayan lament that recalled the moment when they were overwhelmed by that horror.

> The blond-bearded strangers arrived, the sons of the sun . . .
> Ah how sad we were when they arrived . . . The white man's
> stick will fall, will descend from on high, will strike every-
> where . . . The hangings will begin, and lightning will flash from
> the white man's hands . . . and tribute will be demanded after the
> grand entrance of Christianity, and the Seven Sacraments will
> be established, and travail and misery will rule this land.

When the artist Georgia O'Keeffe first encountered the plains of the Southwest in 1929 she said they were 'the biggest thing I know'. And crossing them today, with empty grassland laid out as far as the Sangre de Cristo to the east, the Carson National Forest to the west and the Rio Grande running between, one initially enjoys the same sense of unrestricted promise. In 1540, when Coronado's army first explored the land, there was nothing here but the sun, the wind, the buffalo and the game. The Pueblo Indians were further south or in the foothills. Then, shortly before the full Spanish invasion of 1595, two nomadic tribes, the Navajo and the Apache, moved into northern New Mexico, and began to prey on the settled peoples.

The Franciscan missionaries could make no headway at all with these nomads, but they had been able to force their beliefs on the Pueblo Indians. In 1633 a Franciscan friar, representing the Inquisition, toured the pueblos of the northern territory to conduct an investiga-tion into witchcraft. Fra Esteban de Perea found that the Indian converts to the Faith were refusing to abandon their old gods: they persisted in dancing, wearing masks and handling venomous snakes. The Inquisition's solution was to condemn the native priests as sorcerers. They were flogged and enslaved or hanged, the *kivas* were destroyed and masks and fetishes burned. The Indians then abandoned their superstition and became orthodox Catholics, or so the Spanish missionaries thought. In fact, they continued to follow both religions, one in public and one secretly.

In 1680 there was a great uprising, known as the Pueblo Revolt and the Spanish were driven out of New Mexico. The mission stations such as Santa Fe became pueblo settlements and the *kivas* were rebuilt everywhere. When the Spanish returned twelve years later to reconquer the land, it was on different terms. The Franciscan priests never regained their full power; relations between the Spanish and the Indians improved in consequence; Christianity and the Indian faith were allowed unofficially to coexist. The Pueblo people and their *kivas* were treated with wary respect, though Indian numbers were reduced from 50,000 to 15,000 by European disease. By 1700 it looked as though Pueblo and Spaniard might be able to live together, defending themselves against the regular raids by Navajo and Apache, on terms of guarded peace. But six years later another nomadic nation arrived from the north and looked out over O'Keeffe's 'biggest thing' and knew that it was theirs. They were called the Comanche and they instituted a reign of terror that spread right across New Mexico and deep into Texas and lasted for 170 years.

The Comanche, who have been described as the greatest horsemen in the world, first fell on the Apaches of north-eastern New Mexico and within twenty-five years had driven them off the plains and forced them to take shelter among their hereditary enemies, the Pueblo Indians of Taos. The Comanche then started to attack both the Pueblos and the Spanish settlements and throughout the eighteenth century they became the dominant force east of the Rio Grande. Before long Apache tribes in southern New Mexico had also taken to the warpath and were creating just as much destruction in the southern province, the part that was directly linked to the more peaceful central regions of New Spain. As a result the Spanish and Pueblo people were driven closer together, but by 1776 the situation had become so bad that the governor of New Mexico informed the viceroy that the province might have to be abandoned. There is a sign outside the Galisteo Pueblo today which bears witness to those desperate times, noting that its people were eventually driven out of this village by 'drought, famine, disease and Comanche raids'.

It was only in 1779 that a competent Spanish general managed to outwit Green Horn, the Comanche leader, and inflict a heavy defeat. The Spanish then offered the Comanche a permanent peace – and the prospect of joining in an endless war against the Apache. This agreement was signed at a solemn council in Pecos Pueblo in 1786 and it lasted, unlike most other treaties with the Indians, for 100 years – until the Spanish had departed and the Mexicans had in their turn been colonised. The Spanish had used missionaries, warfare, bribery and finally alliance with the nomadic Indians, and so found a way to live among them.

The first notable Anglo penetration of New Mexico came from Louisiana in the last days of Spanish empire. The Spanish governor was alarmed, but delegations sent to Spain to warn of the Anglo danger returned empty-handed. With the coming of Mexican independence, the new Mexican governor of New Mexico opened the frontier for commerce. The first Anglo trader, an ex-Indian fighter called William Becknell from Missouri, arrived with a pack-train in 1821, having picked a way through the Sangre de Cristos that would later be called the Santa Fe Trail. From the start of this new incursion the Comanches made a distinction between the Mexicans and the Anglos, continuing to observe a truce with Pueblo Indians and with Spanish-speakers, but treating Anglo travellers and other Easterners as trespassers and fair game. Apart from Indian attacks, one of the commonest forms of death on the Santa Fe Trail was snakebite.

At first, while it was a matter of trade, there were few problems between the Mexican government and those incomers who survived the journey. In 1825 the United States was authorised to open a consulate in Santa Fe, and the Mexican governor was able to pay most of his administrative costs out of the taxes imposed on imported American goods. An early attempt by neighbouring Anglo-Texans to move on into New Mexico was defeated, but the demographic pressure to move west was building and by now the newcomers were arriving in Texas with slaves. In 1821 the first constitution of newly independent Mexico had outlawed slavery. Thus, the Mexican provincial government had granted Anglo immigrants to the province of 'Coahuila-Texas' 5000 acres of land each for growing cotton, but without the right to use slaves. This considerably limited the immigrants' possibilities, although it did not stop the influx. Then in 1836 the 30,000 Anglo settlers of Texas saw their opportunity and conspired to overthrow its Mexican provincial government and declare the area to be an independent republic. They soon started to import slave labour. By 1845, when the United States annexed Texas, there were 160,000 Anglo-Texans; the slave labour had wonderfully added to the possibilities of life in the new state. During this period the governor of the southern neighbouring state of Chihuahua tried to stir the people of New Mexico into some appreciation of the danger they were in, and sent them an open letter. 'Do you know who the Texans are?' he asked.

They are adventurers who despise you as barbarians, weak-minded and corrupt men. They blaspheme your religion and scoff at your pious customs; they are grasping merchants who envy the fertility of your lands, the richness of your mines, and the clemency of your weather; some are men who distinguish their fellowmen by the colour of their faces in order to impress the stamp of slavery on those who are not white . . . And they come to take possession of the land with their sword.

And the Anglos were not only armed. They had God on their side. According to the *New York Morning News* in 1845, 'Our manifest destiny is to overspread and possess the whole continent which providence has given us for the great experiment of liberty.'

In the opening scenes of the epic western *Red River*, a youthful John Wayne playing Thomas Dunson, a pioneer settler, arrives on the banks of the Rio Grande in southern Texas after beating off an attack by Comanches, and lays claim to 'the greatest ranch in Texas'. He looks around the glorious landscape, the river, the mountains and the empty grassland and he imagines the spread that he will build in the years to come. Just then a horseman appears over the horizon. This turns out to be the steward of the established landowner, a Mexican don. The steward, who is a most courteous grey-haired man, tells Dunson/Wayne that he is welcome to stay on Don Diego's land for days or longer, but that he will be a guest, since the land has belonged to Don Diego's family for over a hundred years. Dunson, who has not had time to unpack his saddlebag, says that the land is now his. The steward says that Don Diego will not agree. So Dunson provokes the steward into drawing his gun and then shoots him dead. Argument settled, the land *is* now his.

Watching *Red River* today one can see that the director, Howard Hawks, had no illusions about the winning of the West. In one sequence he established Thomas Dunson's courage in fighting off the Indians, his excitement on seeing the 'empty' land, which entitled him to own it, and his speed on the draw, which confirmed him as a man prepared to defend his rights and enabled him to murder the courteous old Mexican. The death of the Mexican is not a drama. The Mexican is an opponent of manifest destiny, no longer a person, just an impediment to 'the great experiment of liberty'.

One year after the annexation of Texas, in 1846, the US 'Army of the West' crossed the border into New Mexico and provoked a confrontation with the army of Mexico. Washington then declared war on Mexico and occupied Santa Fe. Mexican patriots fought back in 1847 in what became known as the Taos Revolt. This brief episode ended after US forces shelled the church in Taos pueblo, where the Mexicans had taken refuge, and in 1848 Washington annexed New Mexico.

The struggle between the Anglos and the Indians of North America raged on for 250 years, on battlefields that stretched right across the continent. In 1600, the 1 million Indians who lived on the Great Plains north of the Rio Grande are said to have spoken over 2,000 languages. They had no horses and survived by hunting or growing maize and vegetables. The Anglo settlers, unlike the Spanish, made comparatively little attempt to convert them. Whereas in New Mexico the Spanish had complex and sometimes mutually beneficial relationships with Indians, the Anglos tended to a simpler solution characterised by extreme violence. The wars began in New England in 1636 and as they continued the Indians were driven steadily west. By the time the last battle was fought in South Dakota in 1890, the Republic had become the world's leading industrial power.

Until 1830 the Plains Indians still dominated the centre and west of the United States. But as the pressure of settlement grew, the Anglos' methods became more ruthless. Between 1831 and 1837 President Andrew Jackson breached a ruling of the Supreme Court and introduced both the concentration camp and ethnic cleansing. Forty-six thousand Indians were rounded up and driven into camps. In 1838, 15,000 Cherokee were sent on a winter march for 1,000 miles out onto the icy plains; 4,000 of the marchers died from exposure and starvation and 25 million acres were thereby made available for settlement. The Anglos did not just want the use of the land, they wanted an empty land, and to acquire it they set out to destroy its occupants. This was the first empire of the North Americans, the continent itself. Over fifty years a puny republic was transformed into a prosperous and powerful nation. Some of the land was purchased, some of it acquired by negotiation, some by fraud and some by conquest. Where treaties were employed they were systematically broken. It was an unstoppable process, carried out with absolute ruthlessness in one of the most beautiful landscapes in the world.

For some time New Mexico was protected from this devastation because it lay to the west of the Rocky Mountains and its people were largely settled and prepared to defend themselves. Ethnic cleansing, the method applied to the Indians of the north Atlantic coast and of Florida and Louisiana, could not work in Texas and New Mexico because the Comanche and Apache would not be pinned down and concentrated into camps, they moved too quickly. During the years of the Civil War, between 1861 and 1865, the Comanche even managed to regain lost ground on the plains of the Texan and New Mexican border, and in 1865 the newly victorious Union government signed a peace treaty with then. This guaranteed that 'perpetual space shall be maintained between the people and the government of the United States and the Indian parties hereto', which of course it was not. The Spanish had succeeded in signing a peace treaty with the Comanche nation that lasted 100 years. But the Spanish were prepared to share the land. The post-Civil War Republic had different plans.

The Declaration of Independence had declared that all men were 'created equal . . . with [the] unalienable right to Liberty'. The Constitution then tolerated slavery. This situation was sanitised by the Unionist victory in 1865, and by the subsequent passage of the 14th Amendment guaranteeing civil rights to all men, including freed slaves. But a congressional bill of 1866 promptly excluded Indians. Following the Civil War, and armed with the six-shooter and a renewed moral authority, a Righteous People resumed its advance on the West. By 1865, the railroad had reached Texas and the buffalo herds were already being wiped out. According to some estimates, 13 million animals were shot. One of the Unionist heroes of the Civil War, General William T. Sherman, promoted the railways precisely because he foresaw that they would result in the extermination of the buffalo and the consequent extermination of the Plains Indians, a policy of which he wholeheartedly approved.

Deprived of buffalo, the Comanches started to eat their surplus horses and were able to keep fighting for another ten years. But in 1874 a young US cavalry officer managed to trap over 2,000 Comanche warriors in the Palo Duro Canyon in Texas. Many of the Indians could climb the cliffs and escape, but their horses were corralled and the cavalry officer had all 1,400 animals shot. One year later the Comanche, after a 200-mile forced march, entered a reservation. The Apaches of New Mexico under Geronimo fought on for another ten years. The cavalry officer who shot 1,400 horses died insane.

The heroic myth of the American West has enabled the people who won this land at any cost to come to terms with the violence of their victory. All nations need myths, they restore our health and freedom, and link us to that ideal past when we lived in an ideal land, a place with abundant food and shelter, what Octavio Paz describes as the place 'where opposites are reconciled . . . in the days when animals could talk'.

In Santa Fe I had spent time in the Georgia O'Keeffe Museum and I wanted to visit the Ghost Ranch, where she lived and painted, about two hours north of Santa Fe. Approaching the ranch the landscape began to imitate her work, I started to see the surroundings through her eyes. Where the first settlers saw hardship and emptiness, O'Keeffe saw an alternative beauty. The rust-red geology, jagged cliff forms and desert-animal skeletons of coyote and rattlesnake became her chief inspiration. Towards the end of her life she moved off the Ghost Ranch and some miles away, to Abiquiu, into a house that stands alone on a ridge above the road. Uninvited visitors are not welcome and when I visited the house was shuttered and padlocked. It is a long, narrow adobe building clinging to the rim of a cliff. Just behind it, three stark and brutal wooden crosses, tall as trees, have been erected and beyond them, hidden in the scrub, is a meeting house of the Penitential Brotherhood.

In 1820, after the Mexican Declaration of Independence from

Spain, the Franciscan missionaries lost their influence and for a second time withdrew. The secular priests who succeeded them were not impressive replacements; many were ignorant, greedy and corrupt. The Indians could respond by withdrawing into their original faith, but this was not possible for the Mexicans, the children of Spain, who had only their Christianity to sustain them and no adequate priests as ministers. Instead they developed a sub-denomination of their own. Known as *Los Hermanos Penitentes*, the Penitential Brotherhood, it was a secret religious society that mingled Catholic practices with magic and witchcraft. It still exists and today it is strongest in the mountainous regions of north-central New Mexico and southern Colorado. The Brothers habitually built their meeting houses, known as *moradas*, in remote places.

The Brothers do not use the road to reach the meeting house at Abiquiu. There are foot trails winding through the bush towards it from the far side of the dried-up river bed. Inside the *morada* is the meeting room and a chapel. The ritual tools – a flute, a rattle, flints for cutting the skin and a whip for self-scourging – are locked away with a tub for washing penitents' wounds. Poking around behind the house I found two great timber *maderos* leaning against a rail, the huge penitential crosses that are carried on Good Friday during the re-enactment of the procession to Calvary. This ceremony culminates in the crucifixion of the penitent who has dragged the *madero* for some miles. Ropes bind the penitent to the cross, but nails are also used, and death may result from the rites. There is no water and no sign of life on top of the *mesa* among the thorns. But the place is rarely silent, the winds – 'the terrible winds' as O'Keeffe called them – still rattle through the brush, day and night. And the sense of an overwhelming desolation that marks much of the artist's work is never far away.

The Brothers have been and still are the subject of many lurid tales. But Marta Weigle, who investigated the Penitentes of the Southwest, concluded that they were chiefly religious men who were determined to keep part of their Spanish heritage alive, and that their order had played an important role in regulating and enriching Hispanic village life. Where the Brotherhood was in decline 'village life . . . was marked by vandalism, factionalism and conflicts between families'. There are many points in the Brothers' practice that recall the traditional Catholicism of Spain. When they are undergoing penance they wear hoods. They enjoy a close acquaintance with the saints – whom they treat as family members, even to the point of locking images of unhelpful saints into a trunk until they have been reminded of their duties. They reproduce the wounds of Christ in images, and they are devoted to the scourge. They do this in secret because the modern Catholic hierarchy, which has no link with Spanish tradition, has sometimes attempted to ban their practices. I was reassured by Marta Weigle's research until the morning, standing by a road bridge over the river, I was approached by a friendly janitor who said he lived in a village above Taos. The name seemed familiar so I asked whether there were many Penitentes over there. 'Oh no, señor,' he replied, 'not in my village.' Then he moved off rather quickly.

Continuing on the road north towards Taos, we crossed the Rio Grande and pulled up by a log bridge, suspended on rusted iron cables. Down by the water there was a sandy bank covered in tall grass, cacti and thorn bushes. Puny black cattle were picking their way across the sand. Scattered between the cacti were the remains of somebody's feast, Vienna sausage tins, polystyrene cups and Slush Puppie soft-drink containers. There were the embers of a fire. On a granite boulder written in glowing white letters were the words 'The Wrath of God is coming, Jesus is Lord' – belief lying in silent ambush amid the garbage.

We reached the border of the land of too much food at a railway junction called Antonito, which is about twelve miles north of the Colorado state line. Here, set up in a wooden cabin, was a solitary truckers' diner that served the world's most challenging chicken enchiladas. Not even the cold beer could wash out the taste. Beside the road across the grasslands to Tres Piedras, Route 64, we had passed scattered groups of people living in abandoned yellow school buses. It was hard to tell which buses they were living in and which ones they were breaking up for the metal. From a distance the little circle of vehicles out on the plains looked like horse wagons drawn up together against savage Indians. A hippie veteran in a rusting camper van had driven up to the Rio Grande Gorge Bridge to sell his white metal trinkets to the few travellers who were looking down onto the river, 660 feet below. Having made a few sales he started to pack up. 'That's it folks . . . heading back now . . . my turn to clean house!' Then he started cackling at some private joke. His bracelets and necklaces polished up well, but were more likely to have been made from carburettor wire and hubcaps than Taos silver; the school-bus people were eating their own homes.

On either side of the gorge the flaky, stony ground seemed to stretch for hundreds of miles. Out on the plains there was just the continuous wind and the rim of the road, the fence and the power line cutting straight through the grey sagebrush. The land was fenced off to stop people squatting on it, but entrances cut through the wire appeared at intervals. We drove through one of these gaps to reach a railroad wagon parked amid disused farm machinery. There was a nailed-on porch and a wire screen door banging open and shut. A dog started to bark and eventually a man appeared at the door. Asked if he would like to speak to us he said he would not. We were interrupting the television news. 'I'd appreciate it if you would get your truck off my drive and I'd advise you to be careful. There's a lot of touchy people out here. That's why they're out here.'

The next entrance we tried, a couple of miles further on, led to the cabin of Carlos and Patty, who were entertaining Murray, a Vietnam vet. We said we would like to make his acquaintance and Murray said he was drinking beer and that was fine by him. He was enjoying life 'off the grid'.

'One thing is we have wind here, y'see. We get ninety to one hundred mile-an-hour wind. Last night I lost my TV antenna and my horse got scared and jumped the fence.' Murray's horse, a palomino, had been recovered and was standing nearby, tied to a pick-up. Patty said, 'That horse is valuable. It has papers.' She explained that the land around them was common property and that the roadside fences should never have been erected. 'This is still open range – you could ride all the way to that mountain over there and not hit a fence.' She said that she had electric light, water from a borehole, a refrigerator and the sun paid for it all. 'Twelve-volt solar panels. We don't depend on nobody. We don't hardly pay taxes. In the city people are always paying bills. They can keep the city. All of us out here is off the grid.'

Carlos said that he had Navajo and Jicarilla Apache blood in the family and invited us in for a beer. He said that his grandfather had been a German prisoner-of-war 'who got Grandma pregnant', but that originally they had been Vascos from Spain. He wore a broad-brim hat with an eagle feather stuck in the ribbon, Indian-style. There was a woollen bobble cap hanging on a stick beside his chair and, after opening another beer, he removed the cap to reveal that the 'stick' was a double-barrel shotgun.

Murray had another friend, John, who was camera-shy – he described cameras as 'odious and obnoxious' – but who eventually confided that he had 'put the thrust of his entire life, everything he had', into planting trees. He had planted over a million of the damn things, coast to coast . . . He offered us a beer and said, 'You guys were lucky it was Patty you called on. You could have knocked on the wrong door. Life gets pretty *intense* round here, a lot of violence.' When we left Patty's place after several more beers the wind had got up again, the palomino had once again taken fright and taken off and the last we saw of Murray he was running for his pick-up shouting, 'Where's my horse?' When we next heard from Patty, five months had passed and we were crossing the Congo River in a dugout canoe. 'Still waiting for my box of Belgian beer,' was the message she texted.

*

Just outside the diner at Antonito we crossed the tracks of the Denver and Rio Grande Western Railroad running north, stretching up the spine of the continent. A 1940s steam locomotive was parked on some broken rails as a museum piece. The tracks running west were heading towards the Toltec Gorge; a notice urged tourists to ride a scenic railroad that would enable them to relive the heroic myth of the West.

There was a young man in the diner who was not a tourist and who was trying to make it with an older woman who was paying for his beer. He was drunk, she wasn't. He was telling her about the place he had, and suggested they should go there. She said that she had heard he lived in what was more or less a wooden box. He somehow managed to smile and then said yes, but if she came with him he could find somewhere better. So she ordered two more beers. Her car was parked outside the wood-cabin diner. Beside it was the steam locomotive on the broken rails, a memento of the iron road that cut through the buffalo-migration trail and carried the hunters with repeating rifles who wiped out the herds. And there was the thin sunshine and the bitter wind, and the empty grasslands stretching south as far as the eye could see; the black hole at the centre of an imperial explosion, a landscape without life or purpose, a place where idealism ran out of territory and destiny became manifest. Off the grid.

CHAPTER SEVEN

Snake Dance: Lightning and Rain

'The nature of reality is intolerable for as long as it is devoid of any spiritual or metaphysical dimension.'

David Gascoyne

The descendants of the people who once lived in Frijoles Canyon now live in the San Ildefonso pueblo, which is on the banks of the Rio Grande, just below the Los Alamos Plateau. In 1895 it was one of the first settlements that Aby Warburg visited. Driving north from Santa Fe the land on either side of the road seems to empty out. The river is an occasional presence snaking over the boulders as the hills close in. The road starts to climb and you have the feeling that you are driving back through time. There are no towns, no fields and no houses. If men once lived in this landscape, their lives would have been brutally different. This is stony ground, unsuitable for crops or ranching. The sun over the high desert of the Southwest casts no ground shadow; this – according to an air-force veteran I encountered in Albuquerque – makes the region suitable for training military pilots preparing for Afghanistan.

The entrance to San Ildefonso lies off State Road 502. To the far side of the pueblo the view north is dominated by Black Mesa, a sinister-looking rock table. In 1694, after the Great Pueblo Revolt, when the Spaniards returned in force, they attacked San Ildefonso and the people fled to Black Mesa. There they were eventually crushed. Today it is holy ground and off-limits to visitors. The centre of the pueblo is a sacred plaza that is marked by 'Big Tree', a cotton-wood that Warburg photographed; it was here that he first saw an Indian dance.

During our tour of San Ildefonso the settlement remained closed. There were no children outside the school, and the museum was locked. We saw only two men, who were tending graves in the church-yard. They turned their backs as we approached. The cemetery, too, is off-limits, the graves cannot be photographed and the inscriptions face away from the visitors' footpath. For the Pueblo Indians of New Mexico, control of their Catholic buildings has finally been won after a struggle lasting hundreds of years. They accept the new religion, but strictly on their own terms. Even the parish priest has to negotiate his right to enter the church. The little whitewashed chapel surmounted by a dome and a cross has become an overground *kiva*.

Visitors to the Tewa-speaking pueblo of San Ildefonso are handed a welcome leaflet which is issued by 'the governor, tribal council and people of the Pueblo'. The title of Governor was conferred by the King of Spain in 1620 and has never been replaced. The leaflet shows a clearly marked trail which visitors are strictly forbidden to leave and advises everyone to

Stay off the Plaza; No Tripods Allowed; Close snapshots of the *kivas* are Prohibited; May you have an enjoyable visit; Do Not Wander; Individuals taking photos without permits will have their cameras confiscated by the Tribal Police; Do Not Enter the Church; To Avoid an Embarrassing Situation . . .

and so on. The leaflet made no mention of the fact that within the pueblo, US law does not usually run. The tribal police apply a mixture of customary law and local habits. But the young lady working in the Visitors' Center who handed me this leaflet was charm itself. She said that the Los Alamos National Laboratory had recently returned 4,000 acres to San Ildefonso. I asked whether they had decontaminated the land first.

She laughed and said, 'As much as it ever will be.' That was a rare moment of contact. The chief's initial enthusiasm about the arrival of a film crew bearing sacks of gold had cooled when our American executive producer, Steve Westheimer, explained that we were just 'five guys from Belgium in one van'.

While Aby Warburg was in San Ildefonso he was able to watch and photograph the Antelope Dance, which the people dance even now on the pueblo's feast day, 23 January. 'When I first saw the antelope dance,' he wrote, 'it struck me as quite harmless and almost comical.' He added that there was no moment more dangerous for the student of human culture than when he is moved to laugh at popular practices. 'To laugh at the comical element in ethnology is wrong, because it instantly shuts off insight into the tragic element.' He concluded that the pantomime animal dance was an act of sincere devotion to an alien creature that the Indian considered to be a higher being, a far more gifted creature than man. 'For the Indian the antelope *is* speed, the bear *is* strength. Men can only *do* in part what the animal *is*, totally.' The pagan Indians demonstrated a reverential awe towards animals, which they regarded as the mythical ancestors of their own tribes. For Warburg, this was 'an attitude not so far removed from Darwinism'.

After visiting San Ildefonso, Warburg interrupted his study of the pueblo Indians and took the train to California. Then in March 1896 he returned to New Mexico and attended Mass in a church in Acoma pueblo at the request of the priest, who was acting as his guide. He noticed, to his amusement, that this priest, Père Juillard, a follower of the French missionary bishop, Jean Lamy, was treated with reverence by his parishioners, but also robbed by them, and that his flock had to be ordered into church by their governor. Père Juillard spoke not a word of Keresan and so 'had to employ an interpreter who translated the Mass sentence by sentence'. Warburg added drily that the interpreter 'may well have said whatever he pleased'. He did not mention, and may not have been aware, that Acoma was the pueblo where the Indians sometimes claim to have tossed two Spanish priests over a 300-foot cliff, saying that since they believed in angels they should be able to fly.

After leaving Acoma, Warburg crossed into Arizona, where he photographed the Corn Dance of the Hopi Indians and was permitted to enter the ceremonial *kiva* in Oraibi; and it was here that he discovered as much as he could about the Snake Dance. This dance became the central discovery of Warburg's journey, and although he never saw it he later described it at length.

The most pagan of all the Indian ceremonies is the snake dance of the Hopi Indians. The remote villages of Oraibi and Walpi, which were three days' journey from the railway, still sheltered this most extreme statement of the desire for a unity with nature via the animal world.

Here the dancers do not just simulate the animal as in the antelope dance. In the snake dance the dancers and the live animals form a magical collaboration, and the chosen animal is the most dangerous of all, the rattlesnake.

The snakes are caught in the desert in August when storms are imminent and when the crops must have rain or die. Then they are tended in the *kiva* for 16 days by the chiefs of the serpent clan. During this time the snakes, about 100 of them, are washed ceremoniously. Then drawings are made on the sand floors of the *kiva*, depicting clouds and lightning, and onto these drawings the snakes are hurled with great force in a gesture intended to induce rain.

On the final day of the ceremony the snakes are taken out of the *kiva* and enclosed within a bush. A dancer then takes one of the snakes and places its body in his mouth. For half an hour the dancer who wears a fox skin cape and is covered in tattoos, carries the snake while the dance continues to the sound of rattles worn by the Indians. Then the snakes are carried out into the desert by swift runners, and released, as messengers to the souls of the dead.

Since the Indians believe that the good ancestors live in the clouds, the snakes can then return from the clouds in the form of lightning and produce rain.

In April Warburg organised an experiment with the assistance of Hopi schoolchildren and their teacher. He told them a story from *Struwwelpeter*, 'Little Johnny Head-in-the-Air', then the Hopi children were asked to illustrate the terrible storm in the story.

Of the fourteen children in the class, twelve drew the storm lightning 'realistically', with zigzag lines, but two who were less 'Americanised' drew the Hopi symbol of lightning, the serpent with the forked, arrow-head tongue. For Warburg the use of this symbol showed that the children were failing to distinguish between the signifier (the serpent) and the signified (lightning). The resemblance between the serpent's darting forked tongue and the lightning flash in the sky that betokened a storm, and therefore water, had led the Indians to adopt the serpent as the symbol of water – the natural element that was essential to their own survival in 1895, just as it had been 10,000 years earlier. The fact that two of the Hopi children were still using the symbol of lightning as an illustration of the storm, rather than drawing the lightning itself, indicated to Warburg that the Hopi mind was adopting modern rationality, but had not yet lost touch with the primitive. For Warburg this development was of great significance. He considered that the progression in the production of religious and aesthetic images from pagan antiquity to the art of fifteenth-century Florence showed 'an increasing psychological distance' between human and divine. The greater the ability to separate symbol (serpent) from reality (zigzags) the more modern the mind, and the greater the distance 'of the human imagination from the divine'. He believed that this separation constituted a grave threat to the survival of civilisation.

Warburg later developed his argument by referring to 'the geographic constant . . . that is the scarcity of water'. Drought teaches magic and prayer. Among the Hopi's magical practices were the masked dances that were not festive additions to everyday life but an assistance in the struggle for food. The Indian was an efficient tiller and hunter, but to technology he added magic; by mimicking what he desired he believed that he would improve his chances of obtaining it. This was 'applied magic'. Warburg linked these practices with contemporary European harvest customs, some of which were in themselves a survival from Greek paganism.

Unlike other observers, Warburg understood that the Snake Dance of the Hopi Indians was not a circus turn, but a powerful example of 'the projecting cause'. Lightning preceded rain, lightning furnished rain, so for the Hopi it was the most important force in nature. Since the Indian's survival depended on rain he naturally sought control over the cause of rain, control over lightning. The rattlesnake could kill with one bite, so it was powerful. If the Indian could control the snake he could project the snake beyond its form into its twin image and control the lightning. 'Two thousand years ago,' Warburg noted, 'in the very cradle of our own European culture, in Greece, cultic habits were in vogue which in crudeness and perversity far surpass what we have seen among the Indians.' In the cult of Dionysus, the maenads danced with snakes in their hands and woven into their hair. At the height of their frenzy an animal would be sacrificed in honour of the god. For the ancients the serpent was the spirit of evil and of temptation. When the gods sent a punishment, they sent a serpent. The supreme image of the serpent as a destroying force was in the story of Laocoön, immortalised in sculpture, when the priest and his two sons were strangled by the destroying force from the underworld.

For Warburg the Hopi's Snake Dance was both an act of primitive magic and a quest for enlightenment. It was an attempt to master electricity. In linking drought, rain, lightning and the symbol of the serpent, the Indian, 'primitive man', was sketching the image of a structured universe – which contained the germ of science.

*

Years later, looking back on his adventures, Warburg wrote that he had found it extraordinary, as a cultural historian, that 'in the midst of a country that had made technological culture into an admirable precision weapon in the hands of intellectual man, an enclave of primitive pagan humanity was able to maintain itself and engage in hunting and agriculture with an unshakeable adherence to magical practices'. It was no less extraordinary that, only ten years after the high desert of the Southwest ceased being used as a killing ground, an art historian from Florence should have chosen to travel through it seeking the roots of Western civilisation by studying the ritual practices of the American Indians.

In May 1896, with his research completed, Aby Warburg checked out of the Palace Hotel in Santa Fe, took the horse-trap back to the railroad station at Lamy and boarded the train to Denver. Within a month he had returned to his peaceful study in Florence, and his work on the Quattrocento, and he never set foot in America again. He arranged the records of his journey and wrote one brief description of his travels among the Pueblo Indians. But he did not immediately develop his first impressions and insights into any sort of theory. It would be over twenty-five years before Warburg realised the full significance of his discoveries in the Southwest, and when he did so it would save his sanity, and possibly his life.

Aby Warburg lived for the past and he may have failed to notice that the country he was visiting was in a state of political transformation. Over ten years, in the 1890s, the United States changed its identity and purpose just as a snake changes its skin.

In 1890, year of Wounded Knee, the US Census Bureau announced that there was no longer a land frontier between the East and West Coasts of the Union. In the same year the influential military philosopher, naval Captain Alfred Mahan, argued forcefully that 'Americans must now begin to look outward.' Congress promptly voted funds for the construction of a modern, offensive navy.

Warburg's 'admirable precision weapon' was swiftly re-sighted.

The men of the 7th Cavalry, who had won eighteen Congressional Medals of Honor at Wounded Knee, now gave way to the US Marines. The American population had increased by 50 per cent in the previous decade and the pacified continent was no longer enough. In the words of one rabble-rousing senator, 'We are a conquering race. We must obey our blood and occupy new markets and new lands.' God wanted this. 'In the Almighty's infinite plan debased civilisations and decaying races will give way before nobler and more virile types of man.'

The 'debased civilisation' in question was Spain, which was clinging to the remains of a seventeenth-century empire in the Caribbean and the Pacific, and which now became the chosen target of the United States. The long-standing internal political argument between expansionists and isolationists was settled in favour of the former, and the Republic abandoned its founding ideals of the just nation that ruled by consent of its people, shunned conquest and set the example of a better future for the world.

In April 1898, the United States declared war on Spain and on the pretext of assisting native independence movements, invaded both Cuba and the Philippines. By July, Spain was defeated. The Spanish were driven out of Cuba, which was granted nominal independence, while Puerto Rico was simply annexed. But the most brutal expansion took place in the Pacific.

In 1895 Japan defeated China in a brisk little war, leading Kaiser Wilhelm II of Germany to coin the phrase 'Yellow Peril'. The Japanese victory over its giant neighbour caused alarm in Washington and there were calls for the annexation of Hawaii, which was reported to be 'filling up' with Japanese immigrants.* In July 1898, Hawaii was duly annexed, on the general justification of 'protecting US interests'. President McKinley added a further justification, with the old slogan of 'Manifest Destiny'. The question then arose of what to do with the Philippines, where the native independence movement was

---

* In 1887 the United States had acquired a coaling station on the island. They called it Pearl Harbor.

confidently expecting Washington's blessing for the islands' future as a sovereign state. This hope was disappointed: the American imperialist tendency was by now unstoppable. The Philippines too was annexed against payment of $40m to Spain. President McKinley agonised over the decision and spent much time in prayer. Captain Mahan, who was strongly influenced by 'social Darwinism' – the doctrine of survival of the fittest – made up the President's mind for him with the triumphant invocation *Deus Vult* – 'God Wills It' – battle-cry of the Crusaders.

In 1899 the Filipinos rose in outraged protest and the US Marines spearheaded an invasion of 75,000 troops. The tactics favoured by the American generals were as ferocious as those that had been honed on the Great Plains by the US Cavalry, and atrocities were soon the order of the day. 'I wish you to burn and kill,' said marine commander, Brigadier Jake 'Hell-Roaring' Smith. 'The more you burn and kill, the better it will please me.' And the order was obeyed. A soon-to-be familiar arithmetic was introduced. For every dead American sentry a village was destroyed and its people put to death. Entire communities were surrounded and wiped out. Dumdum bullets, happily not yet banned by the Hague peace conference, were issued, and 'water torture' – simulated drowning – was introduced to extract information. Senior officers gave orders to take no prisoners and junior officers arranged summary executions. The struggle lasted for ten years: and during this time a spokesman in Washington said, 'We intend to stay in the Philippines indefinitely in working out this good that we propose to do them.' The philosopher William James – who was one of the leaders, with Mark Twain, of the anti-imperial cause – said, 'We are crushing the most sacred thing in the world . . . a people's attempt to attain freedom.' By the end of it America had acquired 100,000 additional square miles. A mission had been accomplished, new markets gained, and the great experiment of liberty extended across the world's greatest ocean. In the Pacific, as in New Mexico, the United States had become the new Spain.

*

The road to Taos, north out of Santa Fe, passes the entrance to the national military cemetery, 78 acres of neatly tended lawn with 40,000 white gravestones lined up in silent parade. Once, waiting in traffic by the cemetery gates, I read a bumper sticker on the beaten-up Chevrolet ahead – 'We're making enemies faster than we can kill them.'

PART III

THE GATHERING STORM

PART III

THE GATHERING STORM

CHAPTER EIGHT

Warburg at War

*'The 1914–18 War had confronted me with the devastating truth that
unchained, elemental man is the unconquerable ruler of this world.'*

Aby Warburg

'Elemental: devouring, seething, incandescent.' (Dict.)

The three men whose lives or work form this story never met.
The closest they came to meeting was in 1921 when all three
made journeys across Europe along transecting paths. None of these
journeys ended well.

In January, Joseph Conrad, who was both celebrated and hard-
pressed for money, left his house near Canterbury and boarded the
cross-Channel ferry to France. He was travelling with his son, Borys,
who had survived being blown up, gassed and buried alive while fighting
with the British Second Army near Cambrai in 1918, one month before
the Armistice. Borys seemed to be the ideal guide for his father's
battlefield tour but Conrad did not enjoy the experience; he found his
son's descriptions of the fighting to be far too vivid. Joseph Conrad
then continued his journey to Marseilles, where he had once tried to
commit suicide as a young man, and then to Corsica, where the mountains 'got on his nerves' and he found the hotels 'detestable'. He died
of a heart attack, having declined a knighthood, three years later.

Also in 1921, Julius Robert Oppenheimer, a young American,

who had just finished school and was waiting to go to university, sailed up the English Channel in a transatlantic liner out of New York and bound for Hamburg. From Hamburg he and his parents travelled to Frankfurt to stay with his father's German family, and then Oppenheimer continued alone to Joachimstahl, in the former Austrian-Hungarian Empire, to prospect for unusual rocks in the uranium mines. He became seriously ill at Joachimstahl, and nearly died from 'trench dysentery'. A year would pass before he recovered his health.

The third traveller was Aby Warburg, who now lived in Hamburg and whose journey was made very much against his wishes. Since the defeat of the German armies in November 1918, Warburg had been confined to a mental hospital near his home. In the summer of 1921, accompanied by his doctor and a nurse, he crossed Germany and travelled by train to Kreuzlingen, in Switzerland. On arrival at Kreuzlingen he was diagnosed as an incurable schizophrenic and once again locked up in an asylum.

When Aby Warburg had returned to Europe from New Mexico in 1896, he had given a short illustrated lecture to the Photographic Society in Hamburg, after which he published no more about the journey he regarded as primarily of importance for his research into Renaissance psychology. In 1897 he married Mary Hertz, the daughter of a Protestant ship-owner. The marriage shocked the Warburg clan. Aby's father offered to double his allowance if he would abandon such a betrayal of Judaism. Aby declined this offer and furthermore refused to promise to have any future sons circumcised. Following their marriage Aby and Mary settled in Florence. Although he had quarrelled with his family he remained financially dependent on their generosity because he failed to take up any academic appointments. He and Mary had three children and he started to assemble an enormous library of books on dozens of different subjects, in all of which he was driven to find unsuspected connections. A biographer of the Warburg family records that as an interdisciplinary pioneer, an ethnologist, social historian, psychologist and art historian, Warburg mocked the keepers of academic purity as 'border police'.

By 1904 Aby's library had grown too big for his apartment in Florence and he returned to Hamburg to find a suitable building to house it. It was during the decade preceding the First World War that he developed his extraordinary personality – explosive, meticulous, obsessive, absent-minded, occasionally psychic, unstable and increasingly paranoid. He was a brilliant, dominating and impractical man who demanded total devotion from his wife, his brothers and his colleagues. And he had found his life's work: his library. When offered an appointment by the University of Bonn, with residence in Florence, he took so long thinking about it that the university lost patience. He refused to do anything at short notice, and usually declined to finish his books. 'If more books were read,' he would say, 'then fewer would be written.' As a scholar he set his own standards. In 1909 he purchased 1,500 books on astrology, which he saw as the pre-scientific study of the universe and as humanity's recognition of its ultimate helplessness when faced with the cosmos. But what distinguished Warburg's thought was his determination to connect human origins with his own times. The idea that a custom or a technique that had been superseded became redundant, would have been anathema to Warburg.

After he left Florence to return to Hamburg, Warburg started to work on a new line of research: the Flemish influence on the Italian masters of the Quattrocento, exercised through patronage. From this he reached the conclusion that Germany and Italy were the cradles of modern civilisation and that other nations, in particular the Anglo Saxons, were barbaric. At the same time he became increasingly estranged from Judaism. All this meant that when war broke out in 1914 he found himself as the least integrated member of a Jewish family whose livelihood was drawn from a German-American bank. Furthermore the coming of war meant that he had to shelve plans to expand his library, which was in any case paid for with the family's

American dollars. He also felt intensely patriotic, which was one reaction that he did share with the majority of German Jews.*

The pre-eminence of German scholarship and science at the beginning of the twentieth century was the fruit of the *gymnasium* system of a broad education. It produced the concept of *Wissenschaft*, the systematic organisation of knowledge. It also fuelled German nationalism. In the unified German state created by Otto von Bismarck, industrial growth, scientific research and military authority marched in disciplined step. By the time he was dismissed by the new Kaiser in 1888, Bismarck had created the most powerful nation in Europe.

But despite Germany's power, its emperor had no empire. The most powerful nation in the world was Great Britain. And even France, which Prussia had humiliated in 1871, possessed an extensive colonial empire. In 1881 – ten years after the Prussian army marched into Paris and France was forced to cede Alsace and Lorraine – French troops invaded Tunisia and declared it to be a protectorate. Subsequently France seized territory in West Africa, Madagascar and Morocco. This imperial expansion had British support, and in 1890 Britain and France signed an agreement on 'spheres of influence' in Africa. When Germany protested and tried to challenge French influence in Morocco in 1905 and 1911, Britain steadily supported France. Germany's demands for 'a place in the sun' were generally ignored. The sole German success had been the Berlin Conference, summoned by Bismarck in 1884, which had led to international recognition for Leopold II's claims to the Congo. Subsequently, British and French colonial expansion in Africa thwarted German imperialism and made the German leadership even more determined to mount a bid for world power.

In 1892 the German general staff were presented with what became known as the Schlieffen Plan, the secret blueprint for the next

---

* From a total population of 500,000, 100,000 Jewish men volunteered for the German armed forces during the 1914–18 war. Two thousand were commissioned as officers, 12,000 were killed and 30,000 were decorated.

invasion of France. The plan hinged on an undeclared act of war against a neutral country, Belgium, and was adopted in 1905 and successfully put into operation in 1914, twenty-two years after it had been drawn up. German nationalism and imperialism enjoyed popular support. In 1898, Admiral Tirpitz founded the Navy League, a body that lobbied for a naval arms race, and the Pan-German League preached the unification of all German-speaking peoples. But there was another face to Germany, that of a peaceful, industrious and scholarly people, a civilised society dominated by philosophers, classicists and historians. This was the Germany of Aby Warburg, the country that led the world in physiology, biochemistry and medical research. It was governed by the 'aristocracy of the mind'. Then it was swept aside.

Warburg was appalled by the coming of war but desperate for Germany, the defender of civilisation, to defeat the barbarian hordes. He was ill – he suffered from diabetes – and he was too old to fight so he offered to intervene in Italy, where he was very well known, to urge his adopted country to join the German alliance. Warburg went on two diplomatic missions for this purpose, the second in January 1915. Shortly afterwards the Italian government joined the Anglo-French allies and it is a sign of the extent to which Aby Warburg was already losing mental control that he immediately spoke of the personal efforts he would make to 'annihilate' his beloved Italy.

As the war continued and the slaughter grew worse, Warburg became frantic with anxiety. Watching the systematic destruction of a culture he said, 'We are feeding the furnace with pianos.' Day by day, the values of the war destroyed everything in which he believed, every argument he had put forward, every mast to which his colours were nailed. Unable to enrich his library, he started an alternative life as a newspaper archivist, reading, clipping and filing over twenty newspapers every day in order to record the progress of events. His three children and his wife were all put to work, and he told everyone that he was compiling the 'Handbook of Lies' which would expose the role of the press in creating and prolonging the conflict. Italy, the cultural leader of his world, had become 'this bordello' which 'must disappear'.

The Handbook of Lies was always myopic: only slurs against German conduct were recorded as lies; allegations against Allied troops were treated as verified facts. When America eventually entered the war against Germany in the spring of 1917, the contradictions in Warburg's position destroyed his sanity. As a German patriot, he was now engaged in a war against two of his own brothers. When he thought of Washington, he no longer thought of the Smithsonian. The world war had become a civil war within a family, a conflict that engaged his Jewish identity, his love of the Fatherland, his devotion to his brothers. His obsession with press clippings became irrational.

The arrival of American troops in France in June 1917 was preceded by the mutiny of French frontline troops in May, and was followed by the German peace treaty with the Bolsheviks on the Eastern Front in March 1918. That was followed by the final German offensive on the Western Front that lasted from May to July, which in turn led to the Allied counter-attack and the German retreat that started in September and concluded in the Armistice on 11 November. Warburg watched this switchback in despair. Initially he had been convinced that Germany's cultural superiority would guarantee its victory. But his real fear and hatred had been directed against the conflict itself rather than against the enemy. In 1915, disbelieving rumours of an early peace, he had written, 'The unchained beast must first drink up more blood.'

Since his childhood Warburg had needed a strong intellectual and moral framework to shelter his emotional fragility. That may have explained his original attraction to classicism, and his interest in tracing the enduring influence of classicism over 2,000 years on the civilisation of the Quattrocento. The degradation of war destroyed Warburg's moral framework; it was as though his mind had become infested by the nightmare imaginary world of artists such as George Grosz. His obsessive concern with his archive was the sole means remaining to him to keep some hope alive. It became his contribution to the war effort, a justification for the actions his country was forced to take, the raw material needed for the reckoning that would follow, a reassurance that victory lay ahead. His son said that living with him at this time was 'like living on the edge of a volcano'. The war had entered Aby Warburg's world, his library, his house and his soul. Otto Dix's celebrated portrait of the psychiatrist Dr Heinrich Stadelmann, made in 1922, with formal suit, wing collar, manicured nails and bulging, haunted eyes, vividly represented the internal mirror-image of the art historian Dr Aby Warburg.

In 1915 George Grosz made a drawing of a street scene in which a running crowd was being destroyed by an explosion. He called it *Fliegerbombe*, 'Flying Bomb', or 'Aerial Attack', a form of atrocity that had at that stage been inflicted only by Germany on English targets. In October 1915, five Zeppelins bombed London, killing seventy-one. Warburg was visited by Grosz's nightmare. Although no German city was bombed from the air during the Great War, Warburg made drawings for futuristic machines that would harness electricity to destroy the aerial balloons that had been erected over London as a defence against the Zeppelins. This suggests that part of his mental anguish was caused by his realisation that the war was no longer a crusade, a struggle between the German champions of civilisation and the Anglo-American barbarians from the north. Aware of the harm inflicted on Londoners, Warburg imagined the victims' revenge. Fearing an Anglo-French aerial attack on Hamburg he drew up plans for an elaborate system of defence that included air-raid shelters. Despite the partisan editing of his wartime archive he was aware of the comprehensive nature of the horror. But he associated barbarity with the enemy's guns, and conjugated it as Lewis, Browning and Vickers – ignoring the alternative litany of Walther, Mauser and Krupp. The latest guns were mobile and fired fast. Rubber and copper, the wealth of Africa, had been put to military use by German chemical engineers, who led the world. And there was gas.

*

In 1899 Germany and its eventual enemies had signed the Hague agreement to avoid the use of 'asphyxiating gas' in time of war. But on 22 April 1915, only nine months after the outbreak of war, German engineers opened the taps of gas cylinders at Ypres and flooded the British and Belgian trenches with chlorine gas.* It was a night attack and 15,000 Allied casualties were afflicted by the air that choked and burned. Five thousand men died. One of the German engineers who installed the cylinders was called Otto Hahn.

Lieutenant Hahn was a chemist. He worked under Captain Haber who was setting up a special unit for gas warfare. When Otto Hahn mentioned the Hague Convention, Fritz Haber said that the French had already broken it by using tear gas in rifle bullets. (This was untrue.) Captain Haber claimed that gas would break the deadlock of trench warfare on the Western Front and would, in the end, save many thousands of lives. Before long Haber and Hahn were joined by two more physicists, James Franck and Gustav Hertz. Later in their lives, all four scientists would win the Nobel Prize, though not for their work on poison gas.

In the war years, Haber, Hahn, Franck and Hertz developed several new and improved forms of gas. *Klop* was an ingenious mixture of chlorine and phosgene – acid and bleach – and was cheap to produce. Phosgene was a handy little addition: it was ten times as toxic as chlorine alone. These values were worked out in the Kaiser Wilhelm Institute in Berlin. Brilliant men bent over their microscopes and test tubes and retorts and achieved satisfying results. *Klop* got through gas masks and made men vomit, so they raised their masks and then two breaths of the phosgene mixture killed them. In each of these steps the British and French chemists followed their German peers. And in 1917 the Germans released mustard gas. It had little smell, it dissolved rubber and it dissolved the skin. And it blinded you. And it was supposed to save lives by shortening the war.

Clara Haber had a doctorate in chemistry and she was married to

---

* Only one of the German sector commanders who were offered the gas accepted it.

Fritz. She regarded poison gas as a perversion of science and proof of barbarism, and asked her husband to abandon his research. He said that a scientist belongs to the world in peacetime but to his country in wartime. Then he left for the Eastern Front to direct a gas attack. That night Clara Haber killed herself.

The ingenious gases devised in the Kaiser Wilhelm Institute failed to determine the course of the war and in September 1918 the Allies broke through in France and breached the Hindenburg Line. In November, the German High Seas Fleet mutinied. A revolutionary republic was proclaimed in Berlin. The Kaiser fled to Holland and Warburg decided that his family's English governess, who had been living with them throughout the war, was the leader of 'a Lloyd George spy ring'. The barbarian hordes were on their way. They would be coming to Hamburg and to his house. They were going to rape his wife and his daughters. To save his women from this fate he had to shoot them, and then he would shoot himself. Warburg was disarmed before he could use the gun and taken to a sanatorium. But for him the war was not over.

Three years later, in April 1921, Warburg's health showed no improvement and he was transferred from a clinic in Hamburg to Kreuzlingen in Switzerland. The journey did not pass without incident. Warburg was accompanied by his doctor, Professor Berger, his nurse and his valet. At Stuttgart railway station he created such an uproar that he had to be given a strong sedative injection. Professor Berger reported that Warburg had been screaming, telling people that he was the victim of a judicial error, that he was an innocent man and that they were taking him to prison. 'In view of the current political situation,' Professor Berger said, 'I thought it best to quieten him.' He was referring to the state of incipient civil war in post-war Germany. The Treaty of Versailles had been signed and reparation payments had been set at a punitive rate, the German mark was in free fall, there were bloody riots and there were political assassinations provoked by the anti-Semitic forgery, *The Protocols of the Elders of Zion*. Aby's

brother Max, running the bank in Hamburg and an adviser to the
German delegation at Versailles, had a police bodyguard.

Kreuzlingen stands on the banks of the Bodensee, Lake Constance
or *Konstanz*, a lake bordered by three countries. The long, high,
blue-grey line of the Alps provides a common background stretching
to east and west, far out of sight. Around the town the chequered
field patterns of an over-cultivated countryside show that this landscape is fertile, temperate, safe and crowded. In January, between the
low tops of the alpine foothills, there lie thick, white billows of mist.
Viewed from above one can see that the clouds grow thicker as the
ground falls lower, in contradiction to the usual arrangement. Then
a breeze reveals that the thickest clouds are over water. The fields
and orchards have been planted among streams and lakes. They
stood in sharp contrast to the high desert where Warburg had
discovered the Snake Dance. This is a terrain where human effort is
richly and swiftly rewarded, where nature threatens nothing, where
time can be gained, a place where reason and order are easily imposed,
the right place for a psychiatric clinic.

The Heilanstalt Bellevue Sanatorium at Kreuzlingen that
welcomed Aby Warburg in 1921 still exists, although it has been
moved a few miles along the lake shore to the grounds of a former
convent outside the neighbouring town of Münsterlingen. The
patients today enjoy the same view across the lake to the German
shore. On a clear day they may see as far as Friedrichshafen, although
they will no longer see, as Warburg could see, the Zeppelins tethered
near the town above the celebrated Zeppelin factory. The lake is
the source of the Rhine and it would be logical to assume that it
marked the Swiss–German frontier. In fact the German town of
Konstanz stands on both banks of the river and the Swiss border
is half a mile south of the Rhine bridge. Once across the border
Konstanz becomes Kreuzlingen, but the language remains German;
perhaps the trains run a little more punctually and the prices
certainly rise. The other immediate difference is that a lot more
people speak both French and English.

Mental illness is one of the commonest afflictions, but for those who have not – knowingly – experienced it, the popular dread of a mental hospital still prevails. We spent three days filming in the Bellevue and approached it at first in the usual way, slightly apprehensive, peering nervously at the first figures to come into sight. Realisation then came that for most of the time there is no visible difference between patients and staff. In this hospital 400 people are looking after 250 patients. Spread out in spacious grounds on the shore of the lake, the clinic enjoys a relaxed atmosphere that resembles the campus of a small, well-endowed university. There is a sense of reassurance, perhaps linked to the silence of the water, gentle and enveloping. One quickly has the feeling that one could be quite happy here.

One could spend the day in the mist on the shore, watching the great flock of ducks drifting slowly in front of the reeds from left to right, and then from right back to left, some with a head in the water, some with a head under a wing. The lake is mostly flat and still, occasionally a distant steamer passes silently towards the German shore. A slight breeze clears the mist, a blue and white Swiss frontier-guard boat passes, leaving enough wake to move the ducks gently up and down. Most are mallard; there are sheldrake and tufted ducks; there are also a few cormorants, and even a kingfisher. On the shore there are straight poplars and twisted willows and a lawn that runs down to a low wall; beyond there is a five-foot drop onto the stones that line the water's edge. Fifty yards away the figure of a young man, or woman, in a bobble hat sits down on the wall and, motionless, begins to contemplate the water. She, or he, gazes down at the ducks. The ducks gaze back. The surrounding line of poplars and willows keep watch. There is a sense of communion in the stillness which is barely interrupted by the ritual passage of the film crew: alone or in pairs, director and sound, camera and assistant, director and cameraman. Sometimes all five form a group and advance swiftly and with purpose, changing location.

*

'Are you interested in the lake or the institute?' The man who is standing beside me has approached without warning. Which side is he on? Patient or staff? There is no immediate clue. Mad people look just like us. We look just like them.

'The lake.'

'Don't you have lakes like that in your country?'

'Er . . . no.' Unconvinced he leaves as discreetly as he came. Luc, the sound engineer, reappears from behind a building. With his peaked woolen hat and beard, and mildly troubled air, he looks, when he is working, as though he could fit into the category of 'patients who have been given an occupation': to one side the absorbed figure of a man with a mattock who is dragging this tool around the edge of the fresh-ploughed vegetable patch in the former convent garden; to the other side a patient wearing headphones and carrying a boom mike with fur muffle who is walking slowly past a locked ward hoping for a scream.

And then it comes. A long scream, followed by a groan to refill the lungs. And then another long scream. The sequence is repeated. There is a pause and then, from further down the same convent building, an answering scream. Scream groan scream. Scream. Scream groan scream . . . Then a window is slammed shut, the animal noise is once more enclosed, leaving a deeper silence that has somehow become more disturbing. The crew reappear from behind a further building, once more grouped like a *corps de ballet* and moving swiftly, but without the camera and the boom. Must be lunchtime. In the canteen, staff and patients eat together. Goulash, noodles and courgette fritters. No alcohol.

Warburg's behaviour when he entered the clinic at Kreuzlingen was dominated by anxiety and fears of persecution. He thought the staff were stealing from him, that his letters were being intercepted, that his food was being poisoned. He was capable of considerable violence and the noise he made when he was disturbed upset other patients. But he was also capable of lucid intervals, particularly with visitors or people he met by chance. When people visited Warburg, by appointment, they would hear the most appalling screams coming from the locked building in which he was kept. Soon afterwards he would emerge from the building and walk with them in the grounds, in an apparently rational state of mind. He would be considerate and amusing, and then he would ask them if they had heard a lion roaring as they approached. 'That was me,' he would say. Or walking and conversing with his wife Mary and a friend he would point to a lighted window in the hospital building and tell the visitor, without any change in manner, 'That is the room where they lock Mary up and torture her.' He slipped in and out of reality without warning. He was treated with sedatives and hot baths (believed to be soothing). But in view of the diagnosis this treatment must have been regarded as a holding action, a means of delaying the inevitable.

Filming inside the buildings, closer to those who are ill, the original foreboding returns. The sense of tranquillity is replaced by a sense of enclosure. The great wooden swing doors swish together behind us, the clinic's assistant director unlocks the door ahead, and then locks us in. There is a distant noise of raised voices from within the wards, and one waits for the screaming to start. But nothing happens. In a quiet room with a view of the lake there are two beds, a writing table, a little family picture album and a bedside Christmas tree. One of the patients, an elderly gentleman, has been selected to walk down the corridor away from the camera and turn the corner. He has been handpicked by his nurse as the man most capable of carrying out this mission. 'Walk to the end and turn to the left. Keep going.' For the rehearsal he uses the handrail, but this proves to be too distracting and after eleven metres he comes to a halt, forgetting to turn. For the performance, he is on a zimmer frame. He plugs along, turns left and continues. 'Impeccable, Herr Müller,' says his nurse.

Released once more into the vegetable garden we are plunged back into the spirit of reassurance. It is as though the Swiss medical service has learnt how to bottle a powerful sedative and diffuse it into the atmosphere. The director decides to film the man with a mattock, who is still picking away at the edge of the ploughed field. Voices drift across through the mist. 'Can we just leave all the stuff here, the car's unlocked?' 'Of course, we are in Switzerland.' 'Yes, but we are inside a mental hospital.' Then another voice, the director's. 'I want it to look something like . . . death.' I look around and realise that I personally have rarely felt so much at home. There is a familiar look to the place, a lack of unfamiliarity in the setting. The convent buildings seem appropriate. One feels welcome, unthreatened, almost institutionalised, as in a monastery. Perhaps a monastery is simply an unlicensed mental asylum. There is a sudden banging noise as a boy and a girl burst through the exit doors of 'Haus K' and engage in a sort of dancing confrontation or embrace on the steps. An escape bid? One of them must be a nurse. Drawing closer it becomes clear that they are both about fifteen. She has a blonde ponytail and a love bite on her neck. The pair push back through the doors as abruptly as they arrived, releasing a beat of rhythmic music. Haus K is the drug house, for addicts.

It was Warburg's family who, seeing no improvement after he had been at Kreuzlingen for two years, suggested that he should be examined by Geheimrat Emil Kraepelin, the leading psychiatrist of the age, today regarded as one of the founders of the modern science. Warburg was not pleased by the visit of the distinguished professor from Munich. At first he tried to throw him out. Then he asked him to stay longer. After Kraepelin left, Warburg claimed to have eaten the professor in his omelette. He was obsessed with the idea that the sanatorium was murdering his visitors and serving them up for supper.

The director of the Klinik Bellevue at Kreuzlingen at that time, Dr Ludwig Binswanger, was one of a psychiatric dynasty. His father and grandfather had both been psychiatrists, and his son would eventually become one. Dr Binswanger took a close interest in Warburg's case and became attached to him. Warburg once said to him, 'You won't have many patients who are both as intelligent as I am and who know that they are ill,' and Dr Binswanger readily agreed. When Warburg's family suggested that Aby should be examined by Professor Kraepelin, Binswanger was quite confident that his own diagnosis would stand. But Professor Kraepelin, who spent two days with his patient, concluded that Warburg was not schizophrenic; he was a manic-depressive, and the prognosis was 'entirely favourable'. His recommended treatment was morning bed-rest and opium. Warburg became very angry about this treatment and Dr Binswanger was not very pleased either, despite his high respect for Geheimrat Kraepelin. But the medical record suggests that even if the patient's behaviour did not improve, one important change had taken place.

A week before the opium dose was finally withdrawn, Warburg received a visit from a young Austrian scholar, Fritz Saxl, who had been appointed acting director of the Warburg Library. For some time, Warburg and Saxl had been planning an escape bid. Dr Binswanger, who was always glad to humour his patient, had agreed that if Warburg could successfully deliver a lecture before a public audience he would consider him to be on the way to recovery – and the patient might even hope for a day when he would be released. Dr Binswanger did not expect Dr Warburg to pass this test.

There were several reasons why Warburg chose to lecture on his encounter twenty-seven years earlier with the Pueblo Indians of North America. His research was heavily illustrated, he had never before worked up his raw material, and it was a well-focused subject, limited by the period of his journey. He had initially travelled to the American Southwest in the hope of observing man in a primitive state similar to the pagan Greek culture that was the cradle of modern civilisation. He still believed this connection to be valid, but he now had a far more personal reason for returning to the subject. In the psychic life of the Indians he now found an echo of his own dominating fears, and he believed that his illness had given him new insight into that 'universal terror of existence' that was reflected in the magical practices of the Indians. The lecture would not just be a demonstration of professional competence; it would be an explanation of his damaged psyche and so provide the key to his recovery.

The lecture on the Hopi Indians, later entitled 'Reminiscences from a Journey to the Pueblo Indians', had three themes. The first was the role of symbolism in Indian culture. The second was the continuing importance of symbolism in any civilisation. And the third was the destruction of the role of symbolism and the loss of understanding about its importance in the technological society of the early twentieth century. Although the lecture was greeted by its audience of doctors, fellow patients and members of the public as a success, Warburg himself insisted that it was not a scientific paper. Most of it was devoted to the first theme. In notes added to the text Warburg wrote: 'These notes [are] the desperate confessions . . . of a seeker after salvation . . . [a] search for the eternally unchanging Red Indian in the helpless human soul . . . They are the confessions of an [incurable] schizoid, deposited in the archives of mental healers.'*

In the 30 years that had passed since Warburg's visit, the Snake Dance of the Hopi Indians had become a tourist spectacle. D. H. Lawrence described it as a 'circus turn . . . uncouth rather than beautiful . . . [with] a touch of horror'. Lawrence devoted a chapter of *Mornings in Mexico* (1927) to the 'circus turn', without precisely grasping its significance. Warburg, in a dialogue of the deaf (neither Lawrence nor Warburg had read the other's work), insisted that the Indians' magic was 'not child's play, but the primary pagan mode of answering the largest and most pressing questions of the Why of things. In this way the Indian confronts the incomprehensibility of natural processes with his will to comprehension, transforming himself into a prime causal agent in the order of things.' He added:

* Unless otherwise indicated the translation of Warburg's lecture is by Michael P. Steinberg: *Images from the Region of the Pueblo Indians of North America* (Cornell University), 1995.

Our own technological age has no need of the serpent in order
to understand and control lightning. Lightning no longer terri-
fies the city dweller, who no longer craves a benign storm as
the only source of water . . . The replacement of mythocausation
by the technological, removes the fears felt by primitive
humanity. Whether this liberation from the mythological world
view is of genuine help in providing adequate answers to the
enigmas of existence is quite another matter. The American
government, like the Catholic Church before it, has brought
modern schooling to the Indians with remarkable energy. Its
intellectual optimism has resulted in the fact that the Indian
children . . . no longer believe in pagan demons . . . [This] may
well denote progress. But I would be loath to assert that it does
justice to the Indians (who think in images) or to their
mythologically anchored souls.

For Warburg 'paganism' was a psychological state, the surrender
to impulses of frenzy and fear. Because of the terror that had carried
him away in November 1918, and led to his being locked up for most
of six years, he was convinced that he had gained an insight into the
nature of primitive psychology that would enable him to demonstrate
its lasting importance and lead to the mastering of his own fears. So
the audience in Kreuzlingen were not just being treated to a learned
slide show. They were watching a supposedly incurable patient in the
process of curing himself by force of intellect and argument. For
those present who knew Aby Warburg and the challenge that he faced,
it must have been a deeply moving occasion.

Early in his lecture Warburg introduced an arresting image.
'Primitive man', he said, was 'like a child in the dark, surrounded by
a menacing chaos which threatened his survival.' The idea of the
child in the dark, alone and afraid, was familiar to every member of
the audience; they had all lived the experience themselves. But
Warburg of course had lived it more frequently and more recently
than most. In fact he was living it still. Warburg said that a state of

fear led to reflexes of fear, by which primitive man was always ready to respond to real or imagined dangers. When he was faced with an unknown danger he would identify and name some known danger. The wolf at the door, a wolf which had been repelled before, was always less frightening than the unknown. Warburg called this impulse to name, even if falsely, the source of danger 'cause projection' – the projection or invention of a cause. It was a 'prime phobic reflex' that lived on in the subconscious of every individual in modern times, and we were incapable of overcoming it.

He described this compulsive reflex of cause projection as 'the monster', and the history of civilisation was the history of the fight against the monster. In order to liberate himself from magic fears, Man had to deal with his inability to overcome the compulsive phobic reflex. 'The idea of the tangible cause and its compelling force is tragically rooted in our minds,' he stated. 'But if we cannot escape the monster we can sublimate the reaction into something more spiritual. This is our best hope of salvation.' He summarised this part of his argument with the claim that 'all human attempts at spiritual orientation spring from man's primeval reaction to the universal terror of his existence.'

Having described the essential role of symbolism in Indian culture, Warburg moved to his second theme, the continuing importance of symbolism in modern civilisation. In the scheme of evolution, he suggested, religious and artistic activities stood somewhere between 'phobic cause projection' (the Snake Dance) and logical discursive thought. In religion, the projected cause still demanded active propitiation in ritual and sacrifice. In art, the image evoked by the stimulus was still an end in itself. So art and religion belong to the intermediate region of 'symbolic activity', in which the tragic bipolarity of man finds expression and conciliation.

In his clinical notes Dr Binswanger referred to 'rather disordered ideas', too many technical terms and the fact that Warburg's voice was indistinct. He added that the performance had been dynamic and Warburg's intellectual strength had been a surprise. Others who heard it criticised it on technical grounds, as being badly organised in some places and badly argued in others. But its impact was still considerable, it remained the product of what Michael Steinberg has called a 'complex, vulnerable and humorous mind'. Another commentator has described the paper as 'a structure with many entrances'. Steinberg prefers 'a window on the life and work of a great European scholar . . . [and] a quirky document in the history of the ethnography of the Native American Southwest . . . a voice of spiralling and endless mediation: between cultures, between pasts and presents, between the self that is known and the self that is secret.' In April 1923, Aby Warburg remained a very sick man. He was in good hands but he was still at the bottom of the well, still trapped in what he himself called 'the inferno at Kreuzlingen'. Steinberg notes that for Warburg, 'scholarship was a way to maintain rationality in an increasingly complex and irrational world, a means of maintaining control in a world bordering on chaos – to warn, to exorcise, to encourage, never detached from the challenge of the times'.

In the final part of his lecture, Warburg addressed the disadvantages, as he believed, of Man's technological mastery of electricity, the force that the Hopi knew as lightning, for he was in no doubt that the technical advance had a negative aspect. This was one of the most elusive and idiosyncratic turns in his discourse. Haunted as he was by anxieties, Warburg had a constant need for the reassurance provided by distance and detachment. He placed this state of calm detachment in the evolutionary pattern of human psychology. Electricity tamed in the form of the telegraph eliminates distance and therefore annihilates space. 'Telegram and telephone destroy the cosmos,' he said. In the world of witchcraft things act upon each other at a distance, without intermediaries. But in the rational world, Man can contemplate the chain of events. He occupies a zone of detachment, which allows him to identify causes and name them.

This statement does not appear to be particularly original. But the clinicians in Warburg's audience would have realised at once that for the lecturer this was not just a familiar step in a logical argument. It was a description of what was for him a desperate daily struggle to overcome 'the monster'; for Warburg 'the universal terror of existence' was not just an image. 'The zone of detachment' was not a daily given, it was a fortress wall that could evaporate without warning to be replaced by a grey veil that did nothing to repel terror but served only to conceal its exact nature. And so once again the scholarly mind that had mastered philology, philosophy and history, that had pioneered iconography, would be reduced to the level of a terrified child, whimpering in the dark. Warburg had good reason to believe that his illness had afforded him special insight into the mind of primitive man. His life's work was 'to understand the meaning of the survival of paganism for the whole of European civilisation', and by 'paganism' Warburg meant a psychological state of surrender to impulses of frenzy and of fear. As one who had an exceptional need for 'the zone of reasoning and reflection', the space that was assured by distance and detachment, he would have been hypersensitive to whatever threatened it, in this case the lightning speed of electro-technical information. The American critic, the late Roger Ebert, who said that undertaking research on the internet was 'like using a library assembled piecemeal by pack rats and vandalised nightly', would have appreciated Warburg's point of view.

Warburg's lecture was illustrated by slides. He was, among other things, a photographer. Using the primitive equipment available to him, he had made a memorable series of monochrome images of Pueblo Indian life. Most of these pictures were taken out of doors, often of subjects in motion who disliked being photographed. To these he added pictures of Indian children, pictures of children's drawings, and pictures of Renaissance drawings and sculpture. But the final illustration he used was unexpected. This was the photograph he had taken in San Francisco, in the winter of 1895 to 1896, which he may have entirely forgotten – since it had no apparent connection with the life of the native people of the American Southwest – until he found it at the bottom of the box. There it was, and like a good storyteller he realised that it provided him with his peroration.

> The conqueror of the serpent cult and of the fear of lightning, the inheritor of the indigenous peoples [he did not say 'ethnic cleanser of the indigenous peoples'] and of the gold seeker who ousted them, is captured in a photograph I took on a street in San Francisco. He is Uncle Sam in a stovepipe hat, strolling in his pride past a neo-classical rotunda. Above his top hat runs an electric wire. In this copper serpent of Edison's, he has wrested lightning from nature.

We will never know whether Warburg realised the significance of this image in 1923, or whether he had already posed it with a model in 1896. But the fact remains that it was the perfect illustration of his argument.

'The modern American kills the rattlesnake, he does not worship it,' Warburg concluded. His final words ring out, ninety years on.

> Captive electricity has made an end of paganism. What has replaced it? The civilisation of the machine age destroys the space for contemplation, the space that became the zone of reasoning. The modern Prometheus (Benjamin Franklin) and the modern Icarus (the Wright Brothers) are the ominous destroyers of the sense of distance, and of the zone of reasoning, who threaten to lead the planet back into chaos. Telegram and telephone destroy the cosmos. Mythical and symbolic thought strives to forge spiritual bonds between humanity and the surrounding world, and to create the distance and space that is essential for contemplation and reasoning. This is the space that is destroyed by instant electric connection – unless a disciplined humanity restores the inhibitions of conscience.

With the image of 'Uncle Sam in a stovepipe hat', Warburg's lecture came to an end. In his diary that night he wrote: 'Lecture on the journey to the Pueblos took place and was a brilliant success.'

In July 1924, Aby Warburg was considered well enough to be released from Kreuzlingen and was allowed to return to Hamburg to live with his wife Mary and their three children. He had been cured by the exceptional care of Dr Binswanger, the devotion of his family – his wife had written to him every day of his three-year confinement – and his own determination. His illness, at first thought to be schizophrenia, later diagnosed as manic depression, might best be described as 'Great War Disease' if such a condition had ever been identified. It was the sensitive and committed non-combatant's equivalent to frontline shell shock, and in finding the way out of the inferno Warburg insisted on the eternal importance of 'mythical and symbolic thought' and its ability to 'forge spiritual bonds between humanity and the surrounding world'.

When the photograph of Uncle Sam was taken by Warburg the model was merely the likely looking master of some future universe, the United States was a sideshow, the world's dominant culture was European. But Warburg had subsequently seen that 2,000-year-old culture, to which he had given his life, destroyed in four years of mechanised warfare made possible by the industrialised economy that was increasingly dominated by Uncle Sam. As Conrad's North American entrepreneur had prophesied in 1904, in *Nostromo*, 'Time itself has got to wait on the greatest country in the whole of God's Universe. We shall be giving the word for everything: industry, trade, law, journalism, art, politics and religion, from Cape Horn clear . . . [to] the North Pole . . . We shall run the world's business whether the world likes it or not.' Conrad's fictional financier is 'a big-limbed, deliberate man whose quiet burliness lent to an ample silk-faced frock-coat, a superfine dignity. His hair was iron grey, his eyebrows were still black and his massive profile was the profile of a Caesar's head on an old Roman coin.' That he worked in 'an enormous pile of iron, glass and blocks of stone at the corner of two streets, *cobwebbed aloft by the radiation of telegraph wires*'* underlines the extraordinary resemblance between Conrad's fictional San Francisco financier of *Nostromo* and the man of business photographed by Aby Warburg somewhere near his iron and glass office in 1896.

In Hamburg, Aby Warburg once again devoted himself to his Renaissance studies. He died suddenly, alone in his library, in 1929. His journey ended where it had begun, surrounded by his collection. At the time of his death his lecture on the Snake Dance remained unpublished. Five years after his death Adolf Hitler, the elected chancellor of a democratic Germany, began to expel Jewish scientists from German universities.

When asked whether he thought Aby Warburg would have been released from the Klinik Bellevue without the intervention of Professor Kraepelin, Dr Gerhard Dammann – the director of the clinic at the time of my visit – said that he thought it would have happened, but it would have taken longer; he added that if Warburg had been admitted today he would of course have been treated by different methods. One of the innovations introduced since 1921 is the Observation Room.

The Observation Room is in fact two rooms: the first is a small conference hall, and you can pass through this to a smaller interior room where there is a CCTV camera and a large mirror. Behind the mirror is a window into the conference hall. By this arrangement what happens in the interior interview room can be observed by a small group of people watching unseen through the window, or can be projected onto a screen in the conference room for the entire audience to follow.

Alice, faced with a looking-glass, passed through it into a strange, mad world where sheep knitted, flowers talked, and chess pieces flew in a rage through the air. The one-way mirror of the interior room

* Author's italics

plays the same role, providing a material border between sanity and
madness. The mental patient striving for a cure looks through the
window and sees only the reflection of himself; he is enclosed in the
world of his own senses, locked into a reality with no other inhabitants; the only information he receives is the information he himself
transmits, the person locked into the mind, the mind into the body,
the body into the room; total solipsism. The mirror holds just one
face, his face, the image of madness. On the other side of the looking-
glass, grouped unseen, are those in charge, the gatekeepers and inhabitants of the world of sanity and control.

This was the border Warburg was trying to cross. With his lecture
he broke the looking-glass, and shortly afterwards found his way out
of the room with no windows, to the normality that lurked outside.

The road out of the Psychiatrische Klinik Münsterlingen runs beside
the Bodensee. On the lawn between the road and the lake there is a
stretch of concrete wall to which a radio antenna has been attached.
The wall surrounds a concrete staircase which descends into the
ground. There is an iron handrail bolted to the side of the steps, to
enable people to descend more quickly. The steps lead down into an
underground chamber that is large enough to hold 500 people for a
number of days. Some distance away there are armoured air vents to
feed the underground chamber. This is the *klinik*'s nuclear shelter.
Every public building in Switzerland is required by law to have one.
When the whole world goes mad, those who are officially already mad
can retreat into this chamber for a number of days before being
allowed to mount the concrete staircase and emerge into the devastated
world of sanity above.

CHAPTER NINE

Building the Minds that Built the Bomb

'We are living in the heroic age of physics.'

Ernest Rutherford (1923)

A by Warburg was not alone in being seriously affected by the experience of war. Otto Hahn, who had thought of mixing chlorine gas with phosgene to increase its toxicity, was able to confirm the success of his experiment by observing the agony of Russian soldiers on the Eastern Front. He later said that working with noxious chemicals had affected him personally, numbing his mind and killing his scruples. A man, even a military scientist, who has used enemy soldiers as human lab rats in order to make poison gas more poisonous, needs a certain degree of *chutzpah* to complain about his own suffering. Perhaps this ingenious defence showed that Otto Hahn had a sense that his achievements with the German Pioneer Regiment might leave him open to post-war criticism. But Hahn had no need to worry about reprisals. The Allies had also used poison gas, and in 1919 the embryonic Royal Air Force was dropping gas bombs onto Bolshevik soldiers at Archangel.

At the beginning of the conflict in 1914, there had been 18,000 hospital beds in the British Empire. By 1918 there were 630,000. In the first two years of the war, the French army lost 615,000 men. In one battle in 1916, on the Somme, British and German casualties reached 800,000. Meanwhile the Germans were fighting a simultaneous battle against the French Army at Verdun, where total casualties reached 750,000. The

German general who attacked Verdun, Erich von Falkenhayn, said that his plan would 'bleed the forces of France to death'.

When the conflict was over, a monument was erected in London to the glory of the Machine Gun Corps. The inscription selected was, 'Saul has slain his thousands, But David his tens of thousands'. The monument was placed at Hyde Park Corner, just outside the doors of St George's Hospital. Although machine gunners had enjoyed a marked advantage over riflemen, their life in the frontline was not without its hazards. The chief danger was due to the tendency of First World War machine guns to overheat and jam. If the guns were water-cooled they had to be kept topped up like a simmering kettle. When the gun jammed, its crew worked frantically to get it back into action, knowing that if the advancing infantry reached their lines, David, not Saul, would be the first to get it.

By 1921, the year that Conrad was touring the battlefields with his son, Borys, and Aby Warburg was making his disruptive journey to Kreuzlingen, and Robert Oppenheimer was falling seriously ill near the uranium mines of Joachimstal, the world was apparently on the way to recovering its sanity. And Niels Bohr, affectionately known as 'the Great Dane', had just opened his new Institute for Theoretical Physics in Copenhagen, sponsored by the Carlsberg Brewery and the Danish royal family. Bohr's institute quickly gained a worldwide reputation, as the scientific community – divided by the war, and to some extent divided by its wartime achievements – felt the need to reassert its essentially peaceful vocation and its international character. In the immediate post-war period science continued to be dominated, as in the previous century, by the Germans. The war had broken Germany, but it had not broken German scholarship. The Nobel Prize was first awarded in 1901. Of the first 100 science prizes, 35 went to German science, nearly twice as many as to any other country. Twenty per cent of the German scientists were Jewish, although the Jews formed only 1 per cent of the German population.

The leading figure in the German scientific community in 1921 was Fritz Haber, by now the director of the Kaiser Wilhelm Institute for Physics and Chemistry. There was no more Kaiser, but his institute continued unperturbed. Haber had been awarded the 1918 Nobel for Chemistry. Haber's award was given because his work had led to the discovery of artificial nitrates, which had agricultural value.* After the war, the Allies condemned Haber as a war criminal and forbade him from doing any further work on poison gas for military purposes. He was not unduly bothered by this and secretly continued his work in collaboration with the Soviet government. In 1925 Haber abandoned military research and switched to pest control. Here his experiments eventually led to the development of the gas Zyklon B, which was used in the Nazi death camps during the Second World War. Despite his patriotic record, and rather to his surprise, Haber – as a Jew – was eventually put into jeopardy by the Nazis and was obliged to seek refuge in England. Ernest Rutherford, director of the Cavendish Laboratory, sponsored his removal to Cambridge but refused to shake his hand when he arrived. Haber died shortly after reaching his chosen place of refuge, of a heart attack. There is no evidence that he ever became aware of the extent of his callousness, opportunism and hypocrisy, which were also of world class.

By a curious coincidence, Haber's junior colleague in the German Army's poison-gas unit, Otto Hahn, also received the Nobel Prize in Chemistry within months of the ending of a world war, in 1945. In his case it was for a peacetime discovery that had even more sinister military applications: nuclear fission.

The atom was invented long before science. The idea originated with the ancient Greek philosophers, in about 420BC. Democritus proposed that the infinite variety of material substances, from steam to adamant, could

*That his research had in fact been designed to produce unlimited quantities of explosives was not held against him by the Nobel committee – trustees of the fortune made by Alfred Nobel, the inventor of dynamite.

be explained if matter was not continuous but was composed of separate particles that were in themselves indivisible – in Greek, 'atomos'. The idea is an imaginative extension of the transformation of wood into sawdust, and it became a recurring poetic image. Shakespeare counted 'atomies' and Lord Montrose, the Scottish royalist, referred to the atoms of his dead body in eight lines of verse written on the eve of his execution in 1650. Early in the nineteenth century the chemist John Dalton developed the first scientific theory of the atom; he published a list of chemical symbols and a table of atomic weights. As late as 1880 the physicist Max Planck doubted whether atoms existed. All this changed when Ernest Rutherford arrived at the Cavendish Laboratory in Cambridge in 1895, aged twenty-four. By 1908 he had been awarded the Nobel Prize in Chemistry for work on radioactive elements. Working in Cambridge he had established that radioactivity is caused by the decay of atoms. Then, in Manchester, where he was Professor of Physics, he began to work on the structure of the atom. It was known that the atom was essentially empty space; Rutherford suspected that it might have a hard core. Rutherford was an experimental physicist – he liked to see and touch what he thought. To prove one of his theories he once built a model that included a heavy electromagnet suspended like a pendulum on a length of wire thirty feet long. In 1907 he devised another experiment that confirmed that the atom had a centre, which he called a nucleus. Over the next twelve years he constructed a model of the atom in which positively charged particles, which he called protons, formed the nucleus, and negatively charged particles called electrons orbited the nucleus and formed the outer surface. By 1919 Rutherford had hypothesised that the nucleus contained a third neutrally charged particle that he called a neutron. In the course of his experiment he had transformed the chemical element of nitrogen into hydrogen and, as the newspapers put it, 'split' the atom. One of his students during his time at Manchester was Otto Hahn. Another was Niels Bohr.

There was a problem with Rutherford's model of the atom which was that, following the laws of classical physics, it should have collapsed: the exterior electrons should have been attracted to the protons leaving only the nucleus. The next step needed a theoretical physicist such as Niels Bohr. Theoretical physicists use mathematics rather than models. Faced with a problem, they try to devise an imaginary solution and then to invalidate it. If they fail to invalidate it they adopt it as correct. Working in Copenhagen, Bohr was attracted to the ideas of Max Planck, the German physicist at the University of Berlin who in 1880 had doubted the existence of atoms and in 1900 had invented quantum theory. Planck had suggested that light and heat radiation are emitted in little packets, or 'quanta'. Bohr now adapted this theory to explain why the surface and the nucleus of Rutherford's atom did not slide together. First Bohr improved Rutherford's model by comparing the atom to a planetary system in which the outer electrons were orbiting the central nucleus. He then suggested that the outer electrons could only change their orbit in measured steps – quanta – and so could not be sucked into the nucleus, despite the positive attraction of the central protons. In 1905, at the start of his work on relativity, Einstein took Planck's idea and suggested that light did not travel in continuous waves but consisted of quantum particles that maintained their separate existence, not only when they were emitted (as in the case of steam particles) but also when they were travelling from place to place. Einstein completed his work on relativity in 1916, by which time he had established that matter was a form of energy and that it was possible to discover the amount of energy (E) contained in a given body of matter by calculating the mass (m) of the given body and multiplying the mass by the speed of light (c) in empty space, squared: $E = mc^2$. So Einstein had implied that if matter could be penetrated the energy it contained might be released and that this would amount to a very large number indeed.

Rutherford had a golfing partner at the Cavendish laboratory, a wealthy playboy called Francis Aston who was also a researcher and a Nobel Prize winner. Aston spent the war working at the Army (later RAF) research establishment at Farnborough, designing resistant fabric for aircraft wings. After the war, Aston returned to the

Cavendish and invented a machine he called a mass spectrograph, because it measured atomic weights. With this he was able to go right through the periodic table measuring the atomic weights of each element, from the lightest, hydrogen, to the heaviest then discovered, uranium. He noticed that there was a tiny amount of mass missing from each atomic element and concluded that this was the energy spent in holding the atoms together, the 'binding energy'. His measurements showed that the most energy was expended at opposite ends of the table, in hydrogen and uranium, and that this showed that they were the most unstable atoms. Taking the example of hydrogen, he calculated that if it were possible to transform hydrogen into its neighbour, helium, 1 per cent of the mass would be annihilated and the amount of energy released from one glass of water would be sufficient to drive a steamship across the Atlantic and back at full speed. In a conventional steamship burning coal, all that happened was that the coal was turned into ash because the atoms merely lost the weakly bound outer electrons; the material element changed, but the atomic nuclei remained and most of the energy was never released.

So within a year of Rutherford 'splitting' or transmuting the atomic structure of a chemical element, the development had been linked to Einstein's equation and the practical possibilities of nuclear research were within sight.

In the early 1920s quantum theory spawned quantum mechanics, an essential tool to describe and explain subatomic physics and mechanical systems that were so small that classic Newtonian physics failed. The pacemakers in this new discipline were all young men: Paul Dirac, Werner Heisenberg and Wolfgang Pauli. Fundamental contributions were also made by two older physicists, Max Born and Erwin Schrödinger. All these men were theorists, and in 1927 they were on the crest of a wave, part of an international brotherhood of physics. Its members published their research, challenged each other's work, improved on each other's results and argued ferociously in their love of science and pursuit of the truth. And their discoveries came faster and faster. They themselves termed it 'the heroic age of physics'.

There is a wonderful photograph of the 'A team' taken in Brussels in 1927 at that year's Solvay Conference. The physicists are arranged in three rows, like a rugby squad. Seated in the front are the eminent greybeards who have nothing new to contribute. They include Max Planck, Marie Curie and Einstein. In the middle row are the laboratory chiefs and heads of department; they include Max Born and Niels Bohr. Standing side by side among those in the back row are two who were calling the shots, Pauli and Heisenberg. They have a mischievous and disrespectful air about them. Schrödinger, who was having a serious professional disagreement with Heisenberg, stands one away. Paul Dirac, who should be in the back row, has somehow managed to insinuate himself onto the bench in the centre of the second row, behind Einstein's right ear. Beside him, behind Einstein's left ear, sits a man who was not then so well known. A. H. Compton was an American experimental physicist, Presbyterian and pacifist. One of his colleagues later said of him that 'Arthur Compton and God were daily companions.' He once gave a lecture, in the context of his religious convictions, in which he argued that Heisenberg's uncertainty principle confirmed the existence of free will. Fifteen years after the 1927 Solvay Conference he would be one of those who played a decisive role in the Manhattan Project and who eventually advocated dropping the bomb on a living target.

During the 1930s progress in atomic physics slowed down. With most of the structure of the atom understood and the main arguments about quantum mechanics settled, the scientists turned their minds to the next big question: was it possible to gain access to the huge reserves of energy locked within the atomic nucleus? Rutherford, by now the grand old man of the discipline, was quite clear on the subject. In September 1933, he made a speech to the British Association in which he said that the idea of finding 'sources of power in atomic transformation' was 'the merest moonshine'. With hindsight it is possible to see that this comment placed him in the same prophetic category as Einstein, who never accepted Heisenberg's uncertainty principle (that the act of measurement alters the result*) on the grounds that 'God does not play dice.'

* That the exact measurement of the velocity of a sub-atomic particle always prevents the exact measurement of its position, and vice-versa.

CHAPTER TEN

Joining the Brotherhood

'Reading books interferes with thought.'

Paul Dirac (1926)

In the early summer of 1922 two men alighted at Lamy station in New Mexico, arriving on the train from Denver. The first was an athletic-looking adult in his prime, a schoolteacher called Herbert Smith. He was clearly in charge. The other was a sickly looking youth with spiky hair, vivid, pale-blue eyes, rounded cheeks, narrow shoulders, a wary expression and a notably uneasy manner. He was six feet tall, weighed a maximum of nine stone and was called J. Robert Oppenheimer. Before setting out from New York on the journey with his former English teacher he had asked if he could travel as 'Robert Smith' and pass himself off as his tutor's younger brother. Permission was denied.

In 1922 Oppenheimer was aged eighteen. The previous summer he had travelled to visit his father's family in Germany. It was on this holiday, while visiting the Joachimsthal silver and uranium mines in Czechoslovakia, that he had become so ill with dysentery he had nearly died. His father considered him too ill for university so his entry into Harvard had been deferred for a year. The journey to the Southwest with Mr Smith was intended to set him up and restore his health. They were to spend the summer in the Sangre de Cristo Mountains on a dude ranch called Los Piños.

Oppenheimer had grown up in a spacious apartment on Riverside Drive, Manhattan, overlooking the Hudson River. His father, Julius, was a wealthy businessman, a partner in a firm that imported cloth from Europe to supply New York's garment trade. Julius had arrived in New York aged seventeen, speaking not a word of English and by the time war broke out in 1914 he was a multimillionaire. By then he had married a beautiful artist from Baltimore called Ella Friedman, also of German-Jewish extraction. But the Oppenheimers were not observant and they sent their children to the Ethical Culture Society's school on Central Park West. The school was associated with Reform Judaism. It was influenced by the German *gymnasium* system, and encouraged its pupils to face the problems of the world and overcome them. Robert and his younger brother Frank grew up in considerable luxury. From the windows of an apartment on 155 Riverside Drive you have one of the most splendid views in the city. There to the west is the river, the bridge, the shoreline and woodlands of New Jersey, and the sunset. And you have the impression that you are standing with your back to the edge of a great continent and looking out over the full extent of the place, from the island where the story more or less started, and that the end of the story is not yet in sight and that you are in a country and among a people that holds the future of the world in its hands. It must have felt even more like that, looking out from those windows in the years before the outbreak of war in 1914.

Robert Oppenheimer had decided to major in chemistry at Harvard but he had passed out of the Ethical Culture Society's school with high marks in several other subjects, including English literature, history, Greek, Latin, French and German, as well as maths and physics. He was always recognised as outstandingly gifted; the Oxford professor John Carey later described him as being afflicted with such 'prodigious brainpower' that it was difficult for him 'to mix with other people, or even recognise them as the same species'. One of his schoolfriends said that in almost everything he did 'he displayed a great need to declare his pre-eminence'. Several of his teachers, including Herbert Smith, were aware that he was emotionally fragile. He was troubled for one thing by tension between his parents based on differences in personality and background. Julius, his father, was gregarious, 'desperately amiable', outgoing and generous; he frequently made quite a lot of sociable noise. Ella did not enjoy these 'obtrusive manners'. Robert's mother was graceful, discriminating and fastidious. She gave an impression of sadness and silent disapproval. Where her son was concerned she was both over-protective and emotionally demanding. As a child Robert spent a lot of time with Ella and had a very intense relationship with her. But he was never embarrassed by her. He was embarrassed however by his father's connection with the garment trade and the cliché Jewish identity this bestowed on him. Hence his desire to travel as 'Robert Smith'.

Oppenheimer's visit to Los Piños was one of the formative experiences of his life. He turned out to be a natural and fearless horseman who delighted in the physical challenges of the ranch. The property at that time was owned by a young woman called Katherine Page. Katherine had inherited Los Piños from her father, Don Amado Chaves, whose *hidalgo* family had owned land in the region for hundreds of years. Katherine Page and Robert became great friends; he seems to have fallen in love with her and with the mountains and the outdoor life, all at the same time. Herbert Smith, who had always known Oppenheimer as a frail, over-sensitive and withdrawn personality, was astonished at the emergence of this prototype Western cowboy. He decided that, aside from his intellectual brilliance and self-confidence, Oppenheimer was desperate to be accepted as the social equal of people he admired and was morbidly self-conscious about his Jewish background. At Los Piños he was no longer a New York Jewish egghead but an adventurous young American enjoying his pioneering birthright and discovering the extent of his courage and strength. In Smith's opinion his recklessness when out on a horse in the mountains bordered on the suicidal. Another of Robert's friends remembered that he had displayed the same tendency when out sailing his father's boat on Long Island Sound, but he put the display down to arrogance.

By the end of the summer Robert Oppenheimer's health was restored and he entered Harvard. Before he left, Katherine Page took him on a trek of several days and nights down from the Sangre de Cristo, west across the Rio Grande and up into the Jemez Mountains. At 10,000 feet they crossed the Pajarito Plateau and then the Valle Grande. Their route would have taken them through the Frijoles Canyon, with its prehistoric *kiva*, and on the way back east they would have crossed the *mesa* called Los Alamos and noticed the ranch that had been turned into a boys' school and which enjoyed one of the most liberating and life-enhancing views of any school in the United States, eastward to the snow-topped peaks of the Sangre de Cristo.

At Harvard, Oppenheimer withdrew once more into his shell. He had two friends, Fergusson and Horgan, but his emotional difficulties returned. He used up his excessive intellectual capacity in taking extra courses. His arrival at Harvard coincided with that of the English philosopher and mathematician Alfred North Whitehead, who had written *Principia Mathematica* with Bertrand Russell. Anxious to increase his understanding of mathematics, Oppenheimer, with another student, worked through the *Principia* with Whitehead and by the end of the course the other student had dropped out. At this time Whitehead was giving a series of lectures at Harvard which were eventually collected and published as *Science and the Modern World*. This is the work that established Whitehead, according to the *Dictionary of National Biography*, as 'a major philosopher'. The book was concerned to trace the development of the scientific mind since the ancient Greeks. Whitehead linked the idea of fate in Greek tragedy with the modern concept of order, and examined the impact of scientific thought on spiritual ideas. He also proposed a metaphysical proof for the existence of God, although he generally described himself as an agnostic. It is probable that Whitehead had a considerable influence on his brilliant student. Whitehead too had had a classical education and had then switched to mathematics while an undergraduate at Cambridge. Oppenheimer was supposed to be concentrating on chemistry, but he was also ranging beyond the syllabus. He read Gibbon, Racine in the original and *The Waste Land*, which had just been published.

Oppenheimer at Harvard was sufficiently in love with literature to start writing his own poetry. And he was sufficiently impressed by Whitehead to boast for the rest of his life of his achievement in tracking him through the *Principia Mathematica*. It was his understanding of mathematics that led Oppenheimer to realise that he was more interested in physics than he was in chemistry. (Shortly after he left Harvard, he likened chemistry to 'testing toothpaste'.) In 1929 Whitehead published another book, *The Aims of Education*, in which he argued that the purpose of education was to impart the beauty and power of ideas and to produce students who are alive to the world of ideas and able to investigate it. When Oppenheimer graduated *summa cum laude* with *alpha*s in every paper he was offered a research fellowship by Harvard. But, perhaps influenced by Whitehead's principles, he refused and set off instead for the Cavendish Laboratory in Cambridge, England, where he hoped that the second most famous scientist alive, Rutherford, would welcome him to the world of cutting-edge physics; he had never taken more than an elementary course in physics in his life. The professor who recommended him noted his 'perfectly prodigious power of assimilation' but added that 'as appears from his name Oppenheimer is a Jew, but entirely without the usual qualifications of his race. He is a tall, well set-up young man.' While waiting to hear Rutherfords' response Robert decided to return to Katherine Page's ranch.

On this return visit to the Sangre de Cristo, Oppenheimer did not drive up to the ranch. Confident by now of their ability, he and his Harvard friend Paul Horgan rented horses in Santa Fe and followed a trail over the peaks to Los Piños. Horgan recalled that they reached the top of the pass in 'a tremendous thunderstorm [and] pounding rain'. He looked at Robert and saw that his hair was standing straight up in the electrically charged air. It was a vision of the future, for Oppenheimer, for physics and, unfortunately, for the world.

In October 1925, Oppenheimer left New York for Rutherford's Cavendish Laboratory where he struggled to find his feet. The experience made him profoundly unhappy. Within three months of his arrival in the Fens he had become so depressed that he considered suicide. He was sent to a succession of psychiatrists and diagnosed as schizophrenic. And when his concerned mother arrived to care for him he locked her in her hotel room. He then tried to strangle Francis Fergusson when the latter announced that he had become engaged to be married, and subsequently claimed that he had attempted to murder his physics tutor by poisoning his food. Oppenheimer Snr had to beg the Cambridge University authorities not to press criminal charges against his son. Robert confided to another friend that he had decided that the professionals were too stupid to help him, and later claimed to have cured himself in the spring of 1926 when he went on a walking tour of Corsica. Conrad had taken refuge in the island five years earlier, after his distressing tour of the battlefields of northern France. In Corsica, Oppenheimer read *A la recherche du temps perdu*, and he later said that Proust played an important part in his cure, and in particular a passage from volume one which described 'the terrible and permanent form of cruelty' that is the indifference in oneself to the sufferings one causes in others.

On returning from Corsica to what one of his friends called 'frigid England, hellish socially and climatically', Oppenheimer finally started work as a physicist. One of the possible reasons for his mental collapse in the winter of 1925–26 was that he was so hopeless at laboratory work and for the first time in his life felt inadequate and stupid. He talked in later years in vague terms of a romantic complication, but the broken romance may well have been with his own pride and thwarted self-esteem. To find himself fumbling at a test bench when set a rudimentary research task left him feeling very angry. And it was this anger that led him to place a poisoned apple on his tutor's desk and to seize the throat of a friend whom he imagined was abandoning him.* Oppenheimer was fully aware of his own exceptional ability, and he did not enjoy it when others, his competitors and peers, failed to notice his superiority. Now he moved out of his cramped digs into lodgings by the River Cam near Grantchester. He had endured a year of hell.

The first hint that Oppenheimer might have something original to contribute came after he had read a paper by a young German physicist, Werner Heisenberg, who was studying the behaviour of electrons through a method he termed matrix mechanics. Oppenheimer then read another paper on electrons by an Austrian physicist, Erwin Schrödinger, which proposed 'wave mechanics', apparently an entirely different theory of electron behaviour. Oppenheimer understood enough to suspect that the two theories should be connected, although he did not yet know how this might be achieved. But at least he was beginning to understand what everyone else was talking about. He met a very brilliant young mathematician called Paul Dirac, whose work in the field of quantum mechanics was understood by very few people indeed; but at least Oppenheimer could see why Dirac's work was so hard to understand. Oppenheimer, in a friendly gesture, offered Dirac some books to read. Dirac handed the books back, saying that in his opinion 'reading books interferes with thought'.

Before his collapse, Oppenheimer had met a visitor from Denmark, Niels Bohr, whose Institute for Theoretical Physics had already gained an international reputation. Rutherford introduced them and Bohr immediately noticed that the young man was in trouble. He asked him whether his problems were mathematical or physical and when Oppenheimer replied, 'I don't know,' Bohr said, 'That's bad.' Oppenheimer

---

* The tutor in question, P.M.S. Blackett, was a brilliant experimentalist. He had earlier fought in the Battle of Jutland as a midshipman, and was later to be awarded both the Nobel Prize in Physics and the Order of Merit. The apple may have been imaginary, in which case the incident may have been inspired by Blake's poem 'The Poison Tree'.

never understood English manners. He always felt ill at ease at the Cavendish, and considered that Rutherford had a low opinion of him. But when he left the room Rutherford told Bohr that he had high expectations for his American student. And then another visitor passed through Cambridge, Max Born. Born was the director of the Institute of Theoretical Physics at the University of Göttingen and was directly concerned with the contradictions between the theories of Heisenberg and Schrödinger. He was impressed to find that Rutherford's inexperienced student had independently started to think about this problem and he invited Oppenheimer to leave Cambridge and study for his doctorate at Göttingen.

Oppenheimer was happy in Göttingen. At the age of twenty-two he was at last in the company of the leading men in the theoretical field. He was free of the depressing English manner and his German was already good. He worked with his professor on the quantum theory of molecules and his new acquaintances included Heisenberg, Pauli, the Italian Enrico Fermi, and James Franck, who had just won the Nobel Prize, having left his former commanding officer, Captain Haber of the poison-gas unit, in Berlin. Oppenheimer wrote a letter to his old Harvard friend Fergusson, whom he had once tried to strangle, telling him that the science at Göttingen was 'much better than at Cambridge'. Göttingen, under Born, was the centre of theoretical physics, just as Rutherford's Cavendish Laboratory was then the centre for experimentalists. Another colleague was the American Karl Compton, Professor of Physics at Princeton and brother of the God-fearing Arthur. Karl Compton said that he could keep up with Oppenheimer in physics but was completely lost when the younger man began talking about philosophy or literature. Oppenheimer in a letter to his younger brother Frank said that the other Americans at Göttingen tended to be respectable, married professors who were 'completely uneducated'. A fellow lodger said that she frequently saw him lying in bed for half the day, doing nothing. When he eventually got up he tended to talk a great deal, rapidly, for some time. He sometimes fell over unconscious and he acquired and then overcame a stutter. Oppenheimer was turning himself into a physicist, but in order to do it he had to kill off the numerous other personalities that he knew he possessed and that still tempted him.

Many years later, after Oppenheimer had died, his friend the experimental physicist I. I. Rabi, asked himself why 'men of Oppenheimer's gifts do not discover everything worth discovering'. He concluded that Oppenheimer was overeducated in those fields which lie outside the scientific discipline. Rabi added that Oppenheimer's interest in the Hindu religion 'resulted in a feeling for the mystery of the universe that surrounded him like a fog'. Had it occurred to Rabi he might have identified his friend as 'an enemy', like Aby Warburg, 'of the border police'.

At Göttingen, Oppenheimer was strongly attracted to the prettiest physics student around, a German girl called Charlotte Riefenstahl. Here he had a rival, a young Dutch physicist, F. G. Houtermans, whose mother was half-Jewish. Houtermans used to boast of his ancestry by saying, 'When your ancestors were still living in trees mine were already forging cheques.' Charlotte preferred Oppenheimer but she eventually decided that he was too 'locked up'. So Charlotte married Houtermans, who was a Marxist, and they went to live in Moscow. This proved to be a bad idea. Houtermans was arrested by the NKVD in a purge and Charlotte had to flee to America. Houtermans had all his teeth knocked out, and was kept in solitary confinement for almost two years. Then, with the Nazi–Soviet pact of 1939, he was released and handed over to the Gestapo, who put him in a concentration camp. He was freed after the intervention of German colleagues and, following the outbreak of war, was put to work on the Nazi bomb programme, the only Jewish scientist to be engaged in this way.

Oppenheimer's doctorate was accepted in 1927; he had by then, under the guidance of Max Born, gained an international reputation. One of the examiners was James Franck. The oral examination of a doctoral thesis is designed to be an ordeal for the candidate; after Oppenheimer's oral, Franck said, 'I got out of there just in time. He was beginning to ask *me* questions.' By the time he left Göttingen, with offers from Harvard and Berkeley in his pocket, Oppenheimer was a fully fledged member of the international brotherhood of physics.

Oppenheimer returned to America in 1928 and accepted two appointments in California, at Berkeley and at CalTech, the California Institute of Technology. But before taking up these positions he applied for a grant to return to Europe where he wanted to study with Paul Ehrenfest at Leiden in Holland and then with Niels Bohr in Copenhagen. Within six weeks of his arrival in Holland, Oppenheimer had learned enough Dutch to give a lecture. While Ehrenfest was drilling 'Opje' (his Dutch nickname) in mathematics he received a letter from Born warning him that his new post-doctoral student was very gifted, very undisciplined and very arrogant under his modest exterior. Ehrenfest, who was himself emotionally unstable, defended Oppenheimer from these criticisms and persuaded him to abandon the idea of going to Copenhagen to work with Niels Bohr and to go to Zurich instead. He had decided to expose Oppenheimer to somebody who would be a match for him and would be able to help him 'thrash things out'; this was Wolfgang Pauli, the disrespectful face in the back row at the Solvay Conference. He was a very aggressive, witty man who had achieved much more than Oppenheimer and who had far more self-confidence. Pauli said of his student, 'His ideas are always interesting and his calculations are always wrong.' By choosing Zurich over Copenhagen, Oppenheimer also chose to spend the final part of his training with a very clever man – Pauli – rather than with a clever man who was also wise – Niels Bohr. This choice may have influenced him for the rest of his life. Pauli teased him and imitated him when he hesitated in a lecture, but not to the point of unkindness. Oppenheimer's response was revealing. Instead of resenting Pauli's discourtesy he submitted to the authority of his supervisor. He knew that Pauli was a better physicist than he was. Pauli was baffled by Oppenheimer's reaction. 'Unfortunately he has a very bad trait,' he wrote to Ehrenfest. 'He considers all I say as final and definitive truth.'

In June 1929 Oppenheimer left Zurich to return to California. His training was now complete, his international reputation was secure and he never worked in Europe again. Wolfgang Pauli remained working in Zurich, safe from Nazi persecution, until 1940, when he went to the United States. Paul Ehrenfest continued to teach at Leiden. He felt increasingly isolated in the brave new world of quantum physics. In the autumn of 1933, a few months after Hitler had come to power, he wrote – but did not post – letters to Niels Bohr and Einstein, and then killed himself and his handicapped son in a park in Amsterdam.

CHAPTER ELEVEN

The Price of Uranium

'To tear treasure out of the bowels of the land was their desire, with no more moral purpose at the back of it than there is in burglars breaking into a safe.'

Joseph Conrad, *Heart of Darkness* (1902)

Until the discovery of nuclear fission, uranium was an ore of very limited use, and in 1939 it was also in very limited supply. There was one mine in south-western Colorado in the region of a town called Paradox. There was another that had a small but good-quality production at Great Bear Lake in Canada's Northwest Territories, and there were the Joachimsthal mines in Bohemia. Uranium's primary use had been as a dye for the ceramics industry; it produced lemon-yellow, orange and green colouring at various concentrations. When Pierre and Marie Curie identified radium as a source of radiation and demonstrated its use in treating cancer, for which they were awarded the 1903 Nobel Prize in Physics, uranium mines were presented with a second market: radium is a by-product of uranium. Prices reached $3 million an ounce in 1919 and Paradox and Joachimsthal were doing well until 1922, when a newly discovered mine in the Belgian Congo came on stream.

By the time Shinkolobwe had been identified as a source of uranium by the geologist Robert Sharp in 1915, mineral rights in Katanga had become the property of the Union Minière du Haut Katanga which

had acquired them from King Leopold. Sharp made his discovery
by chance. He was working for Union Minière and looking primarily
for copper. One day, while prospecting in the region of Likasi, near
Elisabethville, he climbed a low hill to take his bearings and noticed
that the earth on the hilltop was stained with several colours. One
was yellow, which he associated with uranium. Sharp had heard that
local men used coloured mud to decorate their bodies. He was told
that 'Shinkolobwe' means 'the fruit that scalds'. He sent the rocks
for analysis and they turned out to contain uranium at 80 per cent,
the purest concentration in the world. There was so much pure
uranium at Shinkolobwe that the mines at Joachimsthal and Paradox
in Colorado simply stopped producing it. The Belgian state, through
Union Minière and its parent company, the Société Générale, had
discovered one more 'goldmine' in the province of Katanga.

The day before we flew to Katanga we had lunch at the Cercle de
Kinshasa, an impeccable country club in the city centre with its own
18-hole golf course and 12 tennis courts. There was a young Belgian
university teacher at the next table. Like us, he was due to fly to
Lubumbashi – once Elisabethville – the following morning. He said
that, following the crash at Goma, he had cancelled his reservation
on Hewa Bora. He was on the waiting list for the UN flight. If that
failed he would take the Kenya Airways flight to Nairobi and then
another Kenya Airways flight to Lubumbashi, a diversion of about
4,000 miles and 24 hours. We thought he was rather over-cautious.
He was seated with his wife and small child, enjoying a buffet lunch
in the shade of the club's terrace. Not the time to recall the Kenya
Airways Boeing 737 that had gone down in the Cameroon forest a
few months earlier. It had taken the rescue party two days to find
the wreckage. No survivors.

On our last night in Kinshasa, a Belgian acquaintance from Brussels
joined our party. Bob had been President Mobutu's vet, in charge of
his large menagerie of exotic animals. He was really a horse doctor
but had adapted to dealing with lions, tigers, elephants, gorillas and,

of course, leopards. When Mobutu was overthrown, Bob, who had
been born in Katanga in the days of the Belgian colony, had lost
everything. I asked him what he thought of Mobutu. 'He was a strong
man, a leader. He knew how to hold his country together.' We were
sitting in an Indian restaurant on the top floor of a tall building.
Around us we could see the few lights of the city, we could hear no
noise from the sparse traffic; the darkness covered the unrepaired
wreckage of a civil war that had ended twelve years before. It had
taken quite a time to reach the top floor. The city's electricity supply
was unreliable and nobody seemed keen to trust the lift. The lobby
was protected from the street by scarred steel doors that looked as
though they were designed to withstand missile attack. I asked Bob
how much he had lost all those years before, when Mobutu had fled
the country and the raggle-taggle army had emerged from the forest
and pillaged Kinshasa. 'About fifteen million US dollars,' he said. 'I
was lucky to get out alive. I don't like Kinshasa. "*Ça peut péter à tout
moment.*" It could go up again at any time.'

On the way out, back at ground level, he noticed a hole in the wall
of the lift shaft and peered through. Then he turned on his torch.
'Have a look at this.' Hundreds of bright little eyes peered back into
the torchlight. 'Rats. It's the bottom of the rubbish chute. Hasn't
been cleared for years but the restaurant kitchen is still using it.'

Next morning Papa Thomas drove us out to the airport and I told
him that since we were catching an internal flight to Katanga I
expected no entry or exit controls, no customs, no problems. Papa
Thomas smiled happily when I took this optimistic line. 'We'll see,'
he said. Papa helped me with the luggage and we crossed from the
car park to the door of the Kinshasa Passenger Terminal. The door
seemed to be closed but Papa pushed through the crowd and there
was a man in uniform saying, 'L'entrée est payante.' I am not sure
who he was. I think he was a luggage porter who had decided to
block the door. And there was none of this nonsense about 'Whites
to the left'. Everyone was being excluded. 'I refuse to pay,' said Bob.

Matter of principle. 'How much?' said Papa. 'US$5,' said the porter. 'I refuse,' said Papa. 'These *messieurs* can afford US$5, and you refuse to pay?' said the porter. 'No. I refuse to come in,' said Papa. 'I'm coming in,' said Bob. '*Mission officiel*, nothing to pay, no question,' and he waved a document headed *Ordre de Mission* and bearing the stamp of the Ministry of Culture. The porter gave way, we waved goodbye to Papa Thomas and together with most of the people outside were swept into the terminal.

The *ordre de mission* got us past the baggage porter but that was the limit of its authority. In the departure hall there was turmoil on all sides. 'No suitcases to be checked in unless they are padlocked.' 'Padlocks to be purchased from the porters.' 'All checked baggage carries charges.' The crowd surges backwards and forwards – passengers, relations, pickpockets, airline officials, all closely involved in the ritual of 'checking in'. Faced by the addition of 16, 17 and 19 kilos, the procedure grinds to a halt at the weighing machine, until I tell them my luggage weighs 52. Is it 52? I have no idea. It looks like 52 so we go with 52. Passengers start shouting different figures from all sides. So much for the payload at take-off. For some reason we seem to be the only *blancs* on the flight.

Bob, who was a pilot as well as a horse doctor, passed the time in the departure hall by analysing the previous week's disaster at Goma. He said that the airfield at Goma is at 1,200 metres, so jet engines run at only 70 per cent efficiency. One-third of the runway at Goma was out of action due to a lava flow from a nearby volcano which had never been cleared up. Congolese loadmasters habitually took bribes to overload the planes – fact. So the pilot probably found himself with an overloaded plane that refused to lift on a short runway, and the plane skidded off the end of the runway into a shanty town that was not supposed to be there, with the result that it ploughed through the accommodation, killing dozens of Rwandan Hutu refugees.

Our flight with Hewa Bora was not a great success with Bob. As the crowded passenger cabin became fully loaded his state of alert increased. Standing at his seat he surveyed each new arrival, mothers, children, large men with briefcases, as though they were raving mad to be seeking accommodation on this already over-packed aircraft. When the doors eventually closed he set off up the gangway and I saw him push his way into the pilot's cabin. He returned grim-faced. 'No whites on the flight deck.' We taxied towards take-off with the brakes creaking and banging. As the Hewa Bora DC-9 lumbered into the air, Bob remained on full alert. 'He used the entire runway. What's more his discs are shot. There's no doubt the landing's going to be terrible. There are always problems on the runway at Lubumbashi . . .' As we considered this observation the director of films murmured, apropos of nothing in particular, that it might be a good idea next time to fly via Nairobi.

My immediate neighbour was an elderly gentleman with a delightful smile who had no French and the eager, wondering air of the first-time flyer. Bad weather apart, there were no incidents until the pilot announced our descent to Lubumbashi. Emerging from thick cloud two things became immediately obvious. The first was that we were far too low and flying too flat. The second was that we were moving far too fast. If we did not decrease our speed and gain height we were clearly going to hit the ground some way short of the runway. So the pilot gained height and re-entered the clouds. Then the nose went down and we recommenced our descent. The second time we left the clouds the runway was right there and it was clear that we were going to hit it very fast and very steep and with an almighty bang. For some reason the undercarriage held, the tyres did not burst, the reverse thrust worked and there was huge applause from fellow passengers. Looking at the dreamy contentment on the face of my neighbour I realised what a curse knowledge can be. As far as he was concerned he had just experienced an entirely routine landing, and what fun it had been.

We exited the plane through the rear door, beneath the tail. At the foot of the steps a worried-looking mechanic was holding up a bucket to catch a thin fluid stream that was pouring out from above his head and smelt of aviation spirit. The pilot was coming down the front steps as we passed, a tall elegant man in a smart uniform. 'He looks like a Tutsi,' I said to Bob. '*Oui*,' grunted Mobutu's vet, '*il a une sale gueule de Tutsi*.'

There are many ways to crash a plane in the Congo. And the reason why the Democratic Republic 'holds the world record for air crashes' – to quote *Africa News* – has nothing to do with the nationality of the pilots, despite Bob's embittered convictions.

You can leave a lava flow across a runway (Goma today) and then attempt to take off during a rainstorm along a flooded runway and flood one of your engines – the real reason for the Hewa Bora crash in 2008. Or you can ignore instructions and attempt to land during a violent storm and crash the plane short of the runway (Hewa Bora at Kisangani, 2011 - 101 dead), or even on it (Kinshasa, 2011 - 33 dead, UN flight with Ukrainian pilot). You can under-fuel the plane so that it cannot divert to a safe airfield, but you are able to sell the fuel twice (Kisangani, 2011). Or you can fly in an ex-Soviet Union Antonov.

In 1996 an Antonov failed to take off from Kinshasa and crashed into a local market, killing about 300. In 2003 an Antonov 26 failed to take off from Boende and killed 35 people in the town. In 2006 an Antonov 26 crashed when trying to land at Lubutu, in eastern Congo: 11 people were killed. In 2007, 4 Antonovs crashed in the Congo killing over 100 people. One crashed in Katanga, one in Kisangani and one at Goma. The fourth took off from Kisangani and headed for Goma and then disappeared, leaving no trace.

Alternatively you can fail to check the hand baggage at Kinshasa (2010) and allow a passenger to carry a small crocodile on board, packed into a large sports bag. The crocodile escaped from the bag during final approach to Bandundu causing a stampede of passengers and cabin crew onto the flight deck where the Dutch pilot and his co-pilot, from Gloucestershire, lost control of the L-410 Turbolet – and all on board, except for one passenger and the crocodile, were killed.

Finally you can take off from Kinshasa, in May 2003, with a full load of passengers and land perfectly safely at Lubumbashi but without any passengers at all, since they have all been sucked out of the depressurised cabin somewhere over the rainforest. No one has ever discovered how many people died on that occasion since an accurate passenger list had not been compiled. Air travel in the Congo is just part of the black comedy of daily life, an existence that people accept as routinely hazardous, where each completed day becomes a further excuse for joyful celebration.

The Belgians called the southern province of their colony by its original name – Katanga. Mobutu called it 'Shaba'. The Belgians named the country after its river, the Congo. Mobutu called both the river and the country Zaire. The Belgians called the capital of the province of Katanga Elisabethville, after the wife of King Leopold II. Mobutu called it Lubumbashi. Today Shaba is once again Katanga and Zaire is once again the Congo. And Lubumbashi remains Lubumbashi. Elisabethville died fifty years ago, but the city is still the best regulated in the country, and represents all that remains of colonial order.

The old colonial residential quarter of Elisabethville is recognisable in Lubumbashi today. Many of the houses are built in the Cape Dutch style, long, low buildings with white walls, ornate gable windows and corrugated iron roofs. Other builders have favoured American colonial or Santa Fe boardwalk constructions. In the colonial days there was an internal snobbery within the white community; it was a society that was dominated by distinctions of race and class. Africans needed a permit to enter the residential quarter, and such permits were only given to domestic servants. Within the city there was an Italian quarter, a Greek quarter and a Jewish quarter. There was naturally a Portuguese quarter but no Syrian quarter. The Syrians were not Europeans and so had to settle in another part of town. This does not seem to have caused them much harm. Today the descendants of the Syrian colonial community, now described as Lebanese, remain a prosperous feature of Katanga, and the current governor of Katanga, who is of Jewish descent, is sometimes described as Syrian.

Near the residential quarter is the old courthouse with the words *Justicia Lex* carved into its stone portico, and then the Cercle Matutane which was originally the Cercle Albert. According to our guide, Bernard, who had been born in Katanga, this was a private club where most of the important decisions made in Elisabethville were taken; it was rumoured to have been the haunt of Freemasons. Colonial societies showed great ingenuity in constructing complex systems of exclusion. The Golf Club had been another centre of influence and rejection.

The tour ended at the railway station, where the name 'Elisabethville' is still engraved in stone above the ticket hall. This is the terminus of the line that ran up through Angola from the South Atlantic port of Lobito. It ran more or less straight out west, through dense forest that concealed diamond fields. On the Angolan side of the frontier during the 1960s, the forest became the scene of fierce fighting. The Angolan colonial wars were followed by the Angolan civil war and the railway has long since been abandoned. But the diamonds remained – unharmed – as did the frontier officials, police and military. So in order to facilitate the orderly traffic of illicit diamonds, the officials developed the technique of the moveable frontier. The last Angolan frontier post, where diamonds might legally be lodged, would overnight become the first Congolese frontier post where, as it so happened, diamonds were to be found. This technique was a great deal easier than carrying the diamonds across the frontier. Instead one just moved the frontier over the diamonds.

When the name Elisabethville was carved in stone into the façade of the railway booking hall, such practices would have been out of the question. The Belgian colony was a state under rule of law. Diamonds were dug up by Congolese labourers who were paid a pittance, housed in barracks, beaten if they disobeyed orders and, when they died, buried in a coffin and in due form. And the trains ran on time, in and out of Elisabethville station, carrying the country's

natural wealth away from the Congo and over the seas to the international markets. Now the wealth still gets traded, but the transport
arrangements have changed. On the paving of the platform outside
the booking hall there was another relic of the old order. A large
compass rose, forged in copper, is set into the stone and correctly
aligned with magnetic north. The copper is a reminder of the source
of the wealth that built this railway, and the exact placing of the
compass would have reassured the incoming engineers that they had
reached a terminus where they could count on everything familiar,
measurement, prediction, precision; all they would require to keep
the arsenic out of the milk.

The Congo Free State, until then the private property of Leopold
II, was annexed by Belgium in 1908 and became one of the most
lucrative colonies in the world. But in the early days it very nearly
went bankrupt. The situation was saved by the invention of the
pneumatic bicycle tyre and the discovery of wild rubber. By 1896 the
Congo Free State was exporting 2,000 tons of latex a year and in 10
years during the 1890s the king's annual Congolese income rose from
£60,000 to £720,000 a year.* The rubber turned Leopold from a man
taking a chance into one of the richest individuals in the world. But
by 1906 his violent and destructive system of exploitation had almost
exhausted the rubber supply. Again, the Congo was threatened with
poverty. This time the situation was saved by the discovery of important deposits of copper in the very south of the country, in the
province of Katanga. The mineral wealth of Katanga has since become
legendary, and even today, after more than a century of exploitation,
it remains one of the richest mineral areas in the world. But originally
Katanga was never intended to be part of the Congo at all.

The first time the borders of the Congo were drawn on a map it
was by Stanley in the royal palace in Ostend. There the explorer met
the king in August 1874, on his return from another upriver

* From £23 million to £277 million in today's values

expedition. Using a red crayon, Stanley marked out the proposed frontiers of the future state, stretching from Lake Tanganyika in the east to the Atlantic coast, and from four degrees north of the equator to six degrees south. The king sent this map to Bismarck before the opening of the Berlin Conference, and it was quickly accepted by both the German and the French governments. Stanley's map established the Congo's southern boundary through the middle of the central Kasai kingdom, but during the Conference – on 24 December 1884 – the king had another look at the map and decided to give himself a little Christmas present. He moved his southern border six degrees further south, thereby including the headwaters of the Congo River and the whole of what is now the province of Katanga. Bismarck again approved.

None of this was of much concern to the British government, since Britain declined to recognise the king's boundaries in either their original or their extended form. London refused to accept any 'bold lines drawn through almost unexplored regions'. But in August 1885, when the higher civil service was out of London on summer leave, the Belgian Embassy sent a document round to the Foreign Office in Whitehall that required an acknowledgement.

It fell to J. M. Warburton, an assistant clerk, to deal with the matter. The document, which concerned the Congo Free State, was 'a Declaration of Neutrality', and it included the map of the Congo's boundaries as redesigned by Leopold and approved by Bismarck. Having verified that the map was the same as the one proposed in the final Act of the Berlin Conference, the clerk signed a receipt for the document without adding any further observations and despatched it back to the Belgian Embassy, thereby committing a colossal blunder. For, according to the diplomatic convention of the day, in the absence of any comment, the signed receipt amounted to full agreement with the document, and included recognition of the Congo's boundaries.

In May 1891, the British South Africa Company enquired, on behalf of Cecil Rhodes, whether the northern boundary of Rhodesia might be extended into Katanga, where there were known to be rich supplies of copper. The Foreign Office's Africa Desk could only refer Rhodes's engineers to the receipt signed in August 1885, by the duty clerk, which accorded full British recognition of King Leopold's southern frontiers.

Over the years that followed, the wealth extracted from Katanga acted like a draft of magic potion on the body of Leopold's puny North Sea kingdom.

In a land where planes crash because airline officials have stolen the fuel, you need to be resourceful to survive. We called on an old *colon*, Franz Couttenier. Franz was not born in Elisabethville. He set out from Poperinge in West Flanders as a child, one of a family of nine who were attempting to travel overland to Australia. His father led them on to the wrong boat in Marseilles and they found themselves in Turkey. There they changed course and headed back towards Egypt. Driving south through Africa, still heading for Australia, they passed by the Belgian Congo and decided to stay. Couttenier now lives in a splendid house with a large garden in an unfashionable part of Lubumbashi. It is unfashionable because it adjoins the main army barracks. He said that he had acquired his house cheaply because everyone else was too frightened to live there. 'If the army want to shoot me,' he said, 'they only have to lean out of their window. They don't even have to get out of bed.'

Of the nine children who had travelled from Flanders to the Congo, Franz was the only one left. Some departed after independence, the remainder after the fall of Mobutu. Three of his four children had moved back to Belgium and his wife wanted to go too. But he still had the family farm, 5,000 hectares of good land reclaimed from forest at the heart of the copper-mining belt. He grows maize and raises cattle; he has recorded the lowing of his cattle as his mobile ring tone. He said that by rights the Congo should be paradise. 'Nothing to do with mining but because of the agriculture. Agriculture is a renewable resource. The Congo River crosses the equator twice, so there is no dry season and no low water. And we have incredibly rich soil that is unexploited. Yet today the fields are abandoned and we import food.

'We have the world's worst form of government, a dictatorship without a dictator. No strong man. The DRC has become a society of fraudsters. We have miners who have never run a mine and bankers who have never run a bank. Money-laundering and diamond-smuggling are well established and drugs will follow. I am not sure what will happen after that. You can never tell in Africa. The Africans are good people, but we never really know them.'

Couttenier is celebrated in Lubum for his behaviour in the late 1990s, during the civil war. For twenty-seven days Lubumbashi was at the mercy of rioting mobs who looted everything they could find. His house was surrounded. He decided to sit it out. When the mob broke into his grounds he realised that the best way of dealing with them was to organise the looting himself. He advised the looters what to take and what to leave and what not to break. He told them that they could have water from his supply provided they stayed out of his garden. Grateful for his assistance they accepted his authority and formed an orderly queue. Then one night a young woman with a child came to the house saying that she was from Rwanda and had been turned away by the Belgian Consulate. At that time the Lubumbashi mobs were hunting for Rwandans and beating them to death. Couttenier took the mother and child into his house, and when the mob arrived he got them out of the back gate and into his car. Then he drove them to the house where the child's grandmother was hiding, with other children. Then he took the whole family in his car to the Belgian Consulate and told the consul that he had done his bit and it was now the Belgian government's turn. He said that he was still in touch with this Rwandan family, and that several of the children he had helped to save now lived in Belgium.

The first farm that Franz Couttenier's father owned in the Congo was at Shinkolobwe, and bordered the domain of the uranium mine.

He grew up beside the mine. The current status of this mine is one
of the ongoing mysteries of Katanga. It was officially sealed in 1960,
although it remains one of the largest deposits of high-grade ore in
the world. Today uranium is mined all over Africa, at various levels
of purity, and whether a particular mine is profitable depends largely
on the fluctuating price of the world market. The Shinkolobwe mine
is not only sealed but heavily guarded, and yet it is known to be
mined illegally and dangerously by artisan miners who scrabble
around the entrance digging up what they can. There are frequent
rumours of visiting businessmen in the Congo being offered suitcases
full of black-market uranium ore.

A United Nations report in 2006 found that 15,000 amateur miners
were living in the village of Shinkolobwe and using 'informal' or manual
methods to mine cobalt from what was supposed to be a sealed uranium
mine. Shortly before the UN inspection took place the regional authorities had destroyed the mining village and *les creusers* (the illegal miners)
were dispersed. But rumours of black-market uranium being offered
for sale soon started again. Hacking into a flooded uranium mine to
remove the ore is a dangerous occupation, but at Shinkolobwe children
were said to be employed by the black-market traders and tunnel
collapses were frequent. Article 15 of Mobutu's imaginary constitution
stated 'Art. 15: Others may call it corruption, I call it looking after
myself and my dependants. You all have my permission to do the same.'
As a result of Article 15 thousands of families living in precarious
circumstances were able to make a living by breaking the law.

Hoping to learn more about Shinkolobwe, the director managed
to get an interview with a senior engineer at the Forrest transport
and engineering group, which was founded in Katanga in 1922, and
which had kindly supplied all the traffic lights in Lubumbashi. Forrest
is connected to most of the industrial activity in the province, but
all the engineer would endorse was the official position: the mine was
closed in 1960 and it belonged to the state. The most interesting
result of the interview was seeing inside the group's premises.
The company's security guards wore bright orange overalls, and the

engineer we spoke to spent his working life inside a concrete building that had no windows. The exterior doors were made of solid steel with interior hinges and the interior doors from the corridor into his office were of the same design. There were no pictures on the walls and the place resembled a military facility, with uniform cream-coloured walls. At the corner of every passageway, sensors on the ceiling blinked. The design only made sense if the building was connected to the outside world by a system of underground tunnels. Katanga has had its fair share of violent political disturbances in the fifty years of independence, and this building's architect had apparently intended it to be defended room by room.*

The Forrest Group owns copper and cobalt mines at Kawama, on the road to Shinkolobwe, and they have had troubles of their own with *creusers*. We visited Kawama a few days after a police operation had closed down an illegal mine. The huts built by *les creusers* had been smashed up or burnt down; several people had been killed. The community was disrupted but it had not been driven out, and hundreds of squatters were still living in the wreckage, which they called their '*citée*'. Most of the illegal mining is done by young men, teenagers, and one of them explained how they worked.

We cut a tunnel into the side of the hill and we dig down holding a candle until there is not enough air for the candle, and then we switch on a torch. We have a string with us which runs back to the surface, and this acts like an oxygen tube, it draws in the air. We work for up to four hours and then we return to the surface. If there are enough of us we can cut a big chamber underground, we call it a *salon*. Then we cut side tunnels off the chamber, and this way we do not have to keep going back to the surface because four or five of us can sleep in the *salon*

---

*During the civil war in 1996 Georges Forrest, who ran the Forrest Group, was put up against a wall by drunken 'liberators' and only saved from a firing squad by the intervention of his own African workers.

and eat there. We know we have found copper when the boulders turn green. We live like animals. It's dangerous. The tunnels collapse, and then there's not much chance of rescue. People get killed all the time.

We do this because it is the only way we can make any money. The mine owners are not African. Now they have smashed up our homes and are calling us thieves and looters. The Congo is our country. But the only people who feel at home here are the foreigners.

You can recognise *creusers* from a distance. They move in groups, young, muscular, and, if they have returned from work, absolutely filthy. They wear rags to go underground and from top to toe they are covered in grey mud. They look both angry and exhausted, dangerous and vulnerable. Behind the *citée* where the people of Kawama still lived, the skyline was dominated by the long, flat table of the open-cast copper mine, with the grey-roofed warehouses and bright yellow bulldozers of the Forrest Group parked neatly beside.

On the drive back to Lubumbashi we passed a Chinese doctor's house; there was a slogan painted on the wall outside, 'Together We Share the Wonder of Life'.

It took us three years to get permission to enter Shinkolobwe. Among those who proved attentive but unable to help were the Ministry of the Interior, the Ministry of Mines, the Office of the President of the Republic, Areva, Forrest, the Belgian consul and the head of the ANR, one of the DRC's many intelligence agencies. Eventually help came from an unexpected quarter. We had dinner with a building contractor who lived by a lake in Lubumbashi. The lake was full of frogs. Pretty lake, no mosquitoes, but full of bilharzia. After dusk Luc, our sound engineer, recorded the frogs. I asked our host if this was the lake where a European ambassador had once been eaten by a crocodile while taking a nocturnal stroll. He said there were no crocodiles and anyway that sort of thing only happened in Kinshasa.

The building contractor owned a red Hummer, one of the few in Katanga. He said that he knew the governor of Katanga very well and would have a word. We heard no more. Then one morning the telephone rang and it was our friend with the Hummer who said that Governor Katumbi had called him at 7.30 a.m. and that he was displeased. The governor had given our friend a rocket because the *cinéastes* had not yet paid a courtesy call. We were to be at the palace in one hour.

The meeting lasted less than ten minutes. The governor listened to the director of films, summarised our project as '*un document historique*', and said that it should be seen by every schoolchild in Katanga. The visit would be organised by the Ministry of Mines and could go ahead at our convenience.

We spent the night before we set out for Shinkolobwe in the guesthouse of a Franciscan convent that was attached to a girls' boarding school. The school had been endowed by Union Minière. Sister Bernadine had given us a good supper: meat stew, okra and *frites mayo* with a tomato and cheese salad. No beer, lights out at 10.30. At 5 a.m. the convent bells rang out to rouse the girls. I had not been woken by school bells for 50 years. The girls had breakfast, went to chapel and started lessons at 7 a.m. Our police convoy set out for Shinkolobwe at 9.30.

There were five vehicles in the convoy: the lead car contained a major of police, followed by the Atomic Energy car with Geiger counters. After ten minutes we stopped at police headquarters to take on six more policemen. The mine was supposed to be sealed but was said to be infested with *creusers* who could become aggressive if interrupted. A violent argument broke out at the police station involving fifteen policemen, the major, his wife and his daughter. This was settled when the major's wife and daughter left on some expedition of their own in the major's 4x4. We were now down to four vehicles, one of which we knew would not be able to make it through the forest road. This also meant that we were down to ten policemen.

On the road the major stopped the convoy to arrest another police officer who happened to be passing and who was apparently absent without leave. He was crammed into the back of the Atomic Energy vehicle. At 11.00 a.m. the road began to deteriorate and one vehicle was ordered back. Fortunately this contained both Gento and Victor, our two minders from the ANR. They did not look pleased as we waved them goodbye, and Victor later declared that he would be making an official complaint about this regrettable incident. Shortly after we left them, the driver of the Atomic Energy car drove it into a tree.

We reached the mine at 12.20 after twice losing our way in the forest. The Atomic Energy car, having recovered from the tree, was then turned onto its side in a deep rut. The major seemed to be lost in the forest. Eventually we found the right path by following the wide tracks of a lorry, presumably one that was normally laden with bootleg cobalt and uranium. The forest opened out and we found ourselves in a rather overgrown clearing containing several twisted steel skeletons that marked the site of the world's most celebrated and most secret uranium mine.

There is no shortage of rumours about Shinkolobwe. We had been told that it was staffed by child miners, that it was heavily guarded by South African soldiers, and that the 'South Africans' were actually US marines. A Belgian professor of politics in Lubumbashi had identified the mine as the key to the situation in the Middle East and the target of Sudanese mercenaries working for Hezbollah, which was supplying Iran with uranium. Shinkolobwe had apparently become the focus of an Islamic thrust across Africa. The professor said that he had recently visited the site wearing a lead suit.

We had no lead suits but we did have paper face masks, thoughtfully provided by the Atomic Energy Agency.

The Shinkolobwe mine in its wartime heyday was a single shaft that was entered at the summit of a low hill. The uranium lode took the form of a vertical egg and the shaft ran straight down through the centre of the egg with galleries running off to left and right at intervals. When the mine was sealed by Union Minière on its departure in 1960 the shaft was filled with concrete and a solid ferroconcrete cap was constructed over the summit of the hill. It did not take the *creusers* long to work out that the way to crack this abandoned golden egg was to forget about the central concrete shaft and attack from the sides. Fifty years later the result is a new landscape. The hill has disappeared. In its place there is a raised rim about two metres high encircling a crater about ten metres deep. And lying at the bottom of the crater is the original mine shaft, now visible as a long concrete pillar that has snapped off and tumbled onto its side. Today the mine is derelict and heavily overgrown. Some steel towers and frameworks remain, rusting amid the trees and the tall grass.

Everyone got out of the cars, including the prisoner, and the major led the way to the lip of the crater around the main shaft. As we started to film, Leonard, the unpredictable driver with the Geiger counter, said that we had a maximum of thirty minutes for the good of our health. He obviously had no idea about the length of the filming process. The voice of the director rang out – '*Silence. On tourne.*' Justin, our reliable driver, did not like the look of the Geiger counter and said that he would be getting himself examined by a doctor when he got home.

It was a beautiful day. Towering white pillars of cloud against a deep blue sky. There were black martins hawking low over our heads, and white and blue butterflies in the wind that kept the tall grass rustling, a flame tree was in flower and there was a grove of umbrella thorns, all about thirty metres tall. These trees had had fifty years to grow since independence. Radiation seemed to make good fertiliser.

The first shots of the crater used up twenty minutes of our time, leaving us barely ten minutes to shoot a water reservoir. Leonard said that the reservoir had the highest score on the site and issued more paper face masks as a precaution. The great stone basin was dry, empty and rather impressive with its flights of black stone steps. The radiation score was high because the structure was below ground level. Leonard did not like the reservoir and told us to move on, but not back to the cars. The director and crew disappeared to the far side of the camp to film the rusting steel girders, and did not reappear for forty minutes. Faintly one heard the cry, '*Silence. On tourne.*' By the time we left, thirty minutes had become two hours. Somewhere close by, hidden in the rustling grass, was the site of the slag heap of excess ore that had been packed up in 1939 and sent to America. All in all, that morning Shinkolobwe was one of the prettiest places in Katanga.

In the forest on the road back to Likasi we came across the ghost of a graveyard lost in the trees. There were lines of rusty red iron crosses that seemed like miniature echoes of the rusty iron superstructure of the uranium factory. Each grave was neatly marked and of exactly the same size and design as though these people had all died at the same time. There were no names but these were clearly African graves because on each there was a white enamel food bowl; this was a precaution, placed there to feed the phantoms so that they did not leave the cemetery and return home looking for food. Each bowl had a neat hole drilled in the bottom to make sure that some profane traveller did not steal it and return it to human use. The fact that so many people had died and been buried in military order at the same time had the unmistakeable air of a mining accident.

Back in the bar of the Scala Hotel in Likasi, Leonard sipped his beer, consulted his Geiger counter and announced that we had been exposed to an average of 1.65 microsieverts over the whole 2 hours. The safe limit was 10 and our maximum, by the water reservoir, had been 8. His irreverent colleague Sebastien, who was calling his girl-friend with the news that '*on rentre bien contaminé*', was muttering something about 'Yes, yes, but the counters have not been checked. They are supposed to be calibrated in a laboratory every week.'

Out on the tarmac at Lubumbashi on the day of our departure, an unmarked Airbus was parked to one side. It had flown in from the United States to load unlicensed cobalt but had been discovered and impounded. It carried no registration number. As we queued to identify our luggage and board the plane I looked across the shimmering heat of the runway and saw a lone figure emerge through the haze, a man in a white shirt, carrying a suitcase and going at a steady, easy pace. Nobody else seemed to find this remarkable, and I never discovered whether he was heading for the terminal buildings or just out for a stroll on the runway.

Back in Kinshasa we said goodbye to Thomas, who was sitting under a gum tree, looking over the Congo towards Brazzaville. There was a thick grey haze on the water but one could still make out the swirling flow just above the rapids, the heavy scattering of timber from the forest being swept on towards the sea, and the fishermen with the long poles standing in their *pirogues* and casting their nets. This was where it had all started, the point above the rapids where the river became navigable upstream, deep into the heart of the forest, and the place where Stanley set up his first camp. This had been the Central Station, later Leopoldville, where the king's agents realised very quickly that 'Anything – anything can be done in this country.' And where their successors have been doing practically anything ever since.

There was no direct sunlight in the haze, and it was just as hot under the gum trees as it was on the open river bank. There were seeds falling out of the trees onto my hand and into my hair, and then soldier ants. So I turned back to the car – to discover that Papa had gone for his stroll by the water leaving the vehicle unlocked, with Bob's briefcase and passport visible on the back seat. This led to another of Bob's memorable explosions ending with the words, 'That's why I *hate* them.' It is Conrad's chief accountant at the Outer Station who says, 'When one has got to make correct entries, one comes to hate those savages – hate them to the death.' We seemed to have made little progress in 120 years.

Walking across the tarmac through the night to the A330 Airbus

of ex-Sabena (now Brussels Airlines) that had landed twelve minutes
ahead of schedule, we could see flames and a lot of smoke pouring
from the Arrivals terminal. The fire engine had already arrived. Then
as we drew closer it became clear that the Arrivals building was fine.
It was the fire engine that was on fire.

PART IV

OPPENHEIMER'S JOURNEY

CHAPTER TWELVE

Looking for Mr Oppenheimer

'To each sort of man his own achievement, his own victory, his own consequence.'

D. H. Lawrence, *Mornings in Mexico* (1927)

When Robert Oppenheimer returned to the United States from Zurich in June 1929, his first thought had been for New Mexico. The previous winter his father had signed a four-year lease on a small ranch property that stood at 9,500 feet in the Upper Pecos Mountains above Los Piños, where Katherine Page lived. They called this cabin Perro Caliente ('Hot Dog'); Oppenheimer took out a longer lease on the property and eventually bought it. The family still own it today. For Oppenheimer, Perro Caliente was his ivory tower. It has a superb view north-west across a valley to the Sangre de Cristo range; it was where he went to ride, read, drink and repair his spirit. He had turned from a boy into a man in the New Mexican mountains and the place had become part of his nature.

The Santa Fe that Oppenheimer saw on his first visit had already greatly changed since Aby Warburg's visit twenty-seven years earlier. Until 1912, New Mexico had been regarded as a colony that the United States had acquired because it needed a southern land bridge between its east and west coasts. The territory of New Mexico bore little resemblance to a conventional state; even today it sometimes resembles a conquered land. Its large alien population, which was both Spanish-speaking and Catholic, had been settled there for centuries. The opening of the railroad and the need to popularise the service eventually overcame Eastern prejudice. New Mexico was no longer considered to be dangerous and its image was gradually transformed by Santa Fe Railroad publicists from 'alien' to 'picturesque'. By 1900 Santa Fe had found its new destiny – tourism. The process culminated with the naming of the company's luxury trains. Just as the Sioux chief Sitting Bull – who had defeated General Custer and massacred an entire US Cavalry brigade at the Little Big Horn in 1876 – spent his declining years in a travelling circus, so Navajo warriors endured the ultimate humiliation of seeing their profiles engraved on railway locomotives. In the 1890s, when Warburg passed through town, Santa Fe possessed 3 hotels and 1 curio shop specialising in Indian art. By the time Oppenheimer arrived there were 16 hotels and 16 curio shops. The number of resident artists had grown from 1 to 29 and there was even an art gallery. In the final conquest of the Southwest the tourists replaced the cavalry. And in Santa Fe it was the artists who led the charge.

This came about at a time when there was precious little for a tourist to do in New Mexico. Some came to cure their TB in the dry climate. Some came like Herbert Smith and Oppenheimer to trek and camp and to enjoy the life of the dude ranch. But most of the activities available today were still to be invented. The first tourists came to New Mexico simply to be; that is, to be differently to how they could be elsewhere. They were anxious to be overwhelmed by the place, by the physical power of the wilderness and by the additional meaning this gave to their lives. They sensed that there was something here that they could not experience in their usual environment. They could inhabit a different world. They could be themselves more fully than they could ever have been back home.

In extreme cases, such as Georgia O'Keeffe, this transformation stamped not only their minds but their life's work. O'Keeffe once wrote of the view from her room in the Ghost Ranch, 'I wish you could see what I see out the window – the earth pink and yellow cliffs to the north – the full pale moon about to go down in an early morning lavender sky behind a very long, beautiful tree-covered *mesa* to the west – pink and purple hills in front, and the scrubby fine, dull green cedars – and a feeling of much space. It is a very beautiful world.' Driving for a hundred and fifty miles away from her house towards the Navajo country on the Arizona border she came on a setting that she named 'the Black Place', where a line of grey hills reminded her of 'a mile of elephants'. And she became as absorbed by the objects she found in the desert as she was by the landscape. She began to paint animal bones, a horse's pelvis, a mule's skull. 'To me they are as beautiful as anything I know. To me they are strangely more living than the animals walking around . . . The bones seem to cut sharply to the center of something that is keenly alive in the desert even tho' it is vast and empty and untouchable – and knows no kindness with all its beauty.' She painted in New York as well, and could have found any number of animal bones in the trash-cans and garbage of the city, but they would never have seemed to her to be more living than the animals around. It was a perception that was given to her by the splendour and desolation of the desert. In 1943 she painted a human skull she had picked up from the ground. It still contained the broken teeth and she placed it inside a broken Indian pot. For O'Keeffe the intensified experience of silence, emptiness, light and distance, in New Mexico, opened a window to a parallel vision of life.

D. H. Lawrence found a different way into the same enchantment. Introduced to New Mexico by Witter Bynner, a writer and resident of Santa Fe, Lawrence followed the same path as Warburg and was drawn to the Indians and to Indian dances. 'The American aborigines,' he wrote in *Mornings in Mexico*,

are radically, innately religious. The fabric of their life is religion. But their religion is animistic, their sources are dark and impersonal, their conflict with their 'gods' is slow, and unceasing. This is true of the settled pueblo Indian and the wandering Navajo, the ancient Maya, and the surviving Aztec. They are all involved at every moment, in their old, struggling religion . . . We dam the Nile and take the railway across America. The Hopi smoothes the rattlesnake and carries him in his mouth, to send him back into the dark places of the earth, an emissary to the inner powers. To each sort of man his own achievement, his own victory, his own consequence. To the Hopi the origins are dark and dual, cruelty is coiled in the very beginnings of all things . . . [To us] the Godhead was perfect to start with, and man makes but a mechanical excursion into a created and ordained universe . . . and [yearns] for the return to the perfect Godhead of the beginning . . . God was in the beginning, Paradise and the Golden Age have been long lost . . . To the Hopi, God is not yet, and the Golden Age lies far ahead.

Warburg believed that his study of the Hopi dances increased his understanding of classical civilisation. Lawrence, who had not read Warburg, suggested that knowledge of the Hopi religion provided a key to understanding the origins of all religions.

Lawrence arrived for the first time in New Mexico just a few months after the seventeen-year-old Robert Oppenheimer. He acquired a ranch near Taos, to the east of the Rio Grande valley, and it was there, after his death in 1930, that his widow scattered his ashes.

Beneath the surface of its spectacular beauty, New Mexico was changing at the beginning of the twentieth century in other less welcoming ways. The original notion of manifest destiny was bolstered by the popularity of social Darwinism which according to Eric Hobsbawm had been warmly welcomed in the United States and used there as a justifying ideology for militant capitalism. The righteous people were not merely planting liberty; they now had an eye for profit. Victories in the Mexican War, the Civil War and the Indian Wars had confirmed the Easterners' conviction of their own superiority, in both their society and their race. Since they manifestly ran the world better than their opponents, it followed that they had a right and even a duty to acquire more of the world to run. In New Mexico this was expressed in the struggle for land, which no longer took the form of some crude armed conflict but which could be conducted even more successfully by use of the law.

A legal battle between the Anglo ascendancy and the Hispanic and Pueblo Indian communities for title to the land could only end one way. From owning nothing on their arrival in 1845 the Anglos are estimated, by the regional historian Chris Wilson, to have acquired by 1912 – when statehood was finally granted – 'through judicial and legislative chicanery 80 per cent of the former common lands of the Mexican farmers and ranchers'. Land was New Mexico's primary resource and to win control of it the ruling elite of the American conquest formed a loose confederation of lawyers, state officials and investors who united with the *ricos*, the old rich of Santa Fe, to form what was known as 'the Santa Fe Ring'. In its heyday the Santa Fe Ring was led by Thomas 'the Boss' Catron, a lawyer, land tycoon and cattle baron who bought up most of two counties. The Boss operated in partnership with another lawyer, Stephen 'Smooth Steve' Elkins, and with a justice of the Territorial Supreme Court, Joseph G. Palen.

Catron was a Republican, but he was not narrow-minded and would work with anyone, Democrat, Catholic or Jew, Anglo or Hispanic, who would work with him. The Santa Fe Ring was a professional outfit that used good old-fashioned methods: extortion, trumped-up criminal charges, fraudulent land claims, forgery and legalised violence to increase its wealth and power. 'Boss' Catron, who had unsurprisingly been elected mayor of Santa Fe, was later successful in his campaign to be elected to the new state's first senate. I asked a friend, a lawyer from St Louis, whether any of this founding tradition survived today and he said that he had first felt drawn to Santa Fe during a casual visit to the district courthouse when he heard the following exchange:

Judge: 'Do you have any *law* for me on that point, counsellor?'

Counsellor: 'Oh, I think I could find you some law on that, judge. If you really *needed* it.'

According to a recent edition of the *National Trust Guide to Santa Fe*, which is produced by the National Trust for Historic Preservation:

> Since the Roundhouse (state capitol building) was designed to minimise contact between legislators and the public, it has become traditional for lobbyists to state their cases at the Rio Chama restaurant and bar, 414 Old Santa Fe Trail, just one block down from the State Capitol. Three-margarita lunches are such an institution at No. 414 that it has recently become fashionable for senators and representatives to pledge publicly that they will not show up inebriated at afternoon sessions.

So something of the spirit of 'the Boss' lives on, a century after the old gentleman's death.

Whereas land has been the battleground for the Hispanic people of the state, the Pueblo Indians have had to fight for water. When statehood was granted in 1912, the citizens of the territory necessarily became citizens of the United States, with the same rights, equalities and legitimate aspirations as any other citizen: except in the case of the Indians. A far-seeing federal legislature ensured that they alone would remain at a longer disadvantage, since they were not granted citizenship until 1924. This meant that Indian property remained at the disposition of other interests. In the 1890s the future President Teddy Roosevelt confiscated thousands of acres of forest that were part of the Jemez and Taos pueblos. This was designated thenceforth as national forest, and to add insult to injury Roosevelt named it after Kit Carson, the legendary Indian hunter. Roosevelt justified this acquisition as an 'unfortunate but necessary sacrifice to progress'.

Under the Spanish, Indian land and water rights were stabilised by mutual agreement and, according to one of the first American scholars to study the matter, Adolph Bandelier in 1892, 'The tendency of Spanish legislation [was] therefore marked towards ensuring the preservation and progress of the natives.' When US federal law was applied to Indian lands after 1845, Washington generally accepted the Spanish partition and confirmed Indian rights. But Washington in the second half of the nineteenth century was a very long way away from New Mexico.

The Native American historian Joe S. Sando has detailed the methods by which unscrupulous individuals took advantage of Pueblo Indian goodwill, their ignorance of English and their illiteracy, to swindle the Indians out of much of their land. An investigation carried out by the 67th Congress established that 'there were approximately three thousand non-Indian claimants to lands within the boundaries of the pueblo grants, aggregating about twelve thousand persons'. The response of the heirs to 'Boss' Catron was worthy of his memory. In 1921 a senator from New Mexico called Holm O. Bursum introduced a Washington bill that was supposedly intended to safeguard the right of Pueblo Indians to 'quiet title' in their traditional land and water rights. The bill received the approval of President Harding and was sponsored by the Secretary of the Interior, a rogue named Albert Fall who also happened to be from New Mexico. It was widely claimed in Washington that this bill had the support of the Pueblo Indians. In truth they had not been consulted and knew nothing about it. And a close reading of the Bursum Bill made it apparent that it was actually a well-disguised instrument for depriving the Pueblos of their traditional rights, depriving them of federal protection and delivering them up to the mercy of the New Mexico state legislature. When Robert Oppenheimer first came to New Mexico the Pueblos were in a ferment of anger and anxiety and were in the process of organising an appeal for national support to defeat the bill. The Appeal was signed by leaders of all the New Mexican Pueblos. Part of it read:

Today many of our pueblos have the use of less than an acre per person of irrigated land, whereas in New Mexico ten acres of irrigated land are considered necessary for a white man to live on. We have reached a point where we must either live or die . . . The Pueblo, as is well known, existed in a civilised condition before the white man came to America . . . This bill will . . . rob us of everything which we hold dear, our lands, our customs, our traditions. Are the American people willing to see this happen?

In the event the American people were not at all willing for this to happen. The Pueblos' Appeal launched in November 1922 received national support, particularly from women's movements, and strong support from the growing artistic and writers' colony of New Mexico. After 100 years, following the departure of the Spanish, the Pueblo people had at last found new allies, and the Bursum Bill was defeated. But the struggle over water rights continues to this day.

It is no easy task finding traces of Robert Oppenheimer in the state of New Mexico 45 years after his death. I heard that his son Peter, who had grown up inside the wartime wire of the Manhattan Project at Los Alamos, still lived in the state. He was said to be a recluse who never spoke about his father, but I nonetheless decided to ask for his help. My sporadic attempts to contact Peter Oppenheimer were made over a period of eleven years, at the end of which I had still to meet him. First, I heard that he was likely to be at a party given by some Los Alamos scientists. It was a great party, but he never showed up. Then I was told that he was living in a remote loghouse, working as a building contractor. I visualised a wired-in compound with guard dogs and security lights. Then I obtained his address. It was a post-office box number. To my surprise he answered my first letter promptly, courteously explaining that he would not be able to meet me but would do his best to answer any questions I might have.

At the time I was preparing a biography of his father, a project that received a severe setback when *Publishers' Weekly* in New York carried the astonishing news that my modest scheme had full family co-operation and that I would be drawing on extensive unpublished archives. This provoked a clipped and fully justified denial from an Oppenheimer family spokesman, and cast something of a shadow over any further attempts I might have made to ambush Peter Oppenheimer.

The biography never happened; it petered out at the point when I had decided that the importance of Oppenheimer's work far exceeded my already flickering interest in the mundane details of his life as a university teacher and research scientist. A biographer has to have some empathy with his subject, and I sensed something in Oppenheimer, a hint of false modesty and a blatant opportunism, that repelled me. Engaging with – and at times judging – the life of such a brilliant man is an intimidating task. And when I came across evidence of his cruel streak (he had a habit of amusing himself by bullying less robust colleagues in public) I began to lose any sense that I would be able to understand him well enough to bring him back to life. Then, by chance, the opportunity arose to make a documentary film about the genesis and use of the atomic bomb.

Working through old notes and correspondence I found the first letter from Peter Oppenheimer – and wrote to him again. This time I got a little further. I had three telephone conversations with my quarry. The first was on a mobile telephone from the forecourt of a gas station in Carrizozo in a 30-knot wind, punctuated by the noise of articulated trucks accelerating away from the traffic lights; the second conversation, on a peaceful landline, led to a remarkable breakthrough: Mr Oppenheimer agreed to meet me. I found this hard to believe but he had apparently succumbed to my powers of reassurance and persuasion and was quite determined on the matter. I felt decidedly proud of my low professional skills. The third conversation, once more on the mobile telephone, took place a week later as I was driving towards his chosen point of rendezvous. With less than an hour to go he cancelled the meeting. At the time I was quite annoyed, but in retrospect I admire Peter Oppenheimer's steadfast determination to have nothing to do with people enquiring into the life of his father. In his position I hope I would do exactly the same.

With his habitual courtesy Mr Oppenheimer terminated our telephone relationship by wishing me a 'Happy Thanksgiving'.

There remained the log cabin.

Los Piños, the dude ranch where Robert Oppenheimer first stayed when he came to New Mexico as a puny East-coast school leaver, is today owned by Alice McSweeney, a range scientist working with the Rocky Mountain Research Station. In the course of her work she has investigated the economic and social conditions of the Sangre de Cristo communities – in particular the small farming families, of which the Los Piños ranch was once typical. We met in the dining room of the La Fonda Hotel in Santa Fe. During the war it was a favourite rendezvous for the Los Alamos scientists.

The struggle between the farmers of the Sangre de Cristos and the wave of land-hungry immigrants and homesteaders arriving from the East, was part of the price New Mexico paid for statehood. Alice McSweeney's research into the condition of the small farming communities of the Santa Fe and Carson National Forests, which are established on the slopes of the Sangre de Cristo range, deals with the conflict between conservation in the interests of tourism, and farming. Sometimes the interests of tourism are disguised as 'conservation', sometimes there is a distinct conflict between genuine conservation and farming. But the farmers in question do not regard this sort of threat as unacceptable. An example is loss of livestock. In the Sangre de Cristo cattle, horses and sheep are lost each year. Some are struck by lightning or get stuck in a bog, some are stolen, others eat poisonous plants. But even where animals are taken by coyotes or mountain lions, about 6 per cent of total losses, the farmers regard it as a natural hazard of the region's farming. They are less tolerant of animal losses caused by recreational hunters or through vandalism, which may account for 15 per cent of the total livestock loss.

Over half the farming families in these communities have owned their land for four generations, some six or more, going back to the 1600s. One of the farmers' chief complaints is against incomers who chose to move into their communities because they like the traditional way of life and then start to complain about woodcutting (for fuel) or fencing meadows to confine stock. The farmers who are of mainly Hispanic or Indian descent have ancestral memories of how they were cheated, first by the Spanish, then by the Anglos and then by the US government. The arrival of the affluent leisure crowd is just the latest challenge they face to their demanding way of life. The farmers received little sympathy from the authorities until the 1960s when, driven by poverty, encroachment and vandalism, they turned to violence. Claiming that they had been robbed of 2,500 square miles of territory, they took over and closed down leisure campsites. And in 1967, 40 'Chicanos', bearing arms, invaded a courthouse in Tierra Amarilla intending to carry off a district attorney in a 'citizen's arrest'. Once they had given their hostage back, conditions improved. But despite changes in government policy problems remain, and the potential for violence is still there.

Driving up to Los Piños, the road from Pecos follows the course of the upper Pecos River which eventually runs into Texas and was once the border between the rule of law and the badlands, a sometimes hazy distinction. As the road climbs, the Pecos River gorge narrows, the trees close in, the properties huddle together uneasily; they tend to have narrow boundaries and expansive names: 'Lazy Cougar Ranch', 'Macho Valley' and 'Rancho Pequeño'. Rancho Pequeño runs right along beside the road. There is the usual wire fencing in front of the scrub trees of the ranch, and then the wire turns into razor wire wrapped in the sort of military camouflage netting one usually sees draped over tanks or gun emplacements. There is a sign, white letters on a red background: 'WARNING: NO FISHING. NO TRESPASSING. VIOLATORS WILL BE PROSECUTED.' The word 'Violators' has been crossed out and replaced by 'Survivors'. 'No Fishing . . . Survivors will be Prosecuted'.

We reached the gates of Rancho Pequeño where there was another notice. You had to get quite close to the gates to read it. The small lettering seemed to tempt the traveller forward. When you got within eyeshot you learned that the gate was electrified and the sign read: 'THERE IS ABSOLUTELY NOTHING BEHIND THIS SIGN THAT IS WORTH YOUR LIFE – SO KEEP OUT.' I realised that this was exactly the sort of place I had originally imagined as Peter Oppenheimer's home. All that was missing was the rottweiler behind the wire.

I later asked a former New Mexico law officer whether it was in fact legal to publish random death threats in the area of his jurisdiction. Without a moment's pause he said that it was probably protected by the First Amendment, guaranteeing freedom of speech.

A few miles further up the road Terrero, 8,000 feet, turned out to be no more than a very tall flagpole bearing the Stars and Stripes, and a post office with general store attached. There wasn't a great deal on the shelves, cans of Coke, packets of Fritos and a Hershey bar, but it was here that the rottweiler finally appeared. Whenever I took a step down the aisle the store-owner's giant hound followed half a pace behind.

You don't make eye contact in Terrero with a rottweiler whose snout is four inches from your trousers and which is bored out of its mind, but I did not have the sense that this dog smiled at strangers.

Perro Caliente, which is not an easy place to find, turned out to be a rather pretty log house set back against tall pine trees, with a wooden veranda and a superb view over the mountains north-westward towards Los Alamos. There was a stream near the house, mule deer grazing in the trees and black bear droppings on the pine needles by the front steps. A rubber tyre twisted in the wind, its ragged rope dangling from the branch of a tall Douglas fir that had been struck by lightning. A man could sit on that porch today and swig some whiskey and look out over exactly the same view as healed the spirit of the visionary who gave us the atomic bomb. Needless to say the house was locked and there was no one at home.

*

The only lasting memorial to Robert Oppenheimer in New Mexico is the town that he founded, which stands in the Jemez Mountains on the banks of the Rio Grande about thirty-five miles west of his old ranch house, on a *mesa* above the pueblo of San Ildefonso.

Los Alamos today is an eerie place, and a curiosity, since, contrary to the usual arrangement, it is a town that actually owes its existence to a weapon of mass destruction. At first glance it resembles any other American small town. It has a main street and a diner that serves simple, wholesome food and good cold beer. You can sit there looking out of the window into the sunshine, watching the world go by. There's a yellow school bus, and neat lawns in front of the houses. There's a bookshop and a drugstore. During my last visit they had pinned a little blue and white banner to every lamp-post; it read 'Los Alamos – Where Discoveries are Made!' Just don't ask what they are.

For this is not just a town with a glorious past. The Los Alamos National Laboratory is still the United States' leading nuclear-weapons research facility. The laboratory is now a vast wired-off complex that stands on a low rise at the back of the town, on the way out to Valles Caldera. They take security very seriously at Los Alamos. I once met a nuclear physicist at a party in Santa Fe who worked in the laboratory and said he would be happy to show me around. He said that we could not meet inside the wire as I would have to fill out too many forms. We arranged to meet in the Holiday Inn instead. I spent about an hour and a half waiting for him in the hotel. His office telephone rang unanswered and he never showed up. And I never heard from him again. Perhaps he was devoured by some unidentified security operative on his way to our meeting.

In fact, even while I was waiting for him, sipping another mug of tepid brown fluid that was supposed to be coffee, one of his colleagues was already under arrest and being held in solitary confinement, accused of espionage.

The story of Dr Wen Ho Lee, a nuclear physicist who had worked at Los Alamos for twenty years, turned into one of the great sagas of 'How Not to Catch a Spy'. Dr Lee was originally arrested in 1999 when the FBI discovered that China had obtained top-secret information about the design and manufacture of nuclear weapons from the National Laboratory. Since Dr Lee was of Chinese origin – he was born in Taiwan – and since he worked in the Laboratory's X Division which is concerned with weapons research, and since he had visited China and met Chinese physicists in the 1980s, the FBI immediately realised that they had their man. Dr Lee was arrested, taken to Santa Fe jail and held in solitary confinement. He was only allowed to see his wife for one hour a week, and when they met they were forbidden to speak in Chinese. When the sixty-year-old scientist exercised alone in the prison yard, his feet were shackled. The FBI then discovered that Dr Lee had downloaded top-secret information onto computer tapes and taken the tapes home with him. It seemed to be an open and shut case.

But Dr Lee's friends were unconvinced. They pointed out that several other scientists from Los Alamos had visited China in the 1980s and they were still working at the laboratory undisturbed. A former security chief at the laboratory said that he believed Dr Lee had been selected for arrest purely because he was Chinese. Despite the solitary confinement, the leg-irons and months of intensive questioning, the FBI had failed to produce any hard evidence from Dr Lee. The doctor said that he had destroyed seven of the tapes but could not account for three others. When he offered to take a lie-detector test the FBI declined, on the grounds that it was unsure what questions to ask him.

Now and again Dr Lee was taken down to the Federal District Court in Albuquerque where his lawyers applied for bail. The FBI continued to oppose these requests on the grounds that Dr Lee posed a grave threat to national security and that if he handed the information over to a foreign power 'hundreds of millions of people could be killed'.

The FBI's case began to unravel when it was disclosed that some of the information obtained by the Chinese ten years earlier had not come from Los Alamos but from one of the subcontractors involved in assembling the weapons. Then the missing tapes turned up, behind a filing cabinet, in an area the National Security agency had supposedly searched already. Then the agency announced that it had traced the loss of top-secret information to the activities of computer hackers working for the Chinese government who were operating with advanced techniques from a research institute in Beijing. At a further hearing in Albuquerque a senior FBI agent acknowledged that he had misled the court about the extent of Dr Lee's suspicious activities. Then two weapons experts testified that the information downloaded by Dr Lee would be of little use to a foreign power and that much of it had already been published in scholarly journals. After eighteen months Dr Lee was bailed and held under house arrest with his telephone tapped.

Two weeks after my first visit to Los Alamos a wildfire blew down from the Jemez Mountains, destroying 48,000 acres of forest. It was finally extinguished on the edge of the National Laboratory's security fence. Many of the firefighters were Pueblo Indians, from San Ildefonso, Pojoaque and Hopi.

As the fire approached the town and hundreds of citizens were evacuated to Santa Fe, the laboratory managers told the firemen that for security reasons they could not fight the fire from within the security fence so they would have to extinguish it from the outside. Any fire-fighting needed inside the perimeter would be carried out by the laboratory's own security staff. But by the time the flames reached the fence, and started to jump it, the laboratory's security staff had all disappeared leaving the gates open. The firemen therefore entered the facility to fight the fire. It was a 'hot' area, that is a high-radiation zone, and at least two firefighters became so sick that they had to be taken to hospital for decontamination.

Dr Wen Ho Lee was released a few months after the great fire nearly destroyed the Los Alamos National Laboratory. All charges were dropped and he was able to return to work. He was no longer forbidden to speak Mandarin to his wife. The judge described the behaviour of the FBI and federal prosecutors as 'a national embarrassment'. And twelve months on from that verdict, the atrocity known as 9/11 took place. It aroused at least as much fear in the United States as the attack on Pearl Harbor; 2,996 people died, killed by a dozen religious fanatics armed with little more than sub-nuclear razor blades.

CHAPTER THIRTEEN

A Slow-motion Train Crash

'Scientific man is a doomed species. In the world in which we are living,
there is an active and dominant will towards death which has, so far, at
every crisis, got the better of sanity.'

Bertrand Russell, *Has Man a Future?* (1961)

The developments in fission research between February 1932 and
January 1939 can be viewed with hindsight as the scientific
equivalent of a slow-motion train crash. Within the space of a few
years, highly speculative attempts to unlock atomic energy for the
notional benefit of mankind succeeded at the very moment when the
world was on the point of being plunged into war.

One young scientist from Buenos Aires, Ernesto Sábato, had a
particularly vivid sense of the situation. Sábato was a child of the
Enlightenment. He would have approved the maxim of Antoine
Lavoisier, the eighteenth-century chemist and biologist who said,
'The Sciences are never at war.' He had been working in Paris since
1938 with Irène Curie, and was proud of the part he had played in
'breaking the uranium atom'. Sábato moved to Boston, to the
Massachusetts Institute of Technology, to continue his research in
atomic radiation, but then suddenly abandoned physics altogether. 'I
saw that war was approaching, a war in which science was going to
be the instrument of mechanised slaughter. I thought it was the
beginning of the apocalypse.'

Sábato became a writer and won a worldwide readership and eventually the Cervantes, the most coveted prize in the Spanish language. But his lifelong depression meant that he only ever published three novels. When he was asked at the end of his life why he had published so little he said that he would usually burn in the afternoon what he had written in the morning, because for him 'nothing really mattered, good or bad'.

The potential dangers of nuclear fission were well known. As far back as 1903, Ernest Rutherford had 'playfully' suggested that 'if a proper detonator could be found . . . a wave of atomic disintegration might be started . . . which would make this old world vanish in smoke.' In 1936 his colleague Francis Aston toyed with the same theory. Referring to the possible liberation of subatomic energy, and three years after Rutherford had dismissed the idea as 'moonshine', he compared those who wanted to ban further atomic research with 'the more elderly and ape-like of our prehistoric ancestors' who would have pointed out the grave dangers attending the use of fire. Aston said that he had no doubt that man would one day release the 'almost infinite power' of subatomic energy. He stated that this research could not be prevented and added, amusingly, that one could only hope that it would not be used 'exclusively' in bombs.

By then the crucial breakthrough had already occurred, in Rutherford's own Cavendish Laboratory in 1932, when – working from Rutherford's original hypothesis – James Chadwick 'discovered', that is proved by experiment, the existence of the neutron. The neutron was the highly penetrative particle that would become the bullet needed in the atom smasher if the atomic nucleus was to be shattered. With the discovery of the neutron, what Hans Bethe called the 'pre-history' of nuclear physics drew to a close.

Within seven years, scientists working in Paris, Rome and Berlin completed the task. In 1934 Irène Curie, working with Frédéric Joliot in her mother's laboratory in Paris, forced the nucleus to release some of its energy in radioactive decay; it was the first artificial transmutation of a nucleus. The experiment was observed by her mother, Marie Curie, who was already dying of cancer. Irène saw the old lady pick up the test tube containing the first artificially radioactive element in her hand, a hand that had long since been burnt with radium, and hold it near a Geiger counter to confirm the ticking. Later that year Enrico Fermi in Rome demonstrated that neutrons were more effective at smashing atoms if they were slowed down by passing through a material barrier.

The Joliot-Curies had used the traditional alpha particles for their bombardment of boron. Fermi decided to switch to the newly discovered neutron as the bullet. His methods were so crude, due to lack of competent engineers, that he had to bombard the nuclei in one room and then race down a corridor carrying the test tube to another room where a make-shift Geiger counter had been constructed. In the course of his experiments Fermi believed that he had produced a new element, and shattered the nucleus, but he was unable to prove his suspicions because there were no chemists in Rome capable of checking his results.

In 1937 Rutherford took a day off from the Cavendish to work in his garden and fell out of a tree. He died four days later, following an operation for a strangulated hernia, and so never lived to see the age of 'moonshine' come to life. Just over a year after that the highly experienced chemist, Otto Hahn, conducted an experiment the results of which he could not understand.

It was December 1938, and Hahn, working in the Kaiser Wilhelm Institute in Berlin, had bombarded a uranium nucleus with neutrons, hoping that the atom would split. In fact the uranium atom had been transformed into two atoms of barium. Hahn was puzzled because he was expecting to produce a new 'transuranic element', and all he could find was barium. For many years Hahn had worked in partnership with a younger woman, an Austrian physicist named Lise Meitner. However Meitner, who was Jewish, had been forced to flee from Germany in 1938 – Hahn had smuggled her over the Dutch border, and by December she was living alone in a hotel outside Stockholm. Hahn could only communicate with her by post.

So Hahn sent his baffling results in the mail from Berlin to Stockholm, and Meitner summoned her nephew Otto Frisch, also a physicist in exile, from Copenhagen, and aunt and nephew donned skis and set out to trek through the Swedish snow, working out what Hahn had done. At one point in their discussion Lise Meitner verified her calculations by checking the figures against Francis Aston's packing fractions,* which she kept in her head. Between breakfast and lunchtime the two outdoor physicists realised that the presence of the barium could only be explained by a loss of energy. In other words Hahn had succeeded in releasing the energy contained within the uranium nucleus.

Meitner and Frisch posted their explanation back to Berlin and Hahn published his results on 6 January 1939. Frisch returned to Copenhagen and wrote up the Meitner–Frisch verification. A microbiologist told him that when a cell split it was called 'fission', so that was the word he used. He airmailed his two papers to London, to the editor of *Nature*, who published them in February. Just after his return to Copenhagen Frisch had met his boss, Niels Bohr, who was on his way to board the boat for New York. Bohr could not contain his excitement. Before *Nature* was published his ship had docked in New York, and the news had spread.

The international brotherhood was generally made exultant by the advent of nuclear fission. But one man shared the foreboding of Ernesto Sábato. Leó Szilárd was a Hungarian theoretician who was in New York when Bohr disembarked from his transatlantic liner on 16 January 1939. Within a few days Szilárd had heard of Hahn's discovery and immediately started to worry. Szilárd was an oddity; he had a private income and held no university appointments, but his competence and ability were known to many. He had once worked

* The measurements of binding energy – see p. 123

with Lise Meitner. Since 1933 he had been obsessed with the idea that an element, when split by one neutron, might emit two neutrons, and so trigger a chain reaction.

He decided that the best thing to do would be to contact Enrico Fermi, who was also at that time living and working in New York, and Joliot who was in Paris. Szilárd thought they would be the two men most likely to be thinking about a chain reaction. He also wanted to dissuade them from communicating any further ideas or research to Berlin.

Meanwhile, at the Kaiser Wilhelm Institute, German physicists, thinking along similar lines to Szilárd, were planning to open a new, secret laboratory to study the possibilities of a chain reaction. To discourage casual curiosity they called it the Virus House.

And out on the West Coast of the United States, where news of Hahn's breakthrough had arrived nearly two weeks after it had reached New York, a young experimental physicist read a brief news report in the *San Francisco Chronicle* and passed the information to Robert Oppenheimer. Oppenheimer, who was working in the Radiation Laboratory, said, 'That's impossible,' and started to write on a blackboard the mathematical proof that fission could not take place. His young colleague then returned to his own laboratory, repeated Hahn's experiment and invited Oppenheimer over to watch. Oppenheimer realised his error and immediately started to illustrate the next step, a chain reaction. Later that week he made another drawing on his blackboard. It was a very crude diagram of an atomic bomb.

CHAPTER FOURTEEN

There's a Wop Outside

'But the wilderness had found him out early, and had taken on him a terrible vengeance for the fantastic invasion.'

Joseph Conrad, *Heart of Darkness* (1902)

Leó Szilárd was a maverick Hungarian intellectual, from a wealthy family, with a degree in civil engineering from Budapest, who had fought in the Austro-Hungarian Army in the First World War. After the Armistice in 1918 he was beaten up by anti-Semitic students in Budapest, despite the fact that he had by then converted to Calvinism. He moved to Berlin and took a doctorate in physics with the help of Einstein, who gave him evening classes in statistics. Then he worked as an assistant to Max von Laue, subsequently the only notable German physicist to stand up to the Nazis in defence of Jewish colleagues. Szilárd remained a free agent, with private means. He lectured without pay and on one occasion devised an ingenious system for securing ladies' silk stockings by sewing a metal thread through the stocking top and a magnet into the lining of the dress.

With the arrival in power of the Nazis in 1933, Szilárd moved to London and put up at a hotel in Russell Square. One morning he opened *The Times* and read a report of Lord Rutherford's 'moonshine' remark. This set him thinking as to how Rutherford might be wrong. Later that morning he imagined the possibility of a chain reaction.

This was not science; it was pure speculation. But the idea grew on him and as the succession of startling events unfolded – Chadwick's discovery of the neutron, Joliot's induced transmutation of the nucleus, Fermi's use of highly effective slow neutrons – his private conviction about the eventual possibility of a chain reaction grew into an obsession. In 1935 he even took out a patent on the idea at the Patent Office in London, and assigned it to the Admiralty. When the Munich Agreement of September 1938 was followed by Hahn's discovery of uranium fission in a Berlin laboratory three months later, and by Hitler's military occupation of Bohemia and Moravia three months after that, Szilárd became convinced that he had a mission to save the world. For this, two steps were necessary. The first was the imposition of a security blackout on all nuclear research being carried out in England, Denmark, France and the United States. And the second was the construction of an anti-Nazi atomic bomb, before the Nazi government announced that it had built one.

Although Szilárd was very well connected in the world of nuclear physics, and knew almost everyone who mattered, he himself still had no official status. He was living in New York in 1939, and so while his fellow physicists in Princeton, Paris and Berlin set to work on the chain reaction, Szilárd launched a desperate one-man assault on his chosen profession to persuade his colleagues to stop publishing their results. The first person he approached was Enrico Fermi – who replied, 'Nuts!' When Szilárd asked Fermi to explain himself the Italian said that he was not worried about a chain reaction because there was only 'a remote possibility' that neutrons would be emitted in the fission of uranium. He estimated a 'remote possibility' at 10 per cent. Szilárd said that this was not remote.

To settle the question Fermi and Szilárd cobbled together an experiment that was funded by a friend who gave them a cheque for $2,000. They used this money to rent one gram of radium from a New York company that was a subsidiary of a Belgian concern, Union Minière du Haut Katanga. They borrowed a laboratory at Columbia

University. The last move in the experiment they devised was to flick
a switch and watch a dead television screen. If flashes of light appeared
on the screen it indicated emission of secondary neutrons following
uranium fission. They flicked the switch, and nothing happened. The
screen remained blank. Szilárd was delighted. No lights, no chain
reaction. Then a colleague checked and found that the screen was
not plugged in. Szilárd described the sequel. 'We turned the switch
again and saw the flashes. We watched them for a little while and
then we switched everything off and went home.' Fermi estimated
an emission of two neutrons for every neutron targeted. It was the
beginning of the chain reaction. As Szilárd walked home from the
laboratory he had the feeling that 'the world was headed for grief'.

Quite independently, working in Princeton, Niels Bohr had compared
the results of several other experiments and worked out that it was
the rare U-235 isotope that was the most highly fissionable component
of uranium. Bohr's natural impulse was to publish his results, which
he proceeded to do in February. Szilárd's choice was not to publish,
but to use his results confirming the chain reaction to alert the
authorities to the approaching danger. On 16 March, the day after
Hitler's troops marched into Prague, Szilárd finally managed to set
up a meeting in Washington to warn the US Navy of what lay ahead.
The chosen herald was Fermi because he had a Nobel Prize. But the
Navy were unimpressed; and Fermi heard the naval rating who
announced him tell the admiral, 'There's a wop outside.'

Szilárd's next target was Niels Bohr. The objective was secrecy,
but Bohr had two difficulties with this: the first was that it would be
practically impossible to separate U-235, which formed 0.7 per cent
of the uranium nucleus, from U-238, which formed the rest. And
furthermore, it would be incredibly expensive. Bohr said it could
never be done unless the entire United States 'was turned into a
factory'. But Bohr also cherished a deeply held conviction that secrecy
and scientific research were totally incompatible. In Copenhagen he
had created one of the greatest international research institutes in

the world. His entire career had been devoted to the interests of the brotherhood of physics. The good scientist reported all his results; honesty and co-operation were essential to progress in the cause of truth. Until he was convinced that there was a real danger, Bohr remained utterly opposed to the isolation of German science. And yet, one by one, his lines of defence were being overrun. Einstein's identification of the relationship between energy and matter; Rutherford's discovery of the structure of the atom; Chadwick's discovery of the neutron; Fermi's advance with the use of the slow neutron; Hahn's discovery of nuclear fission; Bohr had rejoiced in them all. Now he took comfort in the fact that there was still no real proof that there would be a chain reaction; he remained reluctant to accept Szilárd's results. Furthermore, he insisted that isotope separation would always be a practical impossibility. Bohr sought every possible intellectual refuge to fight for his fundamental principle of openness, quite unaware that it was already too late.

While Szilárd had been dunning his friends for funds and forcing himself into laboratories where he had no status, Joliot in Paris, with all the facilities of France's new National Centre for Scientific Research (CNRS) at his fingertips, conducted a similar experiment and achieved the same result. He estimated the neutron emission rather higher than Fermi, at 3.5 per neutron targeted. Driven by ambition, and untroubled by Szilárd's visionary terror, Joliot sent his results to *Nature*, which published them two days after Bohr had turned down Szilárd's plea for secrecy. Joliot published a second paper in *Nature* on 22 April and this time his title included the words 'the nuclear fission of uranium'.

On 29 April in Berlin a secret meeting was called at the request of the physicist Paul Harteck to discuss the implications of Joliot's paper. The OKW (German Supreme Command) were more receptive than the US Navy. Harteck was supported by two other physicists, Kurt Diebner, a member of the Nazi party, and Hans Geiger, inventor of the Geiger counter. The Nazi government's response was extremely positive; a research programme into the chain reaction was started,

German uranium exports were banned, stocks from the newly acquired mines at Joachimsthal were laid in, and strict secrecy was imposed.*

In New York, on the same day as the secret meeting took place in Berlin, Niels Bohr, influenced by Joliot's results, announced that he had changed his mind – not about secrecy, but about probability – and abandoned his objections to the possibility of a chain reaction. Addressing a meeting of the American Physical Society, he warned that if it became possible to bombard the uranium isotope 235 with slow neutrons, it would set off a chain reaction, or atomic explosion, that would destroy the laboratory and the entire countryside for two miles around. This was reported in the *New York Times* as, 'A tiny amount of uranium would wipe out the entire city of New York.' Bohr, true to his principles, was publishing his views and warning the world.

Secret developments in Berlin were naturally unknown to Leó Szilárd, but he was still determined to achieve secrecy in nuclear research. Having been turned down by Bohr and the US Navy he switched to Albert Einstein. Szilárd knew that Einstein was on terms with Queen Elisabeth of the Belgians. He thought that this might be a way to persuade the Belgian government to stop supplying the Congo's uranium to Germany. In August, in the company of fellow Hungarian emigrés Eugene Wigner and Edward Teller, Szilárd twice drove out to Long Island, where Einstein was spending the summer by the sea, and won the great man's agreement to help them. Einstein declined to write to Queen Elisabeth but was happy to send a letter to the US President. Worried about making a wrong move, Szilárd and Wigner hesitated for several weeks, and then found a means of approaching President Roosevelt more directly. The outbreak of war in Europe on 1 September delayed matters further, but on 11 October the messenger, who was an old friend of Roosevelt's, was admitted to the Oval Office, carrying Einstein's letter.

* Germany acquired Joachimsthal when the Sudetenland was ceded in September 1938.

Many years later, after Hiroshima and Nagasaki, Einstein said that his letter to President Roosevelt had been 'the greatest mistake of my life'. But in truth he need not have worried. The emissary was an economist and investment banker called Alexander Sachs and he never even showed Roosevelt the letter. Instead he wrote a synopsis of Einstein's argument in layman's terms, which emphasised the ultimate peaceful uses of atomic energy, but made the possible dangers of a bomb perfectly clear. Roosevelt was impressed. He agreed that the matter required immediate action. He appointed a competent committee, just as Sachs had requested, and then turned to other matters. And the consequence was that for over two years absolutely nothing was done at all. Einstein's famous letter had no practical effect.

In October 1939, when Szilárd finally got his man to take up one hour of President Roosevelt's time, it was generally agreed in Berlin, London, Paris and the United States that to achieve a critical mass sufficiently large to sustain a chain reaction would require between 13 and 44 tons of raw uranium and that the resulting device would be far too heavy to deliver in the form of a bomb. This was such an impractical idea that Rudolf Peierls, a German refugee who was by then Professor of Mathematical Physics at Birmingham University, published his calculations in October 1939, one month after the war had broken out. They were read in Berlin and accepted as correct. With uranium out of favour the German physicists began to consider use of a different element, an artificial element that could be chemically separated from uranium: plutonium.

Scientists and political leaders in Europe and America were not alone in following developments in nuclear fission with close attention. In Brussels the Société Générale de Belgique retained physicists to supply information about the latest research into the uranium atom. A warning about the possibility of an early breakthrough in nuclear fission was issued in 1938, so when Otto Hahn's discovery was announced in January 1939, the Société Générale and its mining subsidiary, the Union Minière, were ready.

By this time Union Minière was under the control of one remarkable man, Edgar Sengier. Following the First World War, there had been heavy investment of Belgian capital in the Congo. By 1925 a total of 20,000 African labourers were employed by the Union Minière in the mines of Katanga. At the same time there was a vast programme of forced labour on road and rail construction throughout the colony, to a point where the authorities began to fear that the labour force 'would become so disturbed that they would be incapable of reproducing themselves'. In Katanga the situation was stabilised by the installation of labour camps linked to the mines where families could be housed, dispensaries provided and children given a primary education. These measures secured an adequate birth rate, but discipline in the mines of Katanga remained strict and attempts at political protest were savagely put down.

Although he was officially responsible to the company's main board and to the Société Générale in Brussels, Edgar Sengier ran the Katanga operation as his personal fief, and took crucial decisions on his own initiative. He was effectively in control of 7 per cent of the world's copper supplies and 90 per cent of the cobalt. He also had a near-monopoly of high-grade uranium, then used as the source of radium; but due to advances made in the 1930s, when radium went out of fashion as a treatment for cancer, the price of uranium crashed.

Consequently, Sengier closed the mine at Shinkolobwe in 1937 and was left with a slag heap of excess uranium ore on the site – about 1,700 tons of it lying loose in open sheds. He had such little faith in the future of uranium that he decided not to go to the expense of pumping the mine and Shinkolobwe quickly became flooded. Sengier continued to dribble his surplus uranium stocks at the rate of a few hundred tons a year to Antwerp, London and New York to satisfy demand for dyes for the ceramics industry.

Then in Paris on 22 April 1939, three months after Hahn's discovery, Frédéric Joliot announced that the nuclear fission of uranium led to a chain reaction – and Sengier, like the German High Command, was galvanised into action.

Between 4 and 8 May, Joliot registered three patents in the name of the French National Centre for Scientific Research. Two of these patents concerned a nuclear reactor. The third was secret and dealt with explosive charges. On 8 May Joliot took the train to Brussels to discuss another secret project – his plan to build a uranium bomb on a site in the Sahara Desert. His meeting in Brussels was with Edgar Sengier.

Two days after the meeting with Joliot, Edgar Sengier was in London for a meeting with Sir Henry Tizard, senior scientific adviser on air warfare to the British government. Tizard asked Sengier to grant the British government an option on the whole of Union Minière's existing uranium stocks. When Sengier refused Tizard warned him that if Congolese uranium fell into German hands it would be 'a national catastrophe' for both their countries. The warning was understandable. Germany was the second largest customer for the Belgian Congo's exports, and a major customer of Union Minière. Three days after Sengier refused Sir Henry Tizard's request, Union Minière signed a secret contract with the CNRS in Paris in which the Belgian company guaranteed to supply all the uranium that would be needed for Frédéric Joliot's atomic-bomb scheme. The project was to be funded by Union Minière.

In other words, within four months of the discovery of nuclear fission, the French government and Union Minière were secretly working together in time of peace to develop the world's first atomic bomb.

The French atomic-bomb project was abandoned in September 1939 on the outbreak of war, and the uranium contract was cancelled. But Sengier did not give up. Unknown to both his own board in Brussels and to the American government, he started shipping uranium ore from the slag heap at Shinkolobwe to the city of New York. A first shipment of 598 tons of ore was deposited in a Staten Island warehouse owned by the Central Trading Corporation, the company retained by Union Minière to market its uranium in the United

States. Sengier made the original decision to stockpile uranium in New York five months before the outbreak of war. After the war he said that he had done this in order to ensure that the ore did not fall into German hands. He did not mention that he had at the same time been planning to devote the resources of Union Minière to an atomic-bomb programme.

In July 1940 Sengier ordered managers at Shinkolobwe to ship the remaining stocks of uranium ore to New York, and by 19 December a further 1,139 tonnes had left Lobito in two fast freighters bound for Staten Island. The uranium sat on the quay for over two years, stored in a warehouse in 2,007 barrels while world war raged and Sengier tried without any success to find a buyer for what he knew to be potentially the most explosive material on the planet.

CHAPTER FIFTEEN

The Secret State: Washington 1939–42

'Yesterday, December 7th, 1941, a date which will live in infamy, the United States of America was suddenly and deliberately attacked by . . . the Empire of Japan. No matter how long it may take us . . . the American people in their righteous might *will win through to* absolute victory.'

President Roosevelt's address to Congress

Anyone interested in the question of why the United States government dropped the atomic bomb on Hiroshima and Nagasaki in August 1945 could start by considering another question: why did the United States government build it?

There were various essential elements in the building of the bomb. One was the availability of the uranium. Without access to the Shinkolobwe mine it is very unlikely that the bomb would have been built during the Second World War. Another essential element was the personal contribution of two men. The first of these was Robert Oppenheimer. Without Oppenheimer's intellectual brilliance, quickness of understanding and ability to follow and guide scientists in many different fields, it is highly unlikely that the bomb would have been assembled before the Japanese surrender. The second remarkable individual was an army engineer, Leslie Groves, director of the Manhattan Project. He was given unlimited funds and within the space of three years he had constructed two huge

assembly lines and a third bomb factory. He had also commissioned
work in four other secret laboratories to create an enterprise that,
at its peak, was the size of the entire US automobile industry,
employed 150,000 people and cost $2bn.* Without Groves the
Manhattan Project would probably have terminated its work several
years after the war. The next essential element was the contribution
of Adolf Hitler. Thanks to Hitler's anti-Semitism, most of Germany's
top physicists had taken refuge in Britain and the United States.
Instead of working patriotically for the Fatherland, they put their
enormous pool of talent at the service of Germany's enemies.
Frightened, angry and brilliant, they were prepared to overcome
their scruples and set to work on the most terrible weapon ever
devised in order to avoid the possibility that Hitler should acquire
sole use of it. And the final essential element was the British government. Without the British contribution, there would, again, have
been no wartime bomb.

One night in February 1940 two émigré Berlin physicists working at
Birmingham University were walking home through the blackout.
Both physicists were 'enemy aliens' and banned from access to military
secrets. The first was Otto Frisch who had doubts concerning Bohr's
original conviction that a nuclear chain reaction was not technically
possible. Bohr's calculations had assumed the use of U-238, the
isotope that formed 99.3 per cent of uranium, and reflected his belief
that isotope separation was impossibly slow and expensive. But Frisch
had devised a theoretical separation system, the cost of which 'would
be insignificant compared to the cost of the war'. Now Frisch turned
to his companion, Rudolf Peierls, and said (naturally enough, in
German): 'If you had enough uranium-235, how much would you
need to achieve critical mass and make an atomic bomb?' Peierls, as
we know, had already answered this question in a paper he had
published six months earlier, but he had used uranium-238. He made

* $578bn today.

a quick recalculation and came up with a very different result. 'About one pound,' he said. Both men were horrified and decided that they had to warn the British government; contrary to previous opinion it was clear to them that it was entirely practicable to make an atomic bomb. Following further discussions at their laboratory, they wrote a three-page memorandum that amounted to a technical blueprint for a 'super bomb'; it was brief, clear and turned out to be extremely accurate.

The atomic bomb was conceived in London in March 1940, when Mark Oliphant, Professor of Physics at Birmingham University, sent the Frisch–Peierls memorandum to Sir Henry Tizard, chairman of the wartime Committee for the Scientific Survey of Air Defence.

Frisch supposed that, in Germany, fellow members of the international brotherhood would have made the same calculations and come to the same conclusion. And he was correct: in December 1939, Heisenberg had informed the OKW that uranium 'enriched' by a concentration of U-235 would produce 'the most powerful explosives yet known', while Paul Harteck in Hamburg was already building a separation tube following the same design as the one favoured by Frisch. The first ton of uranium from the Joachimsthal mines was delivered to the OKW in January 1940. Heisenberg had also suggested that a German nuclear reactor would need plentiful supplies of heavy water; this would act as a moderating barrier, to slow down neutron bombardment. Heavy water was a rare commodity which was only produced in Norway. Early in 1940 the Norwegians refused to sell any to Germany, although they happily supplied it without charge to France. Germany invaded Norway on 9 April and captured the heavy-water plant on 3 May. Harteck immediately ordered a significant increase in heavy-water production.

The British atomic-bomb programme led the world, but it did not last very long. An industrial isotope-separation plant was commissioned and a site was chosen on the slopes of the north Welsh mountains. The programme was directed by a specialist committee called the MAUD Committee, which met for the first time at

Burlington House, Piccadilly, on 2 April 1940. A third enemy alien from Berlin, Franz Simon, soon became involved in the research and replaced Frisch's original separation method with a more promising idea, gaseous barrier diffusion, a technique Simon developed after he brought a kitchen strainer into the laboratory. (His wife was in Canada at the time.) Having beaten the strainer flat he experimented with it to see whether it was an effective means of separating carbon dioxide and water vapour. In May 1940, Simon was naturalised and was authorised to undertake secret work. Churchill had been interested in the science-fictional possibilities of an atomic bomb for many years; in August 1940, on the eve of the Blitz, he authorised British research while famously minuting, 'Although personally I am quite content with the existing explosives, I feel we must not stand in the path of improvement.' The Maud Committee issued its final report in July 1941. Its conclusion was that a working atomic bomb could be constructed by 1943 with the use of U-235, and that work should start at once. In a highly significant note the Maud Committee signed off with a reassuring thought for the Treasury. Even if the war ended before the bomb could be dropped, 'the effort would not be wasted . . . *since no nation would care to risk being caught without a weapon of such decisive possibilities'* [author's italics].

So in a brisk, effective series of thoughts and initiatives, the fate of mankind was sketched out. A weapon of mass destruction was possible, thanks to Frisch, the advantages were positively evaluated, thanks to Churchill, and the bomb was to be built as soon as possible, thanks to the assembled ranks of the great and the good, meeting in the committee rooms of the Royal Society. And the cherry on the cake was not a bomb in time of war, but the possibility of blackmailing the world by Britain's post-war possession of a technology that could destroy civilisation. The entire process had taken sixteen months. But there was a problem for the British government. Atomic bombs were not only expensive, they needed a lot of space, and the hillside in north Wales was not the answer. In fact it was not possible to find a site that was both remote and secure within the United Kingdom.

The first British attempt to involve the United States in its atomic-bomb programme came in August 1940, at the height of the Battle of Britain, when Sir Henry Tizard was instructed by Churchill to go to Washington and supply the US government with information about British nuclear research. The country was then facing a strong probability of invasion and the likelihood of defeat. Churchill, whose mother was American, was a US-ophile to his fingertips and maintained a visceral belief in the importance of the Atlantic Alliance. Military aid from the United States was about the only card he had left up his sleeve.

The historian Ferenc Szasz has listed the contents of Sir Henry Tizard's sea trunk when he set sail for Washington on 31 August. It contained designs for the Rolls-Royce Merlin engine, power-driven gun turrets, the proximity fuse, anti-submarine and anti-aircraft devices, jet engines, the cavity magnetron (later used in radar) and the latest breakthroughs in chemical warfare. The gifts would have rivalled in splendour the tribute paid to an oriental potentate. Accompanying Tizard was Sir John Cockcroft, Professor of Physics at Cambridge and a member of the Maud Committee. He was a pioneer of particle accelerators. With instructions to hold nothing back, Tizard and Cockcroft were well received, but once again their visit had very little practical effect.

One reason for the lack of progress in Washington was the inactivity of a scientist called Dr Lyman J. Briggs. Following the Einstein–Szilárd letter to Roosevelt, the President set up an Advisory Committee on Uranium under the chairmanship of Briggs. The doctor was an over-meticulous and slow-moving administrator. The visit of Tizard and Cockcroft escaped his attention entirely. And when he eventually received the final report of the Maud Committee, Briggs put it in his safe and failed to circulate it. He never showed much enthusiasm for the atomic bomb. Mark Oliphant, a blunt Australian, who was sent from Birmingham on a second mission to energise the Americans in August 1941, described Briggs as 'this

inarticulate and unimpressive man . . .'. But Briggs may just have
been squeamish.

There were however other more energetic men at work. Vannevar
Bush was the president of the Carnegie Institution and on his own
initiative had set up a group he called the National Defense Research
Committee (NDRC) which was licensed by Roosevelt in June 1940. Its
purpose was to place the US military on a scientific basis and its members
were to play a crucial part in the construction and use of the atomic
bomb. They included James Conant, the president of Harvard University,
and Karl Compton, the president of MIT. The NDRC absorbed Briggs'
Uranium Committee, but perversely left Briggs in effective charge of
uranium research. By May 1941, Bush, a consummate Washington
operator, had reorganised his brainchild into a more effective formation.
He would head a new umbrella group, the OSRD (Office for Scientific
Research and Development) and report direct to the President. James
Conant would take over the NDRC and report directly to him.

One direct consequence of Cockcroft's mission the previous
autumn followed a demonstration Cockcroft had made in New York
to Ernest Lawrence, Prof. of Physics at Berkeley, California. The
NDRC set up a secret laboratory at MIT, cunningly called the
Radiation Laboratory, since it was actually engaged in radar research.
In both Britain and in the United States, radar – then a purely
defensive weapon – took priority over work on a uranium bomb.

But Ernest Lawrence was not interested in radar. He was the
leading experimental physicist in the United States and the man who,
when asked about the size of an atomic nucleus, first likened it to 'a
fly inside a cathedral'. Lawrence had grown up on the prairie; he was
of Norwegian stock and had paid his way through college by working
door-to-door as an aluminium kitchenware salesman. Lawrence's
specialist field was the particle accelerator, the 'gun' used to fire the
neutron 'bullet' at the nucleus. This was big-machine physics, the
sort Rutherford would have revelled in had he ever acquired more
money to spend on his laboratory. At Berkeley, Lawrence had access
to plenty of money.

American philanthropists did not have to be mathematicians to appreciate the beauty of big machines. They endowed an experimental laboratory generously and when they went to check up on how it was being spent they didn't just see a blackboard with some long-haired fruitcake standing in front of it, mumbling figures, chalk in one hand, cigarette in the other, while a bunch of wild-eyed students struggled to keep up. They saw a proper laboratory, men in white coats carrying clipboards, huge 80-ton magnets and mysterious metal tubes and warning signs – STAND BACK, DANGER, KEEP OUT. In other words, they got some bang for their bucks. Several of the country's leading universities were established in the San Francisco area, and the city had a hierarchy of wealth and influence; the Pacific Stock Exchange, the Bohemian Club, the Pacific-Union Club, oilmen, bankers, politicians – Money. In the 1930s California was already the home of Hollywood, the dream factory, the myth-weavers, it was the focus for America and for the world's future, and Berkeley was the cradle of Californian optimism. The future would be scientific, physics was at the cutting edge, and nuclear physics was ahead of everything else. Lawrence was no slouch. Thanks to his gifts as a salesman he had built his first accelerator by 1931 and improved it so much by 1939 that he won that year's Nobel Prize. One of Lawrence's good friends and protégés on the Berkeley physics faculty was Robert Oppenheimer.

Vannevar Bush received a summary of the Maud report in July 1941, at the same time as Briggs, but unlike Briggs he was prepared to respond. Ernest Lawrence advised him to 'light a fire under the Briggs committee' but Bush did better than that, he bypassed it altogether. Lawrence and Arthur Compton – by now Prof. of Physics at Chicago – were already members of a uranium review committee which had reported on 17 May 1941. In its report it mentioned 'radio-active materials, carried by air planes to be scattered as bombs over enemy territory'. It also mentioned 'violently explosive bombs and the achieving of a chain reaction'. It further mentioned a choice between U-235 and 'plutonium', a new highly fissionable element recently isolated and produced by colleagues of Lawrence's at

Berkeley. In view of the need to concentrate U-235 the Compton
review finished by estimating that a bomb might be ready by 1945.
It was a businesslike and remarkably prophetic report, although it
did not mention problems to do with critical mass. It did, however,
identify the same possibility as the Maud Committee would pick out
two months later: the process, it said, 'may rapidly become a deter-
mining factor in warfare . . . The nation [that] controls the process
will have an advantage which will grow as its applications multiply.'

On 9 October 1941 Vannevar Bush met Roosevelt to discuss the
July conclusions of the Maud Committee. At that meeting Roosevelt
decided that the United States should take over the British
programme. Policy on a uranium bomb would be decided by the
President who would be advised by a new group, called the Top
Policy Group, consisting of Vice-President Wallace; the Secretary
of War, Henry Stimson; the Army Chief of Staff, General George
Marshall; Vannevar Bush and James Conant. Fear of a Nazi bomb
was not the main motive for the programme. The real interest lay
in the long-term offensive advantage whereby, in the author Richard
Rhodes's summary, 'a military development . . . would change the
political organisation of the world'. Vannevar Bush was to implement
the necessary research immediately. And the money, Bush wrote
later, would come from 'a special source' that Roosevelt could
'arrange'. The 'raw material' was to come from Canada and the
Belgian Congo. By the end of the meeting, in the words of Rhodes,
President Roosevelt had set up 'a separate secret state with separate
sovereignty linked to the public state through the person and by the
sole authority of the President'.

Vannevar Bush now had all the power he wanted to develop the
atomic bomb. All that was missing was a summary of American
scientific progress in the field. He accordingly commissioned a further
assessment from Arthur Compton, and this was ready and delivered
to the President by Bush on 27 November. Compton's final report
provided a more exact overview of the possibilities. He referred to 'a
fission bomb of superlative [sic] destructive power' and added that

the effects of radioactive fallout might well be as damaging as the bomb itself. And Compton, too, emphasised the likelihood that possession of such bombs could well determine future military superiority. On 6 December, Bush summoned the Uranium Committee to Washington to announce the new arrangements, Briggs having by this time been deactivated and packed away. The first problem was the separation and concentration of the U-235 isotope. Lawrence would be responsible for electromagnetic separation at Berkeley. Gaseous diffusion was allocated to physicists at Columbia University. And Arthur Compton would direct theoretical research and bomb design. Bush then invited his inner circle, Conant and Compton, to lunch in Chicago where the odd couple, Fermi and Szilárd, were already at work, constructing the world's first nuclear reactor.

And so the decisive step to build a doomsday machine proceeded secretly, possibly illegally, in a country that was still at peace. Roosevelt had approved the scheme on 9 October, he had reapproved it on 27 November, and it had been launched on 6 December. The stealthy Japanese attack on Pearl Harbor took place on Sunday 7 December. The United States declared war on Japan on the Monday and on the Thursday Hitler declared war on the United States. None of these events interfered with the uranium-bomb programme, which was a peacetime scheme anyway.

If anything, the move into war strengthened the refugee scientists in their conviction that their work was justified and of international importance. They remained under the illusion, shared by Dr Einstein, that they were engaged in a desperate race to pre-empt a Nazi bomb. Their dedicated efforts would last for nearly four years, and only in the final months of that period would they realise that they had been working on a completely different programme, designed to accomplish entirely different ends, and that contrary to their reasonable belief, they would have absolutely no say when it came to whether and when their terrible invention would be used.

In March 1942, Roosevelt and Bush conferred again, and once again overlooked or discounted the urgent danger of a Nazi bomb;

SNAKE DANCE

they ended by agreeing that it was nonetheless time for the bomb project, in Roosevelt's words, to be 'pushed'. Money was no object and in May, James Conant decided that all five possible means of isotope separation should move onto an industrial basis, even though this might eventually cost half a billion dollars. He had the luxurious freedom assured by a blank cheque.

Conant was undaunted by the prospect that lay ahead. Before he became president of Harvard he had been a leading organic chemist and had served with distinction during the Great War in the military poison-gas unit. This had not troubled his conscience. Conant used to say that he had never been able to see the difference between 'tearing a man's guts out with a high-explosive shell' and 'maiming him by attacking his lungs or skin'. Not everyone involved was so sanguine. In England, James Chadwick was unable to forget the day in Oxford in the spring of 1941 when he realised that, following his discovery of the neutron nine years earlier, a nuclear bomb had become a feasible proposition. Twenty-eight years later, in 1969, he disclosed that he had been so worried that he had been unable to sleep and had started to take sleeping pills; he had not been without them for a single night since.

In June the US Army became involved and it was decided that it was time for the project to be driven by the Corps of Engineers. And in September 1942 a new commanding officer was appointed. He was called Colonel Leslie Groves. His first request was immediate promotion to brigadier general.

PART V

THE PEOPLE FROM HELL

PART V

THE PEOPLE FROM HELL

CHAPTER SIXTEEN

The Half-life of Human Decency

'*He had taken a high seat amongst the devils of the land.*'
Joseph Conrad, *Heart of Darkness* (1902)

F ew people on first meeting him would have identified Leslie
Groves as an eccentric. He was a huge, pear-shaped gorilla of a
man with a domineering personality whose every word and gesture
underlined the message 'what you see is what you get'. He enjoyed
a level of self-confidence that rose well beyond the point of conceit.
He was an engineer not a scientist and yet the opening words of his
memoir *Now It Can Be Told* were: 'Atomic physics is not an occult
science'. In the same introduction he emphasised his unique importance,
as the officer commanding what was now called the Manhattan Project,
to the US war effort by noting that the four-star generals who were the
joint chiefs of staff were only informed of his activities 'insofar as their
specific duties required'. His second-in-command, Lieutenant Colonel
Kenneth Nichols, described him as 'the biggest sonofabitch I've ever
met in my life . . . an ego second to none . . . absolutely ruthless . . .
I hated his guts and so did everybody else.' The historian David M.
Kennedy has corrected this portrait by noting that Groves 'also embodied
a kind of genius – the peculiarly American genius for organisation and
management and for thinking in terms of stunningly vast enterprises'.

Because of his position at the head of the top-secret, unlimited-
budget project, Groves was without any question from November

1942, for three years, one of the most powerful men in the world. And yet, right at the start of a hugely risky enterprise to equip the United States with a weapon so terrible that it would ensure its possessor world domination, this very conventional human bulldozer made one deeply eccentric decision. He decided to appoint Robert Oppenheimer as the scientific director of the project and place him in charge of its most important laboratory at Los Alamos.

Oppenheimer had never directed any laboratory and the only time he had worked in one he had suffered a nervous breakdown, the consequence of realising his own experimental incompetence. Secondly, he had not won a Nobel Prize, and would be required to oversee the work of many scientists who had. Furthermore, he was notoriously disorganised and there were even questions about his patriotism; the FBI had opened a security file on him before the war because of his pro-Communist sympathies.

Groves just brushed all this aside once he had met Oppenheimer in September 1942. He later said that he had recognised the man's genius. On another occasion he said that he recognised 'Oppenheimer's ambition', which would make him easier to direct. It is also possible that Groves recognised his scientific director's particular mixture of intellectual strength and personal vanity. This would mean that Oppenheimer would be able to handle his fellow scientists but would offer no challenge to Groves. It is clear that beneath his brutal exterior Groves was a far shrewder and more perceptive man than he wanted people to think. In the event, he and Oppenheimer formed a very good working relationship.

By 1942 Robert Oppenheimer's main achievement in life was to have created at Berkeley, California, the leading school of theoretical physics in America. His own pre-war research had concentrated on anti-matter, a recondite field where his theories would not be validated for many years, until the eventual discovery of astronomical black holes. Aside from that, his colleagues thought of him as a political activist, a strong supporter of the Republican cause in the Spanish Civil War and a union militant. In 1940 his mentor Ernest Lawrence had warned him that his political enthusiasms were getting in the way of the science and he should simmer down. Both his brother Frank and his mistress Jean Tatlock were Communist Party members, and Robert himself used his handsome private income to make regular donations to Communist front organisations. In 1940 he had married Kitty Harrison (née Pruening), his first wedding, her fourth, and their son Peter was born in 1941.*

In June 1941 Lawrence had become concerned about the lack of practical progress being made in fission research and – before the Manhattan Project had been launched – drew Oppenheimer into a scheme of his own, using the Berkeley cyclotron to separate U-235 by electromagnetism. He insisted that Oppenheimer be invited to attend a secret meeting in New York in October that year, a meeting called to discuss isotope separation. In New York, Oppenheimer met Conant and Compton, and made his first contact with the leaders of the early drive towards an atomic bomb. One result was that in January 1942, when the US had just entered the war, Oppenheimer became director of fast-neutron research at Berkeley. So when he later became scientific director of the Manhattan Project, he was not entering an entirely new world.

Oppenheimer's first task on his appointment was to recruit a team to assist him. He thought he might need six scientists. Groves had already set up a factory at Oak Ridge in Tennessee that was designed to achieve uranium isotope separation on an industrial scale and was soon to become one of the largest industrial plants in the world. He had also commissioned major new laboratories in Berkeley, Chicago and New York. But Oppenheimer pointed out at their first meeting that this scattering of resources was inefficient and that the separate

* Kitty Pruening was German-born, of Prussian stock. Her mother had once been engaged to the future Generalfeldmarschall Wilhelm von Keitel, who was to be hanged at Nuremberg in 1946, and her aunt had married King Albert I of the Belgians. Kitty's second husband had been a Communist Party volunteer who was killed fighting in Spain.

scientific teams were tending to duplicate each other's work. What was needed, he argued, was one remote, highly secure site where the research could be concentrated on achieving its final objective, the creation of a bomb. And he thought he knew just the place.

Driving past San Ildefonso Pueblo and up onto the *mesa* you are on the way to Los Alamos. First there is a bridge across the Rio Grande and then, almost at once, the track cuts into the side of the gorge and you start to climb. The first glimpse of the town is from well back on the Santa Fe road when the white domes of the Los Alamos water towers stand out against the darker background of the Jemez Mountains. A man can happily spend a day or a week driving slowly through the Jemez Mountains. There's a pretty little place called Jemez Springs that has a bathhouse. The water comes piping hot straight out of the ground, full of mineral salts. The attendant gives you a towel and you draw your own tub and occasionally she calls out to enquire if there is anything else you need. The water is just about the right temperature for falling asleep in. One day I must go back. The little settlement is a time capsule, but Jemez Springs had a lucky escape in November 1942 because it was the site originally chosen for the bomb factory. It was Oppenheimer, with his love of a good view, who rejected it. He looked around Jemez Springs, then remembered his first horse trek with Katherine Page in 1922, and decided to move up to the top of the canyon.

When the railroad reached Lamy, and the Plains Indians were defeated and the settlers flooded in from the East, homesteaders had staked out a claim to the *mesa* and tried to make it work as a ranch. They named it after the cottonwood trees that grew around their log cabin. But the Los Alamos *mesa*, which drains into the Frijoles Canyon and adjoins the Pajarito Plateau, has always been short of water. So in 1916, after less than twenty years, the homesteaders sold up and a man called Ashley Pond, who was a former Roosevelt Rough Rider, established what he called the Los Alamos Ranch

School. This was every Eastern boy's dream – in principle anyway. You went to school on a ranch, every boy was given his own horse, there were Indians in the neighbourhood, you spent most of the day on horseback and you had 800 acres in which to roam around. There was a mounted boy-scout troop and there were elk and black bear and puma in the hills. The class sizes varied from one to eight. For the parents who lived in northern industrial cities the school was just the place to turn their pale and delicate sons into strapping lads, provided that they could afford the fees, which had risen to $2,800 a year by 1942 ($113,000 today). The Los Alamos Ranch School was a living extension of the national myth of the West. It trained boys to take their place in the same pageant of self-sufficiency and conquest, apart from giving them a good education, a healthy lifestyle and practical skills.* Groves closed it down in ten weeks. Oppenheimer was delighted. He thought his colleagues would be inspired by the view.

It soon became apparent that Oppenheimer's first estimate of six scientists was likely to be insufficient. Within two days of Groves's first visit to the Los Alamos school, the US Army had requisitioned the site. The school had to be out by Christmas. The idea was that the laboratory should be up and running by March 1943. By the end of November the *mesa* was covered with bulldozers and military tents.

The choice of this site was, in retrospect, insane. 'Security' did not require Groves to build a laboratory on a site without water, electricity, roads or a railway connection. Any number of suitable sites on the Great Plains, or in Washington State, with much better communications and proximity to the everyday world, already existed. A ten-mile security perimeter would have been more than enough and the high desert of New Mexico could have been left untouched.

---

* Not that every enrolment worked out as intended. The list of notable *alumni* includes the names of William Burroughs (1925–31) and Eugene Gore Vidal, who attended for a shorter period.

But, thanks to the blank cheque, expense was irrelevant, and so by the end of February army engineers had delivered the skeleton of what was neither a laboratory nor a factory, but a small town. The blueprint made provision for married and unmarried quarters, family homes, a school, a community centre, a library, a fire station, a hospital and a rubbish dump. There would be grocery stores, a post office, a cinema and stables for trail horses. There would also be cafés, bars and a restaurant. All this within a security fence that took in almost all of the 800 acres of flat ground available. The reason for the emphasis on comfort was that the scientists who were to work there were essentially being locked up for the duration.

Early in 1943 Oppenheimer, who had accepted the rank of lieutenant colonel despite having failed his Army medical, started to tour American universities, recruiting boffins. The original proposal was that they should all follow Colonel Oppenheimer into the army, a condition imposed by General Groves, who wanted to be sure that when he said 'jump' they jumped. This proved to be an extremely unpopular idea. None of the scientists was interested in wearing a uniform; that was not how science was done in Göttingen. Groves had to concede this point, but several of the objectors also made it clear that an initial reassurance would not be enough, and if they were ever ordered to put on a uniform they would leave. Since not even General Groves could force a physicist to do physics it became clear that the laboratories of the bomb factory would have to be manned by volunteers. They were civilians, many with families, and several of the key members were not even US citizens. If they decided to walk away they would in theory have every right to do so. They had to be kept happy. The facility opened as planned in March, with an advance party of 100. By the time the war ended in August 1945, there were 4,000 civilians and 2,000 soldiers living inside the wire.

After several months Oppenheimer reluctantly agreed to draw up an organisational flow chart and a chain of command. There would be four divisions: experimental physics, theoretical physics and chemistry – roughly corresponding to university departments – and ordnance, for the engineers. The divisional leaders would report directly to Oppenheimer. The divisions would be divided into groups, and the group leaders would report to the divisional heads. An early recruiting success was the entire physics department of Princeton University, which had been omitted from the early atomic work and which included one of the youngest of all the scientists to join Los Alamos, Richard Feynman. Even younger was a physicist called Theodore Alvin Hall, who was recruited on or around his eighteenth birthday in October 1943. Hall had been admitted to Columbia at the age of fourteen and to Harvard two years later.*

The head of the theoretical division was Hans Bethe, who had been working on radar at MIT. He was a refugee from Europe, born in Alsace under Prussian rule, of partly Jewish descent, who had studied at the Cavendish and in Rome with Fermi. Until the Nazis came to power he had been Professor of Physics at Tübingen University and was recognised as one of the most creative theorists of his day. Before he became a US citizen, Bethe produced an important paper on armour plating that was immediately classified so highly that he himself was not allowed to reread it. Another recruit was Edward Teller, one of Einstein's Hungarian visitors in 1939, who despite his brilliance did not play an entirely constructive role in Los Alamos. The reason for Teller's lack of punch was his raging jealousy over Bethe's appointment as chief theorist.

Teller was even more frightened of Communists than he was of Nazis. He regarded his country of adoption, the United States, as a fortress against persecution – it was his duty to man the guns night and day. Following a conversation with Enrico Fermi in 1942, Teller had become absorbed in the possibility of a second-generation bomb that he called 'the super'. This was a device in

---

* By the end of 1944, Hall, then aged nineteen, was supplying critical information to Soviet agents.

which an atomic bomb would be used to trigger a form of heavy hydrogen which would produce a far more powerful fusion explosion. At Los Alamos Teller became so obstructive that Oppenheimer eventually isolated him and told him to get on with his fusion calculations by himself. He was allowed one hour a week to keep the director briefed.

One by one, the luminaries of the physics community dropped their scruples and agreed to join Oppenheimer at Los Alamos. Some, like Teller, came running; others were persuaded by friends or colleagues. James Franck, veteran of the Kaiser's poison-gas unit, was among the first recruits. The roll-call eventually included Victor Weisskopf, Stanisław Ulam and Emilio Segré. At least twenty-one Nobel Prize winners worked on the Manhattan Project. Niels Bohr was never a permanent member of the Los Alamos staff, but he did make several visits, at Oppenheimer's invitation, to talk through problems as they occurred. In every case, those who agreed to co-operate on this terrible weapon mentioned the common fear of a Nazi bomb.

In December 1943, following the Quebec meeting between Roosevelt and Churchill, Oppenheimer's team was strengthened by the arrival of the first of twenty scientists from Britain who had been working on a British bomb. The leader of the British mission was Sir James Chadwick, equipped with his sleeping pills and accompanied by Lady Chadwick, and the party included many political refugees, among them Otto Frisch, Rudolf Peierls, Franz Simon, Joseph Rotblat and Klaus Fuchs. Fuchs was not Jewish but had fled from political persecution under the Nazis because he was a member of the Communist Party of Germany, an important distinction since, like Theodore Hall, he was soon supplying Soviet agents with vital information about progress at Los Alamos. In other words, he was working on two bombs at the same time. Fuchs was a bachelor who became very popular with the ladies at Los Alamos due to his skill as a dancer, in particular at the Viennese waltz. Fuchs always felt intensely grateful to Britain for giving him refuge from the Nazis, but his Communist commitment evoked a higher loyalty.

The other refugees in the British mission were all victims of anti-Semitic persecution and needed no further motivation for joining in the race to create the weapon. Otto Frisch had already lived through the anguish of hearing of his father's detention in Dachau concentration camp after *Kristallnacht* in 1938. But not everyone invited agreed to come.

Thanks to the work of men such as Einstein, Max Planck and Niels Bohr, physics in the inter-war years had enjoyed a unique status, and its theoreticians were regarded by other scientists as members of an elite. Physics was almost a vocation. Bethe, after the war, recalled those years as 'golden times . . . when science was a great spiritual adventure . . . The physicists in all countries knew each other well and were friends. And the life at the centres of the development of quantum theory, in Copenhagen and Göttingen, was idyllic and leisurely.' When Szilárd was urging his fellow scientists to join the bomb project in September 1942, he implicitly referred to these ideals. 'Those who have originated the work on this terrible weapon and those who have materially contributed to its development have, before God and the World, the duty to see to it that it should be ready to be used at the proper time and in the proper way. I believe that each of us has now to decide where he feels that his responsibility lies.' When they set out on their task the brotherhood had no doubt that when the time came to consider whether the bomb should be used, their voices would be heard.

There were two physicists, one German, one Austrian, who did not accept fear of a Nazi bomb as reason for absolving them from their moral responsibility. In Britain Max Born, expelled under anti-Semitic laws from his directorship at Göttingen, had become Professor of Physics at Edinburgh. He was naturalised as British before the outbreak of war and later invited to work on the atomic bomb. He declined to do so and described it as 'a wicked enterprise'. He had earlier in his life refused to work on poison gas during the First World War. Lise Meitner, who remained in Stockholm throughout the war, was also invited to join the British bomb team. She too refused to work on 'weapons of destruction', even though she felt isolated and slighted in her profession after her flight in 1938 from Berlin.

The only other physicist who refused to work directly on the bomb was I. I. Rabi, a close friend of Oppenheimer's who had to resist all his friend's most persuasive charm. In a celebrated reply he said that he did not want 'three centuries of physics to culminate in a weapon of mass destruction'. But Rabi's objection was not as uncomplicated as Born's or Meitner's. Rabi was working on radar, which he believed to be much more important. The bomb might help the Allies to win the war, but without effective radar, he said, they could well lose it. And Rabi *was* prepared to work at Los Alamos on a part-time consultancy basis.

Over in Berlin, scientists faced a far more dangerous choice. Nevertheless, Max von Laue, who was eventually arrested by the Allies and held *incommunicado* in England, played no part in the Nazi 'uranium club'. As a courageous and consistent opponent of the Nazi regime he would never have been invited to join it, and would certainly never have agreed to work on a Nazi bomb. Whether he would have agreed to work on an anti-Nazi bomb will never be known. Otto Hahn, inventor of fission, who worked on the Nazi bomb without much enthusiasm, always thought that it would be dangerous for Germany, as well as the entire world, if Hitler was the only national leader to possess the bomb. When, at the end of the war, he heard that the Americans had actually dropped an atomic bomb on a living target, he was appalled. His reaction did not protect him from the roasting he received after the war from Lise Meitner, his devoted pre-war colleague. Referring to the record of German physicists she wrote to Hahn:

You all worked for Nazi Germany . . . Certainly to ease your conscience you helped a persecuted person here and there.

But millions of innocent human beings were given up to be murdered without any kind of protest being made . . . First you betrayed your friends, then your children because you let them risk their lives in a criminal war, and finally you betrayed Germany itself because you did not rise up against the senseless destruction of Germany when the war had become completely hopeless.

Unknown to the Allies, the Nazi bomb – the possibility of which was the Allied scientists' driving force and justification – had effectively been cancelled in June 1942, when Heisenberg told Albert Speer, Hitler's minister of war production, that nothing could be developed for three to four years, and Speer decided that it was going to take too long. Hitler was intrigued by the possibility of a bomb but he never engaged with the details. (Speer said that nuclear physics 'strained the Fuhrer's intellectual capacity'.) Allied intelligence continued to search for signs of a Nazi bomb programme but failed to find any. Mining activity at Joachimsthal did not increase. The Norwegian heavy-water plant – known to be of great interest to Nazi physicists – was destroyed by Norwegian special forces in February 1943, and top physicists continued their routine work at German universities throughout the war, which was certainly not the case in the United States.

None of this amounted to proof, but in November 1944 proof was obtained. The Alsos Mission, created to investigate Nazi nuclear projects, which worked just behind the Allied frontline, entered Strasbourg and found a German Army physics laboratory in the grounds of the city hospital. The abandoned documentary records proved that there was no ongoing German bomb programme. Five months later, on 22 April 1945, General Groves learned that all German uranium supplies were accounted for, and he immediately informed General Marshall. The Nazi bomb had never existed, and fear of it played no further part in the military and political calculations that continued to drive the Manhattan Project. Nazi Germany, like Britain, had never possessed the necessary resources to fight a total war and build an atomic bomb at the same time. The only country with such resources was the United States, which was also the country where most of the world's finest nuclear physicists were now to be found. The possibility that Hitler might have made one of his catastrophic intuitive decisions and ordered the construction of the bomb anyway, was ruled out, according to Albert Speer, for ideological reasons: the Fuhrer sometimes referred to nuclear physics as 'Jewish physics'. In jocular mood Hitler would wonder whether the nuclear physicists might even succeed in setting fire to the whole world, echoing Rutherford and anticipating Enrico Fermi.

On 9 September 1942, as Groves moved into his new office, a minor outrage occurred on the top of Mount Emily, near the little port of Brookings in southern Oregon. A Japanese pilot called Nobuo Fujita climbed out of a submarine, on Pacific patrol some miles offshore, and assembled a prototype microlight aircraft. Using floats, he took off from a calm sea and when he reached the Oregon coast Fujita chucked an incendiary bomb out of the microlight and returned to his submarine. The bomb hit the mountainside and exploded harmlessly. But this trivial event marked the first time that the US mainland had suffered a regular military attack since the war of 1812.

On 8 February 1942, Congress's Un-American Activities Committee had recommended that Japanese-Americans should be removed from Pacific Coast states for the duration of the war. They should then be interned in camps situated at least 500 miles inland. *Time* magazine referred to California as 'Japan's Sudetenland' and on 19 February President Roosevelt signed Executive Order 9066 which authorised military commanders to exclude anyone they wished from designated areas. This order affected 120,000 Japanese-Americans. Responding to the general excitement, the US army then mistook a weather balloon over Los Angeles for a Japanese bomber and fired a saturation anti-aircraft barrage. Many citizens were injured by shrapnel and three people were trampled to death in the streets. Six days later,

Lieutenant General John DeWitt ordered all Japanese-Americans to move away from the West Coast, immediately and voluntarily, 'for their own good'. This order set off a mass exodus; the obedient Japanese headed towards the interior, only to be greeted by hostile mobs lining California's state lines who beat them up and drove them back. DeWitt cancelled the voluntary movement and ordered the Japanese-Americans to return home and await instructions. The US government then suspended the Bill of Rights and set up internment camps. In the same month, citizens of Santa Fe were alarmed to learn that 60,000 Japanese-Americans were on the way, heading for the north of New Mexico. In the event 2,100 Japanese men were held in a camp just to the west of Santa Fe from 1942 to 1946. The protests of state Governor John Miles were overruled, and local newspapers pointed out that the internment camp would provide jobs for eighty local men as guards.

The day after he was put in command of his country's project to gain world domination, General Groves, with a flourish worthy of King Leopold II, set out to buy up all the uranium in the world. Just as he was formulating this wish he learnt to his surprise that over 1,700 tons was already within his grasp. The Union Minière hoard at Port Richmond on Staten Island had finally been discovered. On 18 September 1942, one day after his appointment, Groves purchased the lot.

Acting on the mistaken conviction that uranium was a very rare commodity, Groves pursued his world-monopoly scheme, which he placed before the Military Policy Committee in June 1943 – though, characteristically, he had been working on it on his own authority for months before that. This ambition in itself showed that Groves was not working on an anti-Nazi bomb. The Germans had their own supplies, beyond even Groves' control in 1942, and the first country he tried to exclude from access to uranium was Great Britain. Groves next demanded and duly obtained the exclusive right to Canadian uranium; the contract was signed in

December 1942. By then the Manhattan Project had exhausted Union Minière's Staten Island reserves, and Groves was putting Edgar Sengier under considerable pressure to reopen the flooded mine at Shinkolobwe.

In January 1943 Sengier was told by his local manager that it would take six months to pump the mine dry, and that it would have to be totally re-equipped. In addition it would be impossible to operate Shinkolobwe without drawing skilled labour from the Katanga copper mines, and the loss of copper production would be very costly. Furthermore, Sengier did not have the company's authority to reopen the mine, and the Belgian government in exile in London were still unaware that Sengier was supplying the United States with uranium; Groves had expressly forbidden Sengier to inform them. In subsequent negotiations the US government demanded the right to send geologists to Katanga to prospect for new uranium lodes, first refusal on the production of *all* Congolese mining activities and a contract that would last for ninety-nine years. Sengier successfully resisted these demands, which he considered outrageous, and eventually extracted the total cost of reopening the mine, $13m, from Washington. From 1943 to 1945 the Belgian Congo exported between 8,000 and 10,000 tons of uranium ore to the United States. This level of production eventually exhausted the most valuable resources of the Shinkolobwe mine.

For the people of Katanga the consequence of being drafted into the front line of the Manhattan Project was entirely predictable. Union Minière used forced labour, and if necessary the *chicotte*, to energise the workforce. The *chicotte* was a whip made from hippopotamus hide. A former Congo district commissioner turned historian, Jules Marchal, has said that, if used lightly, it would leave permanent scars, but if laid on with authority it could kill. It was used, according to Marchal, to deal with cases of indiscipline, but also to punish labourers who failed to meet their production quotas. Marchal added that Union Minière used the *chicotte* as a matter of routine throughout the wartime period, and afterwards. It was only declared illegal ten months before independence in 1960. When the company's workforce rebelled they were met with ruthless force.

In 1941 there had been strikes at Union Minière's mines in Katanga. In Elisabethville a large demonstration was brutally suppressed by the Force Publique. Mutinies within the Force Publique took place in 1944, and these too were put down. A typical casualty ratio was supplied by the Kwilu revolt of 1931, in which 1 European and 400 Africans were killed. Subsequently living standards for workers fulfilling their production quotas were not greatly improved. Uranium ore is radioactive, and mining it hundreds of feet underground is dangerous and frequently fatal. Even in the United States in the 1960s the Paradox mine in Colorado lacked ventilation and radon levels were one thousand times higher than the safe maximum. Consequent deaths among Colorado miners from cancer reached epidemic proportions. That was in an industry that was ultimately governed by the rule of law. At Shinkolobwe during the war, where safety standards as nowadays understood were non-existent, the mine polluted the entire area. The ground became radioactive and the water supply, though contaminated, was still in use. The miners and their families lived in shacks that, unknown to them, were frequently constructed from radioactive materials.

None of this disturbed the directors of Union Minière who were merely concerned to fulfil the terms of the US government contract. The first shipments of uranium from Elisabethville to Staten Island ordered by Sengier in 1940 had been transported in the usual way on the railway that ran more or less due west from Elisabethville to the Atlantic port of Lobito, in the Portuguese colony of Angola. But Portugal was a neutral country and Lobito was full of German spies, so, in 1942, Sengier switched the route. The uranium, loaded in sealed barrels marked 'Special Cobalt', was sent by train north, through the central province of Kasai, to the railhead at Port-Francqui on the Kasai River. There it was transferred into barges and taken downstream to Leopoldville, then by train to Matadi on the line that

Conrad had walked up in the weeks following his arrival. At Matadi the uranium was loaded onto fast cargo ships for the United States.

Within the space of six months, what had started as a military engineering project employing a few dozen scientists grew, under Groves's direction, into a $2bn enterprise that was not only employing 150,000 people but was also building two entirely different bombs. At Oak Ridge, Tennessee, 20,000 construction workers took over 59,000 acres of forest reserve and constructed 300 miles of roads and 50 miles of railway. The electricity facility was large enough to power the city of Boston. Three gaseous-diffusion and electromagnetic plants were opened to separate U-235 for 'Little Boy', the uranium bomb. Meanwhile at Hanford in Washington State, on the banks of the Columbia River, a new town was constructed to house those working there; Hanford had three atomic piles (or nuclear reactors) and four chemical-separation plants that would manufacture plutonium for 'Fat Man', the plutonium bomb.

The first gaseous-diffusion plant at Oak Ridge – 'K25' – cost $100m. When the site's electromagnetic separator ran out of copper, General Groves simply decided to use silver instead, and purchased 13,000 tons from the Fort Knox Federal Reserve. At Los Alamos, where the bomb-grade U-235 and the plutonium would be assembled into the two rival bombs, the brief was reduced to something that sounded relatively simple. Oppenheimer's scientists were given the objective of producing 'a practical military weapon in the form of a bomb in which the energy is released by a fast neutron chain reaction in one or more of the materials known to show nuclear fission'.

A Columbia chemist, Harold Urey, was the first scientist to understand the true purpose of the Manhattan Project. He held the Nobel Prize in Chemistry and was Oppenheimer's opposite number at Oak Ridge. It was his responsibility to advise General Groves as to which uranium isotope-separation method was more satisfactory. The electromagnetic plant – 'Y12' – started to run in February 1943 but was closed down due to pollution in its pipes in December. The gaseous-diffusion plant, K25, started to run in June 1943. It proved to be effective but extremely slow. In December, Groves asked Urey what should be done. Knowing the need for speed, Urey said that Y12 was ineffective so the best solution was to redesign and speed up K25. The engineering firm Union Carbide disagreed. They proposed to repair Y12 and dismantle K25. This would slow down production noticeably. Groves decided to ask the British team, who were experts in uranium-isotope separation, to adjudicate. The British scientists agreed with Urey. They said that K25 would only produce enough bomb-grade product for a limited number of bombs, but would make it available significantly quicker. Groves then overruled the scientists and went with the proposal from Union Carbide, choosing quantity over speed. Harold Urey concluded that winning the race against a Nazi bomb was no longer the top priority of the Manhattan Project and resigned in January 1944.

Nine months after Harold Urey resigned, the method he had rejected, Y12, came on stream. In January 1945, one year after Urey's resignation, the method he had favoured, K25, started to produce fully enriched U-235. General Groves was delighted and on 20 January 1945, *less than two months after he had learned for a fact that there was no Nazi bomb*, Groves started to make plans to triple production of bomb-grade uranium by February 1946.

Robert Rhodes, the dean of atomic-bomb studies, whose magisterial work *The Making of the Atomic Bomb* was described by I. I. Rabi as 'an epic worthy of Milton', has written that, 'one of the mysteries of the Second World War was the lack of an early and dedicated American intelligence effort to discover the extent of German progress towards atomic bomb development . . . Why did the Manhattan Project not mount a major effort of espionage?' But the matter becomes less mysterious if one abandons Rhodes's assumption that the US government's determination to build an atomic bomb was ever based on fear of a German secret weapon.

When the war in Europe broke out in 1939 President Roosevelt, who has gone down in history as a great man, made a public appeal to the belligerents not to bomb civilian populations. Britain and Germany swiftly and absurdly agreed to the President's call for a ban. This relatively new practice, which had been made notorious by the actions of Spanish insurgents and their Nazi allies during the Civil War at Guernica and Barcelona, was regarded by American public opinion as barbaric. On the first day of the war, Roosevelt said that aerial bombing of civilian populations had 'sickened the hearts of every civilized man and woman, and has profoundly shocked the conscience of humanity'. But earlier in the year, despite his fine words, Roosevelt had privately decided to equip the USAAF with several thousand long-range bombers. He had become interested in the offensive capabilities of bombers during the Munich crisis of the previous year, when he had calculated that they were the best means of breaking German civilian morale and defeating Hitler. Roosevelt also saw the advantages of bombers in sparing American military casualties.

Nine months later, on 10 May 1940, the day Germany invaded Belgium and bombed Rotterdam, Roosevelt addressed the Pan-American Scientific Congress in Washington. His message to the assembled scientists was a ringing call to arms. Roosevelt told the scientists that due to modern technology the United States was no longer isolated from European wars, that it was the duty of the scientists to invent weapons to defend freedom, and that *they* would not be responsible for the consequent bloodshed. So it seems that, taken as a whole, President Roosevelt quite approved of aerial bombing as a tactic. Given the interval between the first chlorine-gas attack at Ypres in April 1915 and the atomic bombings of August 1945, one could argue that twentieth-century scientific warfare set the half-life of human decency at just over thirty years. It also sounded the death knell for the international brotherhood.

CHAPTER SEVENTEEN

The Inner Station

'As a boy I lived with my father at old army posts in Indian country and we met old soldiers and scouts who had won the West. And I wondered what there was left for me to do. My question was answered when I saw the dawn of the Atomic Age that early morning in Alamogordo.'

Brigadier General Leslie Groves, *Now It Can Be Told* (1962)

The last five months of the Manhattan Project were marked by two significant events, either of which might have been expected to check its progress. One was the sudden death of the project's chief supporter, President Roosevelt, on 12 April 1945, and the other was the unconditional German surrender of 8 May. But Manhattan sailed past both these obstacles without hindrance. With the death of Roosevelt, political control of the atomic bomb effectively passed from the political leadership of the United States to the military, and in the event to Leslie Groves.

And with Roosevelt's death, the bombing of Japan became more likely. It was Secretary of War Henry Stimson who said, after the attack on Hiroshima, 'I have been responsible for spending two billions of dollars on this atomic venture. Now that it is successful I shall not be sent to prison'. Only Roosevelt, who had given a blank cheque to the Manhattan Project when America was still a country at peace, might have had the authority to cover the spending of $2bn on a weapon that had never been used.

Ever since September 1942, when he was first appointed, General Groves had patiently constructed his personal empire. By April 1945 the laboratory city at Los Alamos had been in existence for just over two years and had developed an intense community life of its own. Later many of the scientists looked back on Los Alamos during the war and described those years as 'the time of our lives'. In Santa Fe the bomb factory was known as 'the Hill', and there was lively speculation as to what was going on up there. For the first eighteen months the scientists, the staff and the guards were for the most part locked inside, although they could ride the Jemez Mountain trails at weekends and could apply for permission to visit Santa Fe. But in the autumn of 1944, to raise morale, longer journeys were authorised. Such journeys were generally made by train – the top scientists had been banned from flying since 1942, as they were considered too valuable to lose. Oppenheimer made one such train journey to San Francisco in June 1943 to meet his former mistress, Jean Tatlock, still a member of the Communist Party. The director of Los Alamos was followed throughout his absence by FBI agents who reported that he had spent the night in Tatlock's apartment. When questioned after the war by security officers, he was never properly able to explain why he had made the trip. On the following evening, ignoring the ban, he took a United Airlines flight back to New Mexico. It was the last time Oppenheimer saw Jean Tatlock. She was found dead in her bathtub in January 1944. She had left a suicide note, and suicide was the verdict – although it has since been suggested that she was murdered by the FBI.

Other scientists who left the camp on unofficial business included Joseph Rotblat, the Polish experimental physicist and member of the British delegation, who made fortnightly visits to friends in Sante Fe. His wife had disappeared after being trapped in Poland on the outbreak of war, and he needed distractions. Rotblat had always had misgivings about working on the bomb, but had agreed to do so for the usual reason: fear of a Nazi victory. One month after his arrival in 1944, Rotblat overheard General Groves say that 'the real purpose of making the bomb is to subdue our chief enemy, the Russians', and was profoundly shocked. Klaus Fuchs and Allen Hall were also able to leave the camp on less frivolous business. Unknown to each other, they were keeping their contacts in Soviet Intelligence technically up to date. Hall travelled as far as New York to do this. Fuchs had a contact in Santa Fe.*

After the war, the FBI investigated Fuchs' secret activities and interviewed over 1,000 people. The Bureau opened 45 subsequent investigations for espionage and arrested 8 suspects. One man received an 80-year prison sentence and 2 American citizens, Ethel and Julius Rosenberg, were convicted of espionage and electrocuted at Sing Sing prison in 1953. Another of the accused, David Greenglass, brother of Ethel Rosenberg, was not prosecuted in return for giving the evidence against his sister and brother-in-law that sent them to the chair. During the war he had been working at Los Alamos as a mechanic.

On the surface 'the Hill' functioned like any other enclosed community, the only peculiarity being the low average age of its inhabitants. It had a town council and in winter it had a ski slope. At one point the military police closed what they described as 'a brothel'. The facility was reopened after it was redesignated as a dance hall by scientists on the town council. Night after night the alcohol flowed. The town had no public telephones and an extremely high birth rate. Groves complained about this but was unable to stem the flood. The Oppenheimers' second child, Toni, was born at Los Alamos in December 1944. There was some interaction with the local community. Many of the scientists' wives worked as laboratory assistants and

* The head of the KGB at that time, Pavel Sudoplatov, later claimed that he had stationed two of his agents undercover in Santa Fe since 1940, when they had taken part in the assassination of Leon Trotsky in Mexico City, and he may have been telling the truth.

employed Indian domestic servants from San Ildefonso. A famous potter of San Ildefonso, Maria Martinez, did very good business on the Hill. Enrico Fermi, the man who had built the first working nuclear reactor in Chicago in 1942, learnt to square dance by watching the steps. He then insisted on leading the dance and astonished the locals by avoiding any mistakes, but his partner said that it had not been an enjoyable experience for her as he 'danced with his brains, not his feet'. Fermi then took up fishing for trout. He insisted on using worms so as to give the fish 'a last meal'. He preferred this method to fly fishing, which he derisively described as 'a battle of wits'.

On Christmas Eve, 1943, Los Alamos acquired its own radio station which occasionally broadcast live concerts. Some of the piano recitals were by 'Otto' – in reality the Austrian physicist Otto Frisch.

The scientists did not suffer from false modesty. Describing the transatlantic crossing of the British contingent Frisch wrote, 'The ship arrived safely, with perhaps the greatest single cargo of scientific brain-power ever to cross the ocean.' And they sensed that they had *carte blanche*. Oppenheimer, encouraging Hans Bethe to join the project in 1943, wrote, 'General Groves does nothing which would attract Congressional attention to our hi-jinks.' The secrecy surrounding Los Alamos deceived Congress just as effectively as it did the Japanese.

Reality occasionally interrupted this idyll. One day the Los Alamos camp vet treated a cat with radiation poisoning; it had been scavenging in the top security 'Tech Area' – first evidence of bad atomic house-keeping. The vet kept the cat alive for some days to observe its symptoms.

Bomb-grade uranium had been arriving at Los Alamos since January 1945 from Oak Ridge, Tennessee. Its long journey from Shinkolobwe was almost over. First it was driven to Knoxville, where armed couriers carried it onto the Chicago Express. At Chicago it was transferred to the Santa Fe Chief for the 26-hour journey to Lamy, the same tourist train taken by Oppenheimer and Warburg when they were young men. Plutonium nitrate manufactured at Hanford in Washington State started to arrive one month later. It was taken by train from Portland to Los Angeles and there packed into metal containers. These were then loaded into army ambulances and driven in convoy across California and Arizona to Los Alamos.

In May, with news of the German surrender, it was agreed in Washington that although there was no longer any possible threat from a Nazi bomb, the Manhattan Project should continue to the point of an experimental test. The Manhattan scientists were untroubled by this progression. Indeed, as Oppenheimer remembered, '[At no] time did we work harder [on the bomb] than in the period after the German surrender.' But Leó Szilárd, an occasional visitor from Chicago, was horrified by Los Alamos. When he first heard of it he said: 'Nobody could think straight in a place like that. Everybody who goes there will go crazy.' And the behaviour of some of his colleagues bore him out. Fermi's bright idea of poisoning the German food supply with radium dust inserted into high explosive bombs came to nothing, despite the initial approval of Oppenheimer. But, in his private office, Edward Teller continued his calculations on the next, and even more terrible bomb, while the rest of the scientists laboured on in common purpose. By the time the U-235 had started to arrive Otto Frisch – who had more or less enabled the atomic bomb in 1940 – was working a seventeen-hour day on 'the Dragon Experiment'. This was considered so dangerous that his laboratory had to be moved out of the factory into the bottom of a distant canyon. At one point Frisch very nearly started a chain reaction with the neutrons in his own body by leaning too close to an assembly of U-235. He received a full day's dose of radiation in two seconds. The luminaries had become totally absorbed in their complex task.

Except for one. In December 1944, Joseph Rotblat decided that he had had enough. He no longer believed that Hitler was going to acquire the bomb and he was haunted by Groves' earlier indiscretion. He requested permission to leave from Sir James Chadwick, who advised him to plead personal anxiety about the fate of his wife, rather than politics. Rotblat's departure made no impression on his colleagues; all the research done in Oak Ridge, Hanford, Chicago and Canada was coming to a head while in the Pacific, US forces were fighting a desperate battle against the suicidally brave Japanese forces, and were taking 'very heavy' casualties.

Harry S. Truman, Roosevelt's successor as President of the United States, was not briefed about S-1 (the final code name for the Manhattan Project) until 25 April, twelve days after he had taken office. When he was told, it was by Secretary Stimson and Groves. The meeting lasted forty-five minutes. The delay in informing the new president is a useful measure of the extent to which control of the bomb, its purpose, its progress and its use, had passed from elected representatives of the people to the military. President Truman came to office only four months before Hiroshima, and he never seems to have fully grasped the scale of the thing. But he realised that if the project succeeded, as seemed likely, then – in the words of his shrewd new Secretary of State, Jimmy Byrnes – that would 'put us in a position to dictate our own terms at the end of the war'. Truman's operational experience was so limited that right to the end he seems to have believed that the bomb would not be used on a civilian target. Two weeks before it was dropped, he made a note in his diary:

We have discovered the most terrible bomb in the history of the world. It may be the fire destruction prophesied in the Euphrates Valley Era, after Noah and his fabulous Ark . . . I have told Mr. Stimson to use it so that military objectives and soldiers and sailors are the target and not women and children . . . He and I are in accord. The target will be a military one and we will issue a warning statement asking the Japs to surrender and save lives. I'm sure they will not do that but we will have given them the chance.

Perhaps the most revealing error in this note is the President's assumption that a peacetime chain of command, leading down from the President to the Secretary of War to the generals, was in place.

The actual chain of command had been established with Roosevelt's approval in August 1942, when Vannevar Bush had set up a Military Policy Committee, a body which was supposedly in charge of General Groves. In fact, the committee had no control over Groves but acted as his rubber stamp, or figleaf. The first time Groves was confronted with it, on the day in 1942 that his promotion from colonel to brigadier general came through, he reduced its size from nine to three with one dismissive sentence.

On 27 April, two days after briefing President Truman, Groves summoned a meeting of a new committee, the Target Committee, which would report directly to him. This was staffed with air-force officers and scientists, and Groves told them that, following discussions he had already held with the Military Policy Committee, he wanted a list of four suitable targets for the world's first atomic bombing, although no such bomb actually existed at the time. When the United States Air Force bombed targets in Japan, it bombed cities, so it was hardly surprising that the new committee's preliminary list for the world's first nuclear attack contained the names of nine cities plus Tokyo Bay. Tokyo itself could not be included since it had by then been more or less completely destroyed by conventional explosives. The inclusion of Tokyo Bay suggests that, in its preliminary list, the Target Committee was making provision for a demonstration attack rather than a live target.

One man who was prepared to stand up to General Groves was Henry Stimson. On 1 May, the Secretary of War took steps to set up a second new committee, to be called the Interim Committee, whose task would be to lay plans for how the bomb was to be used when the war was over. It was Vannevar Bush and James Conant who had first suggested this committee to Stimson as far back as October 1944, further evidence that, in the minds of the originating visionaries, the Nazi bomb had always been a secondary consideration.

Stimson took the presidency of the Interim Committee, which would officially be the body in control of the bomb from May until the war's end in August. It was a civilian group and included Bush, Conant and Karl Compton. The presidential nominee was Jimmy Byrnes, soon to become the new Secretary of State. The first decision of the Interim Committee was to appoint yet another new body, a 'Scientific Panel', which might be able to offer useful advice. The members of this body were Arthur Compton, Ernest Lawrence, Robert Oppenheimer and Enrico Fermi.

These three new committees now moved to prepare the nation and the world for the new order. Oppenheimer's influence was significantly strengthened when he was co-opted onto the Target Committee as well as the Scientific Panel. The dominant figure on the Target Committee was General Groves, who was of course Oppenheimer's commander on the Manhattan Project. The most prominent figure on the Interim Committee was Henry Stimson, but he had few allies. Bush, Conant and Karl Compton had all been members of the original National Defense Research Committee, set up in June 1940. Ever since then, on one committee after another, this triumvirate had worked together smoothly, with Roosevelt's blessing, and with the support of Scientific Panel member Arthur Compton, to provide the United States with the key to world power. Scientific hawks such as Ernest Lawrence had been enlisted from the start. Stimson may have been chairing the most senior of the three new committees, but in fact it was once again run by the old firm – sitting in different chairs.

By July 1945 Oppenheimer and his team knew how to make a uranium bomb, had the necessary materials and knew that it would work. They were so sure that their uranium bomb would work that they did not have to test it. They called it 'Little Boy' because it was a relatively slim object; by 2 July, all that remained was to assemble it. But the plutonium bomb was different. Because plutonium was so much more sensitive to fission than U-235 they could not use the same design. The uranium bomb would explode. An explosion involving plutonium would just fizzle out. So, in a brilliant innovation, the plutonium bomb was made to implode. But the implosion firing mechanism was complex and no one would know if it worked until it had been tested.

A site had been chosen in a region of scrub desert 200 miles south of Los Alamos and 60 miles north-west of the town of Alamogordo, between the Rio Grande to the west and the Sierra Oscura Mountains to the east. Christened the Jornada del Muerto – the Trail of Death – by the Spanish who had attempted to cross it on horseback 250 years earlier, it had by 1945 become part of an Air Force bombing range. By Indian tradition it was Apache territory and it had been used as a refuge by the Indians, Apache and Comanche, when the West was being won. It was, and remains today, thin, dry country, harsh and pitiless with those creatures that make a mistake. There had nonetheless been men so desperate to prosper that they had tried to use it as dry grazing for cattle. And the first time I drove along its fringe, the only sign of life was the half-eaten hide of a dead calf.

The test took place on 16 July 1945. Oppenheimer named the event 'Trinity', for reasons he chose never to explain. He once said that he had used the name of God because he had been reading Donne's sonnet 'Batter my heart, three-personed God'.* The plutonium device was placed in the centre of a site that measured 24 miles by 18 miles, at 'Ground Zero'. At distances of 10,000 yards the Army Corps of Engineers constructed a semi-circle of 3 reinforced bunkers that contained cameras, recording equipment and the firing party. Five miles further out a base camp was established. And ten miles further still, on a low rise overlooking the Jornada del Muerto called Compañia Hill, a viewing point was set up for selected visitors – scientists not involved in the shot, and VIPs. There was a great deal of tension and several hitches in the days leading up to the countdown.

---

* The historian Marjorie Bell Chambers has suggested that he was thinking of the Hindu trinity of Brahma, Vishnu and Shiva, the gods known as the Creator, the Preserver and the Destroyer.

Oppenheimer maintained an exaggerated calm. Groves did not. Dry weather was needed for the experiment in order to disperse the fallout, yet Groves, for political reasons, had overruled the Army meterologist who correctly predicted thunderstorms for the night of 16 July. 'What the hell is wrong with the weather?' the general said when the forecast thunderstorm arrived. The bureau officer said it would clear before dawn and Groves threatened to hang him if he was wrong. Oppenheimer calmed Groves down, then Fermi wound him up again by reviving the physicists' old joke about the likelihood of the explosion igniting the atmosphere and burning up all the oxygen. Fermi opened a book on this possibility and invited the assembled physicists to choose between the destruction of New Mexico and the destruction of the world. When Groves instructed him to cut it out, Fermi switched to speculating what would happen if the bomb did *not* go off. In fact, that would have caused a very considerable problem since a huge area of New Mexico would have had to be evacuated until it could be defused. In the middle of the night Groves decided to telephone the governor of New Mexico to warn him that he might have to declare martial law. The next day, the final countdown was occasionally interrupted by the voices of railwaymen who were using the same radio frequency in a freight yard in San Antonio, Texas.

With five minutes to go Edward Teller, standing on Compañia Hill, recalculated the blast figures, thought they might be an under-estimate and started to rub suntan lotion into his face and hands. Ten miles closer, at base camp, I. I. Rabi lay down in a shallow trench in the darkness, with his feet towards Ground Zero. General Groves lay down nearby, between the president of the Carnegie Institution and the president of Harvard University, Vannevar Bush and James Conant. They made an incongruous trio, locked together in excited anticipation of their success in creating a weapon that could destroy their world. The base-camp siren wailed its two-minute warning. Five miles closer still, and only five miles from Ground Zero, Robert Oppenheimer, standing inside the forward bunker, held on to a post to steady his balance. George B. Kistiakowsky, a White

Russian explosives expert who was Professor of Chemistry at Harvard, recalculated the blast figures in the opposite direction from Teller, walked out of the bunker with forty-five seconds to go and stood on its roof. At ten seconds a gong sounded. Fifteen miles further back Edward Teller, still recalculating upwards, was donning heavy gloves over his suntan lotion.

When the needle on the automatic timer inside the bunker reached zero a voice shouted, 'Now!' Thirty-two detonators at Ground Zero fired simultaneously, and within thousandths of a second a plutonium sphere the size of an orange was imploded. Conditions inside the bomb 'resembled the state of the universe moments after its primordial explosion'. But there was no noise. Twenty miles away the physicist Robert Serber, standing beside Teller, but without suntan lotion, gloves or even sunglasses, was completely blinded for about twenty seconds. With the brilliant yellow-white light came a silent blast of heat 'like opening a hot oven door' in the cold night air, and then a shock wave that knocked Professor Kistiakowsky, standing on the concrete bunker roof, to the desert floor. He had been standing on the roof because he had calculated a blast of 1 kiloton; it was actually over 18 times stronger. The blinding ball rose from the desert, with a great pool of light racing outwards over the scorching ground beneath it. Four seconds after the detonators went off the surrounding nuclear dust was already beginning to form into a bright, blue mushroom-shaped cloud. Nearly a minute later, as the fireball reached over two miles high, the thunder hit Compañia Hill. The noise continued for far too long, bouncing on the rocks, rolling backwards and forwards from the Oscura Mountains. Robert Oppenheimer's brother Frank, who was standing beside him, said, 'It went on and on. It never seemed to stop. It was a very scary time.' Thirty-four years later Otto Frisch claimed that he could still hear it.

What people said after watching Trinity has gone down in history. Oppenheimer said that he thought of, but did not recite, a line from the Bhagavad Gita, 'Now I am become Death, the destroyer of worlds.' Rabi watched Oppenheimer step out of his Jeep when he got back to base camp and got a different impression. 'His walk was like *High Noon* . . . this kind of strut. He'd done it.' Rabi added that he himself was scared because he realised that this new force 'represented a threat to mankind and to all forms of life, to the seas and the air'. The director of the Trinity test, Kenneth Bainbridge, put it very well. Thinking perhaps of Groves, he said to Oppenheimer as they climbed out of the forward bunker, 'Now we are all sons of bitches.' He later added that it had been 'a foul and awesome display'. Stanisław Ulam, a mathematician who declined to witness Trinity, remembered the faces of his colleagues as they returned. 'I saw that something very grave and strong had happened to their whole outlook on the future.' For the scientists, the spell of Los Alamos had finally been broken.

But not for Groves, who was jubilant. Not only had he managed to deliver a successful atomic test, he had delivered it in time for President Truman – who was in Berlin at the opening of the Potsdam Conference – to inform Stalin that the United States now had a new weapon 'of unusual destructive force'. Unknown to Truman, Stalin, who had at least three agents inside Los Alamos, had known about the bomb since 1942. That night, somebody said to Groves, 'The war is over,' and he replied, 'Yes, after we drop two bombs on Japan.'

Unlike many there, the general knew that Little Boy, the uranium bomb, had already set out on the start of its journey towards Hiroshima, leaving Kirtland Air Base, Albuquerque, two days before the Trinity test.

The Jornada del Muerto stands on the extreme northern rim of the Chihuahuan Desert, a long barren stretch of land that runs south, deep into central Mexico. It was a death trap for the Spanish who tried to reach Santa Fe by what seemed to be the easy route – travelling north along the banks of the Rio Grande. Where the river disappeared into a long series of impenetrable canyons the only way forward was a passage across the desert for three or more days, without water. A man could die of thirst or snakebite, or become the victim of Apaches – watching from the San Andres Mountains to the east. A Spanish map of 1680 shows the river running north between hills with a few scattered missions and settlements named after saints, and the warning word 'Apaches' in bold black letters ringing the edges of this barely discovered world. Any survivors of the northward journey across the Jornada del Muerto would have regained the Rio Grande at a marshy plantation known now as the Bosque del Apache. In the 1840s this became a hideout for renegades and scalp-hunters. Today it is a wildlife refuge notable for the winter flights of thousands of geese and Arctic cranes.

At dusk in the Bosque the big birds descend out of a low sun; coming from behind they cast shadows that make you flinch and duck. An entire lake of geese rises as the dusk thickens, with a roar like a distant bombardment. During the day the deep silence of the wetlands is broken only by songbirds or sage sparrows. Then there is a rumbling sound as a four-engined USAF fuelling tanker and two attendant helicopter gunships, black in the sky, pass slowly overhead. The interruption seems to symbolise the contradictions of the American empire. Below, the twitchers and idealists, building their bird sanctuary, teaching their children how to live happily beside diamondback rattlesnakes and lions – 'You are in lion country. If you see a mountain lion, lift arms and shout loudly' – above, the impervious war machines, practising how better to kill.

The wartime bombing range is now a missile range that takes its name, White Sands, from a site that is sacred to the Indians. It is said to be the target for missiles that are fired from as far away as Kansas. A road follows the northern boundary of the range directly across the Jornada del Muerto. There are no settlements on this road and even the few isolated farmhouses seem to have been abandoned. Twelve miles out there is a turning to the range's northern gate. At the double security barrier to the missile range there is no one in sight, although there are plenty of cameras. Silent control. 'Every month the US government adds around 20,000 names to the terrorist watch list,' a recent edition of the *New York Times* had announced.

Just inside the gate, and to the west, stands Compañia Hill, where the observers who were assembled twenty miles from Ground Zero were momentarily blinded by the initial flash of Trinity as the terrible light – that people called green, purple or yellow – and its pursuing mushroom cloud rose to 41,000 feet through the night. Then the darkness returned and a minute later came the unbreaking roar of the explosion as it moved across the Sierra Oscura and filled the plain. And there was a hot wind, and the ground trembled. And then in the land of the Ghost Dance and the Snake Dance the watching crowd of scientists and soldiers began to howl in triumph. They formed a chorus line and danced their own snake dance.

The light from the explosion was seen in Albuquerque, Santa Fe, El Paso in Texas, and up to 180 miles away. In at least one case it was seen by a woman who was completely blind. A few windows were broken, one of them 125 miles distant. Radioactive material was subsequently located as far away as 120 miles. Kodak camera film was contaminated in Indiana, 1,000 miles away.

In reply to enquiries General Groves put out a statement saying that a very large munitions dump had gone up.

From the foot of Compañia Hill there is a long view south-east across the death plain that terminates after thirty miles with the Oscura Mountains. The site of Trinity is somewhere down there on the Sierra. The bright sunlight on the distant peaks was cut by several distinct weather patterns. Black sheets of rain lay like a thick veil directly over Trinity, and immediately behind Ground Zero a flat yellow light stood vertical like a tombstone in front of the southern rim of the Oscuras.

It takes about an hour to traverse the Jornada del Muerto on Route 380. On the night of Trinity this road was the scene of events that verged on both farce and panic. The area around Ground Zero was believed to be uninhabited, but a shepherd dozing fifteen miles from the explosion was blown out of bed. The crew of a mobile searchlight were ordered to evacuate the area and one of them forgot his gas mask. As he drove into a cloud of radioactive sand he resorted to breathing through a thick slice of bread. Cattle grazing near the town of Bingham that were exposed to a plutonium cloud (which has a half-life of 24,000 years) changed colour, from red to white. So did half the beard of one of the ranchers who happened to be in the area. The town of Vaughn, 115 miles from Ground Zero, became so polluted with radiation that at one point evacuation was imminent. The worst polluted area, just to the north-east of Route 380, was dubbed 'Hot Canyon'. The monitor estimated that it had received 230R (roentgens) per hour, against a safe limit of 0.2R per day. In the weeks that followed two unlisted but inhabited ranches were discovered in the area and some years after that a number of people living beside the red and white cattle died of cancer. In 2010 a ten-year research project organised by the Los Alamos National Laboratory concluded that everyone living between Tularosa and Socorro in July 1945 may have been at risk of harm from the Trinity test. The two towns are ninety miles apart.

In 1946 General Groves told a Senate Committee that the best cure for exposure to radiation was a short vacation.

Today on Route 380 one can drive straight through Bingham without noticing that it is there. Careful inspection reveals one shop advertising stocks of 'trinitite' – the green-tinged glass formed from sand by the fireball as it flashed into the half-mile-wide Ground Zero crater – but the shop is generally closed. Eventually the road reaches the Valley of Fires, a slow lava flow where it passes between heaps of flaming pitch. And then there's the town of Carrizozo, which is the first settlement beyond Trinity. Here in 1945 they felt the explosion like an earthquake and one man ran down the street shouting, 'It's the Japs!'. This is an old coal-mining town, associated with Billy the Kid. It has three gas stations, three motels and Elsie's Burger Bar. It was

getting dark, and the lights were on at Elsie's, a family business, a
fine burger bar and the only eating house I have ever patronised
where the proprietor tried to sell me the premises while I dined. He
was sitting behind the cash till, within earshot, and was polite enough
not to ask what I was doing there. He said that he had a house in
Albuquerque, 120 miles away, that he was retired, and that he spent
the week camped in a trailer that was parked behind the diner. He
was clearly more than ready to quit.

We had a couple of cheeseburgers, some cold beer and a side order
of peanut butter and jelly, and he told us that his wife was doing the
cooking and that was her sister waiting tables. He said Elsie had been
their mother's name, and added, 'It just happens that this place is
for sale. Only $280,000 and you'd make money from day one. My
wife's doubled her turnover in each of the last three years. All the
machinery is new. This town is booming. There's a nine-hole golf
course that is about to get another nine holes. We're on a major
truck-route intersection, just two miles from a new sub-division that's
ninety-five per cent sold, and the nearest casino is only thirty-five
miles away. It's a goldmine!'

The director and I ordered some more beer, then moved on to
share a quesadilla supreme and discuss the idea of putting less than
half the film's budget into this venture; then we drove round the
boom town to inspect our goldmine and found that parts of it were
totally abandoned. In the back streets the paint was flaking off the
empty front porches, the fly screens banging in the wind. All the
shops were locked up, their windows empty. One convenience store
that was open advertised 'Horseshoeing' and 'Alcoholics Anonymous'.
A silver object leaving a vapour trail flashed across the sky much
faster than any aircraft, then zigzagged and disappeared behind the
Oscura; and shortly afterwards there was a series of window-rattling
bangs. Another missile fresh in from Kansas. Two miles outside
town the Valley del Sol sub-division, which was supposedly 95 per
cent sold, contained hardly a construction, although several roads
had been laid out behind the imposing billboard. A line of flags

snapped straight in the wind and the tumbleweed blew down from the hills.

Back in Carrizozo the lights went out at Elsie's. A coal train that must have been a mile long and was powered by four locomotives passed over the intersection, taking nearly five minutes to snake through the silent town. The lights at the intersection flashed orange, beat out a rhythm – 'sub . . . prime, sub . . . prime' – changed colour in the roadside rain pools, but the trucks were few and far between. The boom town was a retirement park without any customers, a place where the generation that fought the war would not even come to die.

CHAPTER EIGHTEEN

Nagasaki! American Empire

'Bombs can be made in large numbers . . . There is no defence against them . . . Fear of them will destroy our liberties.'
Harold Urey, Nobel Prize in Chemistry, project director, the
Manhattan Project (1946)

'There is no uranium in Russia.'
Brigadier General Leslie Groves (May 1945)

Exactly three weeks passed between Trinity and Hiroshima, and it was an extremely busy period for General Groves. The ground war had reached a pause in the Pacific, although the USAAF remained active, fulfilling its mission of bombing Japan and 'not leaving one stone standing on another', to quote Air Force General Curtis LeMay. But Groves was chiefly occupied with his committees.

Curtis LeMay had a short definition of warfare. 'I'll tell you what war is about,' he said. 'You've got to kill people. And when you've killed enough, they stop fighting.' He remained confident that conventional air raids would end the war without any need for a land invasion. As the leader of XXI Bomber Command, LeMay had over 350 B-29s available. Each had a crew of 11, a bomb load of 20,000 pounds, and incendiary bombs which sprinkled the target – usually a city – with burning, jellified petrol that started fire-storms, stuck to human skin and was almost impossible to extinguish. XXI Bomber Command had put up an outstanding performance on the night of 9 March when 334 Superfortresses, practically the entire force, had bombed Tokyo for 6 hours, leaving 1 million people homeless and up to 100,000 dead. By the time the atom bomb was ready, 66 of Japan's largest cities had been destroyed, and the only important centres remaining untouched were those on the Target Committee's atomic bombing list.

US ground forces numbering 183,000 had won the battle for Okinawa Island on 22 June, after 83 days, with casualties of 12,600 killed and 36,000 wounded.* The Japanese, outnumbered two to one on the ground, had started with 97,000 soldiers; only 7,000 survived the battle. In addition over 100,000 Okinawan civilians had died. The invasion of the Japanese home islands was planned for November. Following the invasion of Okinawa on 5 April the Japanese prime minister resigned, and the new cabinet, with the Emperor's support, decided to start negotiating an end to the war through its Moscow embassy. On 18 June President Truman had met the Joint Chiefs of Staff to consider how a Japanese surrender might be accomplished without the need to invade. Two methods for obtaining a peaceful surrender were suggested by the military leadership. Admiral William Leahy objected to the insistence on 'unconditional surrender'. The other method considered was to warn the Japanese about the atomic bomb. So by the end of June both Washington and Tokyo were trying to find a swift end to the conflict.

Even before this, Secretary of War, Henry Stimson, who loathed the aerial bombing of civilian targets, was urging President Truman to spare the civilian population wherever possible. In May the Target Committee, meeting at Los Alamos with Robert Oppenheimer present, had considered whether to follow the atomic bombing with a conventional raid, in case the 'yield' from the new weapon proved

---

* This was approximately 9,000 losses fewer than the British Army suffered on the first day of the Battle of the Somme in July 1916.

disappointing. This suggestion – one of pure evil – was rejected due to fears that radioactive clouds might harm the second-wave bomber crews. Stimson's efforts did not deter Curtis LeMay, who on 25 May carried out a second fire-bombing raid on Tokyo, this time with 464 B-29s, burning out 16 square miles of the city. Stimson's response was expressed at a meeting of his Interim Committee when he spoke in great distress of 'the appalling lack of conscience and compassion that the war had brought about . . . the silence with which we greeted the mass bombings in Europe and, above all, Japan . . . As far as degradation went, we had had it.' The bombing continued. Secretary Stimson had lost control of his air force.

But Henry Stimson did enjoy one victory over the generals, and in particular over General Groves. Five cities had eventually been placed on a reserved target list, ready for an atomic bombing. They were Kyoto, Yokohama, Niigata, Kokura Arsenal and Hiroshima. Henry Stimson knew Kyoto and loved it. It was a beautiful place, an intellectual centre, the ancient capital, and – then, as now – the spiritual centre of Japan. For the Air Force, its cultural importance made it even more valuable as a target, and Groves selected it as the number one choice for the first atomic bombing. He liked it because of its size. It had a population of 1 million, which was being swollen by many refugees from the bombing elsewhere. And it was 'large enough to ensure the damage . . . would run out within the city'. When Stimson asked to see the target list Groves tried to put him off, and the Secretary of War had to tell Groves that he had all day and neither of them was going to leave his office until the list was brought to him. Stimson then removed Kyoto from the list.

The first choice of target thereafter was Hiroshima, which Groves liked because the surrounding hills would produce a focusing effect that would considerably increase the blast damage. But it still did not match Kyoto in experimental value. On 21 July, Groves tried to put Kyoto back again. This time Stimson got a ruling from President Truman, which Groves surprisingly accepted. Kyoto was safe. After the war, Groves referred to 'the wisdom' of Henry Stimson's decision.

Meanwhile, in Chicago, there was a scientific uprising. Unsurprisingly the man who led it was Leó Szilárd. With Germany out of the war, Japan forced back to the last ditch, and the United States in possession of the two different designs of atomic bomb, Szilárd concluded that the time had come to regain control of the monster. Szilárd had observed Fermi's triumphant experiment, the first induced chain reaction, in Chicago in December 1942, and had summarised it as 'a black day in the history of mankind'. The work of the Chicago scientists was finished once Hanford started to produce reliable supplies of plutonium. In June 1945, Szilárd held discussions with Einstein, Harold Urey and James Franck, among others, and then formed a committee to produce a report which argued that within a very short time a nuclear arms race would begin between the USA, Britain, France and the Soviet Union. An international agreement was urgently needed whereby research could be shared in peaceful co-operation. The bomb should not be dropped on a living target, since this would destroy America's moral credibility; it should be demonstrated in some uninhabited place.

This prophetic 12-page report, known as the Franck Report, was taken to Washington by James Franck, who carried it to Henry Stimson's office, where he was told that Secretary Stimson was out of town. This was untrue. Franck left his report with the Pentagon who undertook to lay it before the President. In fact it was dropped into an army safe and never seen again.

Initially, trying to approach Roosevelt, Szilárd had managed to get an appointment to see Mrs Roosevelt, but after the President died Truman's office had sent him to see Secretary of State Byrnes instead. The meeting did not go well. Byrnes considered Szilárd to be presumptuous and out of order. He was unimpressed by Szilárd's belief in 'the republic of science' and his assumption that only scientists were qualified to decide the proper future of the bomb.

Szilárd's personal mission petered out with Byrnes. The scientists had one last hope of an intervention with the new President; Niels Bohr, officially attached to the British mission to the Manhattan Project, was still in Washington. In June, Bohr made a last solo attempt to see Mr Stimson, but the answer was again negative, and Bohr left America with his personal dread of a nuclear arms race and his belief in the importance of international control unrecorded.

News of the concerns in Chicago reached Los Alamos at the end of June when Szilárd drafted a petition and sent it to Edward Teller on 'the Hill'. The petition, which was circulated before Trinity, was highly political in that it urged President Truman not to use nuclear weapons on Japan without a public statement of the terms of surrender, and a public rejection by Japan of those terms. In other words, the United States would have to publish reasonable surrender terms which Japan would have to reject before resorting to the bomb.

At Los Alamos this petition was signed by 155 scientists, with only two signing a counter-petition. A subsequent army poll of 150 Manhattan Project scientists showed that 72 per cent preferred a demonstration of the bomb to military use without warning. Oppenheimer was very angry when he was shown Szilárd's petition. He persuaded Teller not to sign it, and persuaded those who had signed it not to send it directly to the President. Instead it went through 'military channels' and disappeared from view until after the bombings had taken place. Oppenheimer took one further action. He privately sent a copy of Szilárd's petition to General Groves, with a critical covering note. Since the general hated Szilárd, and had done everything he could to drive him out of the Manhattan Project – including having him tailed for over two years, forcing him to surrender his patents on the chain reaction without proper compensation, repeatedly accusing him of being a German agent and then trying to have him arrested – this was not a friendly act towards a brother visionary on Oppenheimer's part. The dumping of the Los Alamos petition into 'military channels' marked the end of the scientists' revolt.

There was only one question left unsettled, and again Oppenheimer played a crucial role. On 31 May, Stimson's Interim Committee, advised by Oppenheimer, talked about some harmless but effective demonstration to convince the Japanese of the bomb's power. After a discussion lasting ten minutes Oppenheimer said that he was unable to think of a demonstration that was sufficiently spectacular. On another occasion, at Los Alamos on 16 and 17 June, the Scientific Panel pondered an apparent choice between 'a technical demonstration' intended 'to outlaw the use of atomic weapons' on the one hand, and 'an opportunity of saving American lives by immediate military use', believing that such use would improve the prospects of the prevention of future wars. The panel, whose members knew nothing of the new Japanese move towards surrender talks, answered this loaded question in the only way possible. 'We find ourselves closer to the latter views . . . we can propose no technical demonstration . . . We see no . . . alternative to direct military use.' Stimson had asked President Truman to consider giving Japan a warning on 2 July, and on 24 July had asked him to assure the Japanese that following surrender they could keep their Emperor; both requests were ignored.

President Truman never gave a specific order to drop the atomic bomb, but on 31 May he had endorsed a recommendation made by the Interim Committee which said that the final selection of targets was a military decision and that the bomb should be used as soon as possible 'on a war plant surrounded by workers' homes', and without prior warning. Truman confirmed his approval of Groves' draft order on 24 July. No precise decision was taken to drop the bomb because those in charge of the project never really considered that there was a choice.* The project initiated by Roosevelt, on the advice of Vannevar Bush, James Conant and Karl Compton in the autumn of 1941, had acquired an unstoppable momentum. On 24 July Stalin was informed

---

* This conclusion nullified the agreement reached in London on 19 September 1944, between Roosevelt and Churchill, that the new atomic weapon '*might perhaps after mature consideration be used* . . . [once] . . . against the Japanese'.

that the bomb existed. On 26 July, the Potsdam Declaration called on Japan to surrender 'unconditionally' without delay. On the same day, Little Boy was unloaded from the heavy cruiser USS *Indianapolis* at Tinian, a tiny island in the Pacific Ocean, 1,500 miles from Tokyo, 'with a very long airstrip'. In fact Tinian had 6 runways, each as wide as a 10-lane motorway and each 10,000 feet long.

On the afternoon of the same day the order went from Washington to the new Commander of the Strategic Air Forces in the Pacific, General Carl Spaatz. The 'first special bomb would be delivered as soon as the weather permitted visual bombing, after 3 August, on one of the targets: Hiroshima, Kokura, Niigata or Nagasaki. Additional bombs would be delivered as soon as made ready.' This order* was issued in the name of the Secretary of War, Stimson, and the 'Chief of Staff, USA', General Marshall. But it was initiated and written by General Groves. The order should have gone through the Joint Chiefs of Staff, but they were ignored. However, Groves was not acting without authority. He was responding to anxiety expressed by Secretary Byrnes that Stalin, in reply to the news that the United States had acquired a new 'weapon of unusual destructive force', had said that Soviet forces were gathering on the Chinese frontier, and would be ready to invade Manchuria by 15 August.

Hiroshima was chosen as the target for the first attack, on 6 August 1945, because it was the only one of the four cities on the shortlist which contained no prisoner-of-war camps. The B-29, named *Enola Gay* after the flight commander's mother, was carrying one 9,700-pound uranium bomb, Little Boy, and a crew of twelve. A military chaplain blessed the crew at the final briefing, and a large force of photographers took everyone's picture many times before they boarded

---

*General Spaatz had insisted on written orders for the Hiroshima bombing. He was a veteran of the air war in Europe, where he had commanded the Eighth Air Force. Following the Dresden raid on 14 February 1945, USAAF Mustang fighters of the Eighth Air Force had been ordered to machine-gun 'targets of opportunity', that is refugees in the streets of the city. Such attacks were reported more than once.

the 'ship', whose radio call sign was 'Dimples Eight-Two'. The commander, Colonel Tibbets, was one of the finest bomber pilots in the US Air Force. Due to the extra fuel and Little Boy, his plane was 15,000 pounds overweight. They took off from Tinian at 02.45 on 6 August using most of the two-mile runway. At 07.30 the weaponeer climbed down into the bomb bay and screwed live fuses into the bomb. At 08.30 *Enola Gay* climbed to 31,000 feet and 20 minutes later the plane was over the outlying islands of 'the Empire'. They reached the city of Hiroshima shortly after 09.10, flying at 328 miles per hour. The weather was clear, the crew had a good view and could see the delta and the seven rivers and count the big ships in the harbour. From the ground a few people looking up could see just one plane, obviously not on a bombing raid, just one silver speck in the sky. The bombardier, using the celebrated 'Norden Precision Bombsight', took control and searched for his aiming point, which was not a military facility but a T-shaped bridge in the centre of the city. The bomb-bay doors opened and at 09.15 and 19 seconds the 4-ton bomb went down. As Little Boy was released the *Enola Gay* leapt in the air and Colonel Tibbets turned the aircraft into a 155-degree diving turn that would take them over 10 miles in 40 seconds. At 09.16 and 2 seconds Little Boy exploded at 1,900 feet, not above the aiming point but 183 yards off, directly above the Shima Hospital. *Enola Gay* was hit by a flash of blinding light, and then by two shockwaves that made a noise like sheet metal snapping and caused the crew to think of anti-aircraft fire.

A while later Tibbets turned back and circled nearer to the target to see what had happened. Where there had been a city in the sunshine, there was nothing, just smoke and fires, a huge mushroom cloud and, on the ground, what Tibbets described as 'a pot of boiling black oil'. The chain reaction was in working order.

On the morning of the attack Hiroshima had a population of 280,000 civilians and 43,000 soldiers. It had 76,000 buildings of which 48,000 were totally destroyed and only 6,000 were undamaged. Thousands of people died within an instant, many leaving no trace of their existence. By the end of August the death toll had reached 70,000; by the end of the year it had risen to 140,000. A further 130,000 survivors were listed as wounded, of whom 43,500 were severely wounded. Only 16 per cent of the population was unharmed.

Survivors have left accounts of what it was like to live through the bombing of Hiroshima. One child, who lost everyone he knew, recalled looking around and seeing nothing but people who were burning or burnt. That night, long before any assistance reached him, all he could hear were voices from beneath the rubble, crying for help and begging for water.

The *Enola Gay* returned to Tinian and landed safely. The crew received a heroes' welcome. Everyone was convinced that the war was over. President Truman was at sea, returning from Potsdam, and was told about Hiroshima over lunch in the battleship's mess. He described it as 'the greatest thing in history'. Robert Oppenheimer heard the news in a telephone call from General Groves. Oppenheimer's first question was whether the attack had taken place after sundown. He was probably thinking that, if so, many civilians would have been sheltered to some extent. Groves' reply was revealing. It betrayed both mild embarrassment and a swift ability to pass responsibility. 'No,' said the general, 'unfortunately it had to be in the daytime on account of the security of the plane and that was left in the hands of the Commanding General over there.' (This does not seem to be exactly correct. The order from Washington, drafted by Groves, had stipulated 'visual bombing'.) But Groves found just the right words when asked to say how it had gone. 'Apparently,' he said, 'it went with a tremendous bang.'

Later that day Otto Frisch was at work in his laboratory in Los Alamos. There was a sound of shouting and running footsteps and someone threw open the door and cried, 'Hiroshima has been destroyed!' One hundred thousand people were said to be dead. Fortunately, a public telephone had been installed on the Hill, and there was a rush to book tables that night at La Fonda Hotel in Santa Fe. And in Los Alamos, Oppenheimer, in jubilant mood, walked through a cheering crowd of scientists to accept a standing ovation with a boxer's victory salute. As the audience whistled and stamped its feet he said, 'It is too early to determine what the results of the bombing may have been, but I am sure the Japanese didn't like it.'

Even today, old men such as the novelist James Salter, who were young men at the time, in his case training as a combat pilot, remember their relief when they realised that the war was over, they were still alive and the last and most terrible battle of all would never have to be fought. The arguments in favour of the decision to use the atomic bombs have been lucidly summarised by A. J. P. Taylor, who described it as 'a fateful act of terrifying importance', and noted that the justifications were 'almost entirely practical and strategic': blockade and conventional bombing would not force unconditional surrender; invasion would be too costly and prolonged; although the Japanese had been putting out peace-feelers they flatly refused unconditional surrender; the use of the atomic bombs was expected to strengthen the influence of the peace party in Japan; the A-Bombs would be less costly in human life than high explosives and fire storms; Soviet Russia was due to enter the war against Japan, and this did not suit US interests; the use of the A-Bombs would discourage future wars; there was a need to show Congress that the money had not been wasted; and finally the scientists had a legitimate desire to pursue their experiment to the end. Taylor added that in August 1945, it was an easy step from killing and maiming men to doing the same to future generations, and that nuclear weapons were seen as 'just another big bomb'. He summarised his own summary with the words, 'War suspends morality.'

And other arguments have been advanced. The heavy American casualties on the Pacific islands such as Okinawa and Iwo Jima had brutalised men's judgement and given them a thirst for revenge. A swift end to the war, at whatever the cost, would mean a swifter end to the sufferings of the Allied POWs held by the Japanese in atrocious conditions. And the bombings, however great the suffering they caused, took place against the background of a war that had already resulted in the death of 39 million people. So Hiroshima and Nagasaki were a cheap price to pay for an end to all that.

In fact we can set aside some of the arguments justifying the attacks because it is clear that there were men in Washington in favour of using the A-Bomb on a live target without warning who were not totally brutalised by the experience of leadership in war. They included President Truman, General Marshall and Admiral Leahy, Robert Oppenheimer and, of course, Henry Stimson. But if the point of the bombings was to persuade the Japanese that it was futile to fight on, there is still one word that turns the key and opens the door to the opposite argument – Nagasaki. If the A-Bomb was used for exact military reasons to pre-empt a difficult negotiation, why was a second city destroyed before the Japanese leadership had time to react to the destruction of the first?

Four men could have intervened to stop the Nagasaki bombing. The first, President Truman, was literally and metaphorically still at sea. He was an unelected president and a stranger in the secret state, and as such could never hope to assume the genuine authority of his predecessor, Roosevelt. By May 1945, when Germany surrendered, the Manhattan Project had become the central component in America's military drive. And it was directed by five men: Vannevar Bush, James Conant, the brothers Compton, and Brigadier General Groves. Their secret authority was cloaked by the public authority and wisdom of two other remarkable men, General George Marshall, US Chief of Staff, who signed the orders they wrote, and Robert Oppenheimer, who dutifully provided them with the scientific advice they required. Groves, with characteristic truculence, once described President Truman in this situation as 'a little boy on a toboggan'.

Below the President there was the Secretary of War, but Henry Stimson's influence was waning. He had shot his bolt. Next in the chain of command was General Marshall. After the war, Marshall said that in Washington they had been shocked that the Japanese had not immediately sued for peace. 'What we did not take into account,' he said, 'was that the destruction . . . of Hiroshima was so complete that there was no communication at least for a day and maybe longer.' But General Marshall had signed an order that had set in chain a process of continuous atom bombing. When something unexpected occurred, such as silence from Tokyo, it would have been possible to delay the next attack. That would have been a logical step if the primary purpose of the bombing was to enforce Japanese surrender. No such delay was discussed. And fourthly there was General Groves, the de facto commander of the operation, from whom the idea of interrupting the Nagasaki countdown would certainly have provoked another memorable subatomic explosion.

Fat Man, the plutonium bomb, had been arriving in sections on Tinian since 27 July. It was originally scheduled to be dropped on 11 August but the day after Hiroshima, 7 August, the assembly team and Colonel Tibbets decided that it should be dropped on the first day it was ready, 9 August. So while in Tokyo the Japanese leadership moved towards surrender, and Washington pondered the silence, Nagasaki was effectively consigned to oblivion* – with General Marshall's blessing – by the Fat Man assembly team: an army colonel, Tibbets, who was influenced by weather reports; a naval captain, William Parsons; and a junior Los Alamos physicist, Norman Ramsey.

On 9 August, the second B-29, known as 'Bock's Car', took off at 03.47. The operation verged on fiasco. The weather was stormy and the plane soon developed a fuel-switch problem which meant that an emergency landing would eventually be inevitable. Then more fuel was wasted at a broken rendezvous. The pilot, Major Charles Sweeney, reached the primary target, Kokura Arsenal, at 10.44. He found that it was covered in smoke and cloud and after three bomb runs he was unable to locate the aiming point. He said that this was why he decided to switch to the secondary target, calculating that he had just enough fuel left to make one bomb run. Kokura Arsenal was the biggest

*General Carl Spaatz did intervene and suggested that the second A-bomb should not be dropped on an inhabited area.

munitions manufacturing centre in Japan, and a classic 'war' target in Truman's definition. The secondary target, Nagasaki, had only been placed on the list when Kyoto was removed. It met Air Force target criteria as a large port which had never been bombed, and which contained a torpedo factory, but it was in many ways similar to Kyoto in being a symbolic city, though for different reasons. Nagasaki was the first point of contact between sixteenth-century Japan and Christian Europe. It had a long history of openness to the West. It was the spiritual home of Japan's Christian community, a small but well-educated minority who were radically opposed to the war cult of imperial Japan, and who had suffered fierce persecution for centuries.

When Bock's Car arrived over the secondary target it was to find that once again the city was covered by heavy cloud. Major Sweeney was by now very short of fuel. He was under strict orders to carry out a visual bombing using the Norden bombsight. But he was left with the choice of making an imprecise 'radar run' or dumping the bomb in the ocean. The bomb was a wonder of technology; it was worth hundreds of millions of dollars and fashioned according to a remarkable new implosion design. Major Sweeney decided that if he was going to dump it, it might as well be close to the target. As Bock's Car started its radar run the bombardier saw a hole in the clouds above a sports stadium, and, believing he had found the original aiming point, released the bomb. In fact they were 1½ miles out. The bomb exploded at 1,650 feet at 11.02 with the epicentre just in front of the Catholic cathedral, three schools and two hospitals. Fat Man's force was 22,000 tons of TNT, almost twice that of Little Boy, but the steep hills surrounding the dropping point contained the explosion and it caused relatively limited damage. Nonetheless, 30,000 people died instantly, including 1,310 children and teachers at Shiroyama Primary School and about 1,300 at Yamazato Primary School. Over 1,000 patients, doctors, nurses and students died in the medical college and college hospital. About 3 per cent of those who died in Nagasaki were military personnel; 13 per cent of the dead worked in the munitions factories; 84 per cent were civilians, mainly elderly, female, students or children. By the end of the year 70,000 people had died; 140,000 within 5 years. If Hiroshima spelt 'atomic bomb', Nagasaki spelt 'nuclear arsenal'. Bock's Car eventually made a successful crash-landing on Okinawa.

Back in Washington, General Groves told General Marshall that he had 'gained four days' on the production schedule and that he expected to be ready to deliver 'Fat Man II' to its target by 18 August. Carl Spaatz, the Strategic Air Force commander in the Pacific, favoured Tokyo for the next one. On 10 August, the Japanese war cabinet decided to surrender. Conventional bombing continued until 14 August when Washington abandoned the demand for 'unconditional surrender' and accepted Tokyo's request that Emperor Hirohito should remain on his throne.

The Historical Museum at Los Alamos is in a very different style to the National Atomic Museum in Albuquerque. There is no sense of triumphalism about it. The visitors' book would never retain comments like 'Bombs are Fun. Let's drop more!' One section illustrates the national reaction to the news of Hiroshima. There is a T-shirt printed with a mushroom cloud, and the words 'Los Alamos – Atomic City'. But replicas are not for sale. They have an atomic-bomb lamp and US Mail commemorative first-day covers, atomic cheddar cheese from Wisconsin, and locally made red table wine that is labelled 'La Bomba Grande', so associating the Hispanic population in the general rejoicing. There is also an exhibit showing the 'atomic cake' that was baked when the news broke, and was described by a Unitarian minister as 'a monstrous obscenity'. *Time* magazine commented that these were 'probably the harshest words ever spoken of a dessert', and the baker added, 'I intended the cake as something to eat.' *Time* magazine's final comment was, 'Non-Americans have long regarded the US public's attitude toward the Bomb as callous to the point of idiocy.'

The museum contains excellent photographs and relief models of the *mesa* and of the Jemez mountain region showing the extent of the wartime camp that grew into a hilltop town. But there is no

mention either of the reckless manner in which the scientists and the
military scattered radioactive waste around what had been one of the
most beautiful landscapes in America, or of the laboratory accidents.
The wife of one of the British scientists was irradiated while she was
pregnant. Her daughter was subsequently born with spina bifida. And
on 15 September 1945 Harry Daghlian, aged twenty-four, became
the first American casualty of the project. Three weeks earlier he had
been working in the lab late one night, alone, and trying to assemble
a quantity of enriched (bomb-grade) uranium, when he dropped a
12-pound metal weight onto the assembly. He thereby triggered
a chain reaction, the air turned blue and in separating the metal and
the uranium he gave himself a lethal dose of radiation. Daghlian was
rushed to hospital in a state of collapse but nothing could be done.
His body dissolved before his horrified doctors' eyes. He had suffered
third-degree burns, gangrene set in, his blood count collapsed and
after several weeks of agony, he died the same death as thousands of
Japanese citizens of Nagasaki had been suffering in the days preceding
his accident.

The Historical Museum, which is a private institution run by part-
timers and enthusiasts, does give a strong impression of the dramatic
impact of the bomb on New Mexico, which was the youngest American
member of the Union, only recognised and accepted as a state in 1912,
and after thirty-three years' full membership quite unused to being at
the centre of national attention as the scene of a heroic endeavour that
had finished the war in a week without further casualties. In the initial
euphoria the governor declared that the Bomb would henceforth be
listed as an honorary citizen of the state of New Mexico. The Bomb
had finally validated the state's integration into the Righteous Land.

The scientists who built the atomic bomb thought that, because they
were essential to the creation of it, they would be able to influence its
use. In Szilárd's words, they had the duty 'before God and
the world . . . to see that it should be ready to be used at the proper
time and in the proper way'. But when the time came to decide on its

use the scientists were brushed aside like a coach-load of bright sixth-formers. After the war, Oppenheimer learned about the secret, detailed knowledge Washington had acquired of the debate within the Japanese war cabinet and said that he had been kept in the dark. Weeks before Hiroshima the US government knew that the 'November blood bath' that would surely follow landings on the shores of the empire was as much of a threat as the Nazi bomb had been.

Five senior American commanders criticised the attacks on Hiroshima and Nagasaki. General Eisenhower and Admiral Leahy condemned them; Admiral Nimitz, General Arnold and General LeMay said they were unnecessary. Even General Marshall said they had little effect on ending the war. And this conclusion was supported by the US Strategic Bombing Survey of 1946. In the words of Eisenhower, 'The Japanese were ready to surrender, and it wasn't necessary to hit them with that awful thing.'

The official proposition was that, in order to save American and Allied lives, the United States government was justified in inventing and using a weapon that could one day destroy our world. If the Nazis had dropped the atomic bomb on London or Moscow and still lost the war, that proposition would have appeared as an addition on the Nuremberg charge sheet. The real aim of the attack, world power, was equally compromised. By November 1945, the Soviet government was accusing the United States of an intimidating use of atomic weapons. In the words of Ferenc Morton Szasz, 'The arms race had begun.'

Many years later, when General Eisenhower – a Republican – had become President of the United States, he returned to the subject: 'Let me point out that we never had any of this hysterical fear of *any nation* until atomic weapons appeared on the scene.' In 1991, the Los Alamos physicist Victor Weisskopf said, in a lecture at MIT: 'Nagasaki, the second bomb, I don't hesitate to call a crime.'

Washington had endowed the Manhattan Project with an unlimited budget, in time of peace, because the American leadership was attracted by the new weapon's offensive capacity. And after spending

$2bn, the project took on its momentum, and had to be tested . . . on people.

The atomic bombing of two Japanese cities, two living targets, was carried out when Japan was already beaten, and three months after the Japanese leadership had started to seek terms of surrender. And Nagasaki was not destroyed to end the war. It was destroyed as an essential step in an experiment. The development process of two different atomic weapons required two separate living targets. The experiment had to provide exact information about the relative efficiency of these devices. Exact information was required about thermal radiation, fireballs, gamma rays, fallout, strontium-90, blast injuries, flash burns, whole-body radiation doses, ovarian and testicular damage, and induced mutations.

There was a wealth of knowledge to be gained.

The Last Train to Hiroshima

The uranium used in the atomic bombs dropped on Japan in 1945 came from a mine in the Belgian Congo. Within a few hours of hearing the first news of nuclear fission in February 1939, Robert Oppenheimer – a cultivated American liberal – started to sketch the blueprint for a primitive nuclear weapon. Several of the physicists who eventually created this weapon were accomplished classical musicians. The second bomb, which was dropped on Nagasaki, missed the target and exploded almost directly above the city's Catholic cathedral. And since the war, the United States Wildlife Service has developed a bird sanctuary near the test site in New Mexico where the first atomic explosion took place.

These were among the haphazard details which became a welcome distraction from the narrative of science, death, deceit and cruelty that occupies the foreground of any research into the atomic bombing of Hiroshima and Nagasaki. What started as a biography of one scientist became a history or counter-history, and then a travel book, the account of a journey from the uranium mine to the target area. The link between Africa and the atomic bomb grew into the basis for this story and then the inspiration for a film. And it was while we were filming in the southern Congo that the Japanese government announced that at Fukushima, a nuclear power station damaged three weeks earlier by a tidal wave, there was a national emergency.

*

In Tokyo the rainy season had washed away the cherry blossom. Farmers in the region of the Fukushima nuclear power station, 130 miles north of the city, had been banned from marketing their vegetables, milk and beef. And levels of radioactivity in Tokyo drinking water and in seafish were reported to be higher than normal, and rising. According to our guide, the concert pianist Jun Kanno, the city was noticeably quieter than usual. 'There is a sort of mass psychosis,' he said. 'People have closed in on themselves.'

The drive in from the airport to central Tokyo had taken us through the morning rush hour. But although there was heavy traffic few people were visible on the pavements. Later I discovered that this was because they were already at work. First impressions of a city of 35 million people were confusing. Viewed from inside the bus, the highway seemed to have been hacked though a maze of high-rise concrete canyons. These were formed from a brutal jumble of shapes and materials, without any grace or individual style. The only evident priority had been to cram the maximum number of units into the smallest available space. Sections of the city were multi-level, the base – composed of a network of canals – sometimes appearing far below. Occasionally, through the mist of exhaust fumes, a fishing boat or a motor launch could be made out, moored to the bank, bobbing in the murky waters. Tokyo, once known as Edo, is a city that has been destroyed by fire many times. During the 'Flowers of Edo', the great fires of history, thousands of houses had burned down in a single night. The canals once offered protection. Then came the wartime B-29 bomber raids that brought the most terrible fires of all. Citizens who jumped into the canals to escape the flames boiled to death. These misshapen structures of the modern city were what had grown back later, like crust over scar tissue.

The complex rituals of Japanese public manners awaited us at the hotel, where the porters bowed on our arrival and then bowed again to the empty coach as it departed.

Jun Kanno was not only our guide; he had a major part to play in the film. To cheer us all up he proposed we start our first evening in the piano bar of the Hotel New Otani. It was generous of him since in order to avoid actual physical pain he usually had to request the pianist in a piano bar to take a break. Jun ordered beer and whisky and said, 'Welcome to my country.' The walls behind the long, high counter were decorated with brightly coloured frescoes of louche *café terrace* characters in a style that was vaguely reminiscent of Paris and La Coupole.

Jun lives in Paris with his wife and their three daughters in an apartment directly opposite the little stone pavilion where Marie Curie accomplished the early experiments on uranium, radium and radioactivity which won her the Nobel Prize and eventually killed her. Japanese artists have been drawn to Paris for over a century, ever since Foujita set to work in Montparnasse. But the piano bar of the New Otani had not been chosen because of its Parisian frescoes. Jun explained that he thought it the best place to introduce us to his homeland since it was where the novelist and latter-day samurai Yukio Mishima had ordered his last drink, before attempting the *coup d'état* that ended with his ritual suicide. This explanation seemed to raise more questions than it answered, but I decided not to ask them.

Mishima, I learned, had sipped a Scotch in the piano bar, smoked a cigarette, and on the following morning had set out for the Ichigaya army barracks to harangue the troops. First he and his followers stormed the office of the base commander, General Mishita, tied the general up and gagged him. The novelist then stepped out onto the general's balcony and addressed the garrison assembled on the parade ground below. When, in response to his call for an uprising and a military coup, the soldiers laughed at him Mishima insulted them. 'You don't agree with me because this nation has no spiritual foundation. You are just American mercenaries living in a tiny world. You do nothing for Japan,' he cried. Then he withdrew to the general's office to commit *seppuku*, known to us as *hara kiri*, the ritual disembowelling by sword that is reserved for the samurai.

Mishima's chosen lieutenant, Morita, stepped forward to administer the *coup de grace* – by beheading – but on this occasion, despite several attempts, the beheading was a failure, and a third samurai had to finish the job. Morita, the failed swordsman, then demanded the same death, and his head too was removed by the third samurai with one blow. Yukio Mishima's last words were, 'Long live the Emperor of Japan.'

As we settled back in deep leather armchairs and sipped our cold beer in the piano bar of the Hotel New Otani, Jun suggested that Mishima's attempted coup had always been a pretext. He was too intelligent to think that it ever had any chance of success. Sitting in this bar he was already resolved on *seppuku*, but he needed an appropriate setting for his final act. The army barracks was merely the backdrop. Mishima choreographed his death to give it the value of a political statement. However in Jun's opinion, the writer had another motive. He had been driven by the realisation that he was never going to win the Nobel Prize. Mishima had frequently been described as Japan's leading contender, but in 1968 the Prize in Literature had been awarded to Mishima's master, Yasunari Kawabata, and Mishima concluded that it was unlikely to be awarded to a second Japanese writer for some time.

Mishima's failure to win the Nobel Prize limited the influence of his political message and weakened his ability to reverse his country's decline. His suicide took place in 1970, two years after Kawabata's triumph. In an unexpected coda Kawabata joined him, committing suicide two years after his disciple, in 1972, in his case more neatly by placing his head inside a gas oven and turning on the tap.

After more cold beers the successive suicides began to look like another form of ritual exchange. Was Kawabata in some sense returning the compliment, perhaps acknowledging that he should not have accepted the prize, which should have been awarded to the worthier man? Yukio Mishima was both anti-Communist and anti-American. He believed that the Emperor was the sole symbol of Japan's national community and racial identity, and that it had been an error for Hirohito to declare, as one of the unwritten conditions of surrender in 1945, that he was no longer divine. Mishima became convinced that American rule and the imposition of democracy had feminised the character of the Japanese male and suppressed the impulse to action and violent death. Without the martial spirit, Japan was inevitably untrue to itself and condemned to moral confusion.

The solution in Mishima's opinion was to return to the moral purity of the samurai code. This is set out in the eighteenth-century text *Hagakure*, a book that was available to a national readership during the war; it inspired the kamikaze pilots and later, after the war had ended, was concealed from the Americans. Needless to say Mishima's ideas have never been well received by the Japanese left.

Nonetheless they are extraordinary, almost the inversion of every Western assumption about the desirable life. For Mishima, struggle was the essence of life, while democracy and the welfare state were two systems designed to bore people, literally, to death. Death is something that a man must ponder daily and risk at regular intervals. Otherwise he cannot be truly alive. The greatest joy in a man's life is to choose the place of his own death. If the chief end of a man's life is comfortable survival, he is condemned to monotony and impotent decline – a premature living death.

One might assume on taking a seat in a piano bar in Paris or Chicago, looking around, seeing a number of men in suits, some in noisy groups, some drinking alone, that one had some general idea of the outer parameters of their inner preoccupations. In the case of Mishima, sipping his Black Label among the Tokyo *boulevardiers* while contemplating the bloody demands of a medieval code of honour, one would have been wrong.

Most places in the world become less strange the longer one spends in them. Daily life in Japan seems to push the visitor in the opposite direction. The anthropologist Claude Lévi-Strauss seldom visited the country but he was obsessed with it; he compiled a book of reflections on Japan entitled *The Far Side of the Moon* (*L'Autre face de la lune*).

Through the early morning streets of Tokyo in the gently falling rain the people walked in uniform, most without umbrellas or coats, the schoolchildren dressed in white shirts and black trousers or skirts in one direction, the office *cadres* in the same uniform walking in the other. No neckties. 1 June was 'Cool Business' day, when air-conditioning thermostats are moved up to 28°C to save energy, and formal clothes are abandoned. The pedestrians waited patiently beside the traffic lights; they were neatly spaced, slim, mostly young, briefcase or satchel in hand. For a visitor from the land of Anglo-Saxon Protestants, there seemed to be a mystifying lack of urban hysteria in the air. On the airport bus a quietly modulated female voice had said: 'Do not use mobile telephones, as this may annoy others.' So no one used mobile telephones.

As the days passed it became clear that in public spaces where strangers confronted each other, Japanese society was enveloped in a complex, unstated web of courtesies and conventions that governed most people's behaviour, most of the time. The individual gave way before the collective. The notion of personal defiance had low priority. In Western Europe this would be a stifling experience, but in Japan it seemed on the contrary to enhance a sense of personal freedom. An elaborate code of behaviour that everyone knows everyone else will follow means that you actually spend less daily time and concern on the casual, distracting, promiscuous commerce of existence. You can think about most other people less, and think about matters or people you want to think about more. We took the *Shinkansen* (Bullet Train) to Sendai, north of Tokyo, the centre of the tsunami zone, and the ticket inspectors bowed to the passengers each time they entered or left each carriage. Nobody paid any attention, but one had the sense that people would have noticed if this gesture had been omitted. Several days after the great earthquake of 2011 an old lady, who had been dug out of the wreckage of her house, is said to have struggled to her feet and bowed to her rescuers.

The 2011 tsunami zone on the east coast of Japan extends from north to south for 300 miles, and the wave of 11 March, travelling at about 20mph and sometimes rising as high as 130 feet, submerged a coastal strip that was up to 6 miles deep.

The epicentre of the earthquake was 70 km off the Tohoku coast, almost opposite Sendai. At magnitude 9 it shifted the axis of the earth by 9.8 inches and moved Honshu, the main island of Japan, by 12 feet. Natori had been a coastal settlement just south-east of Sendai and we were driven to see it by a local taxi-driver, Mr Watanabe, who knew the district well. It was a Sunday so the bulldozers dotted across the landscape were still. But there were many visitors. Their vehicles moved along the strips of tarmac that had once been roads very slowly, almost as though they too were in shock. Their occupants looked out in disbelief at what remained of their once familiar world.

Standing at the centre of Natori, one could see that in all directions the ground was covered with a thick mulch of rubbish. Factories, schools, clinics, leisure centres and houses, thousands of buildings, had simply been cut off at ground level, smashed into pieces and pulverised. The terrain was flat as a polder, like land reclaimed from the seabed, which was what in a few terrible moments it had become. It hardly mattered where one stopped the car and started to search because on the surface everywhere looked the same. One could see the outlines of buildings because the foundation lines were there. And there were glass shards, a plastic measuring jug, crocks, a blue baby seat, ceramic wall tiles, a chimney pot, a metal grille, a kitchen knife, a toy Bullet Train with the driver's compartment snapped off, some fresh blue wildflowers growing out of the sand and a small piece of metal on which a motto had been stamped, in English: *It's impossible to define impossible – Camus.*

There was also a fishing reel and a swipe card for the 'Natori Orthopaedic Clinic'. And a few yards on I could see a 78-rpm Bakelite gramophone record that lay deep in the rubble, mysteriously unbroken. There were sparrows and a few crows in the blue sky and I could hear a skylark. A young woman who was combing through the mess said that this had been a kindergarten where she had been a teacher. But she could not find any of the children's toys and she did not recognise the junk on the ground as coming from this building. Just beside her lay a metal pole that had been snapped in two. One piece carried a sign, TSUNAMI ZONE, with the figure of a running man and an arrow that must have pointed the way of escape. But when the sea arrives without warning at 20mph and at a height of 60 feet, there is nowhere to run. In this area just one building, a three-storey block of flats, was still standing, but Mr Watanabe said that everyone who took shelter there had died.

Only one spot appeared to have survived more or less undamaged. This was a low earth mound a few hundred yards from the three-storey building with a single pine tree still growing from the top of the bank. Thirty-five stone steps led up to its flat top, and on the summit was a grey standing stone that bore a carved inscription: 'Attention – If there is an earthquake this place could receive a tsunami.' Then there was a list of the names of those who had died in the tsunami of 1933. Three other standing stones had been snapped off by the wave of 2011 and thrown down the side of the bank. Since the disaster this mound had become a holy place and a focal point for visiting survivors. They had bought flowers and offerings of instant coffee, bottled spring water and yogurt. Joss sticks placed in front of a small Shinto figure were burning in the wind, and new memorials in the shape of little wooden sticks with names on them and cartoon images of children's faces rested beside miniature plastic dolls. Incredibly, three men who scrambled up the mound and climbed into the pine tree were said to have survived. From the top of the mound there was a clear view of the devastation stretching for miles in every direction – except one. To the east, just half a mile away, one could see the low waves breaking peacefully on the orderly beach.

At the crossroads below the mound a brightly painted school bus had been pushed off the road and onto the grass verge. Mr Watanabe said that this had been washed there from the school car park over a distance of two miles. Opposite, a heap of twisted iron bodywork and wheels turned out to be two entire school buses that had been rolled over and over and crushed together. Mr Watanabe told us that they had been driven by two of his former colleagues. For hundreds of miles around it was more or less the same. Rice fields littered with fishing boats and buses, towns scrubbed flat like castles in the seaside sand. And where there had been life, purpose and urgency there was nothing – just silence, rubble and mass destruction.

Inside one surviving building, neighbouring apartments told different stories. The first had been smashed in, the exterior wall ripped out and swept away. The building was steel-framed, designed to withstand earthquakes, which it had done. But its girders were now exposed and some had been twisted to 45 degrees and thrown onto the ground. The visible power of the wave was hard to believe. The wrecked apartment had sheltered another, slightly downstream, where very little damage had been done. The fly screens still ran smoothly along the aluminium window frames and the doors were in place, swinging easily on their hinges. This had been a family home. Inside, it was a peaceful scene; the sun-filled rooms looked as though they were waiting for their occupants to return. In one room alphabet tiles were set out on the floor. It was clear that on this side of the building the water had not burst through the walls and windows, it had come quietly, under the closed door, leaving a tide mark that was only eight inches above floor level. When the water seeped away it left most of the contents of the apartment in place. The rubbish was still neatly bagged by the kitchen door, ready to be put out. The ashtray on the low table in the sitting room still contained cigarette butts and cotton buds. Only the lower end of the white towel dangling from a cupboard handle was stained by the floodwater. These people had been packing up after the earthquake, then they had left in a hurry. If they had stayed in their apartment they would still, astonishingly, be alive. Clean bedding and clothes were folded into cardboard boxes, and the boxes were lined up on tables and beds, ready to be loaded into a car. Perhaps the mother had been waiting for a lift and had then made a run for it. What was clear was that everyone who had lived in this apartment was now dead, because three months after the water drained out beneath the door and back into the sea, no one had returned to collect the neatly packed contents. The washing machine was full and ready to go, but the soft toys left on the play-room floor were now covered in other people's waste.

When a tsunami strikes it comes in like a storm. Somewhere outside, on the road, the car had been overtaken by the wall of moving water, and disappeared into the tempest that followed, its height fluctuating wildly, its depths thick with tree trunks, lorries, railway carriages and corpses. Over 18,000 people died or disappeared in the tsunami of 11 March 2011. A mile inland from the neatly packed apartment, in the shattered window of what had once been a supermarket, someone had stuck up a poster showing a baby's cheerful face: 'Missing – 8 months – 70 centimetres – 9 kilos – just cutting first milk teeth', followed by a telephone number.

It was a relief to leave Natori. It looked like the end of the world.

The literal meaning of tsunami is 'harbour wave'. Japan experiences about 1,000 earthquakes a year and on the eastern coast the consequent tsunamis are not uncommon. The tradition of commemorating these devastating events with standing stones is widespread. Two of the worst tsunamis in recent times were in 1896 and 1933, and the standing stones mark the limits of the danger zone. Because the onrushing water, faced with the same natural contours, follows the same valleys, plains and hills for century after century, many of these standing stones date back for hundreds of years. Since 1945 these ancient warnings have been widely ignored. In a high-technology era folklore has been replaced by international prediction systems, sirens and well-marked evacuation routes, with the consequences the world has recently seen. Where National Route 45 and the *Shinkansen* railtrack followed the coastline they were smashed up. Entire trains disappeared. But the old northern highway, also following the coastline, loops around the danger zones, keeping inside the standing stones, and once again was largely undamaged.

In the little fishing port of Aneyoshi, which was totally destroyed by the wave of 2011, no lives were lost. The tsunami rolled in and built up to the incredible height of 38.9 metres (127 feet), but the water came to a halt only 800 metres inland, just a few feet short of the standing stone. There were no victims because the people of Aneyoshi had respected the historical warning and built their houses outside the danger zone. The fishing ports that ignored the warnings were the places that lost more than half of their populations. Nobiru, a harbour and leisure area, was one of them.

Here the port and marina were wiped out and even the railway station, which is over a mile from the sea and protected by a line of hills, was submerged. Three months after the event the stationmaster's smart grey cap with gold braid round the peak, was still lying on the railway platform. Beside the platform the booking hall was a total wreck and the railway's electric power cables still festooned the platform roof. Smooth round stones the size of footballs that had been carried up from the seabed and then over several miles were scattered along the tracks. And the neat lines of holiday villas beside the station remained standing. They were upright but wrecked, silent and empty. On the gateway of one of the houses the search-party's log was still pinned up: '1st visit – 18 March – Call out loudly. 2nd visit – 22 March – Interior search.' In other words it had taken rescuers seven days to reach this prosperous, busy settlement. Other areas were not searched for four weeks.

Outside another house a Roland upright piano had been washed through the front window and thrown into the garden, where it lay inverted. Behind the piano, in the front room, a fair-sized tree trunk remained, draped across the sofa. On the wooded hillsides just above this scene of devastation a badger trotted through the pine trees and maples, showing no fear. And a grey tabby cat hunted through the unkempt gardens. Where was this domestic pet when the water arrived? Up a tree? Asleep on the top floor? Or perhaps like the elephants of Sri Lanka, and a few humans, it sensed what was coming and retreated to a place of safety in good time. Whatever happened, no one had returned to collect it. On the way back we spoke to a man living in a metal cabin that had once been a transport container. He was waiting for a permanent home; his own house had been destroyed. He said that after the earthquake he had heard the tsunami warning sirens and returned home to check that everyone was out. He had had to push his wife and their dog into the car and drive for his life, with the wave 500 metres behind him.

It was in Sendai that we experienced our first earthquake. It took place at 1 a.m. and amounted to nothing untoward but it was enough to make my bed on the eleventh floor of a twenty-storey hotel tremble and pitch. Reflexes first awakened many years before in Guatemala City caused me to leap out of bed and load a bag with passport, torch, mobile telephone and water bottle, and poke my nose outside the bedroom door into a deserted corridor, before falling back into a wary sleep. The correct procedure would have been to stand in the bathroom doorway. The Japanese only respond to earthquakes if they are forced to do so. On the following afternoon there were further tremors while Jun and a pupil were rehearsing a Mozart piano sonata, KV 381. 'Earthquake!' he cried across the empty concert hall, and continued the rehearsal without missing a note.

Jun had a friend in Sendai, Mr Teshigawara, a prominent lawyer, now semi-retired at the age of eighty-six. The lawyer was a widower who lived with his daughter, Michiko, also a professional musician. Mr Teshigawara would only have been sixteen when Japan attacked Pearl Harbor, but would nonetheless have served in the war. He smoked like a chimney and was thought to be unintentionally responsible for the death of his wife, a non-smoker who had contracted lung cancer. Despite this sad turn of events Mr Teshigawara continued to smoke like a chimney. As a widower he had resumed the bachelor life. He intended to end his life as he had started it, in high spirits and irresponsible behaviour. He spent the hours after work smoking and carousing with his friends, often returning home to his daughter's house very late at night. I asked him about the previous night's little earthquake but he said he had been in a bar at the time and had quite failed to notice it. During his lifetime Japan had experienced roughly 90,000 earthquakes, so perhaps this was not surprising.

From the tsunami zone around Sendai we travelled south, back to Tokyo, and then on to the city of Nagasaki, where Jun was due to give a performance of works by Bach, Beethoven and Chopin in an empty concert hall.

Jun's involvement in the film of *Snake Dance* came about because the course of his life seemed to have been ordained by the success of the Anglo-American Manhattan Project. He was born in 1956, in Matsue, and moved north with his family to Sendai where he was educated until 1971, when he moved to Tokyo. While studying in Tokyo he converted to Catholicism, a religion he had first encountered at his primary school which had been run by French-Canadian missionaries. He was baptised five months before he left his homeland to study music in Paris on a French government scholarship. He has never lived in Japan since.

When in August 1945 the Emperor of Japan announced his country's surrender it was the first time he had ever spoken on the radio, and the first time his people had heard 'the Voice of the Crane'. One of the great spectacles of the wildlife refuge at Bosque del Apache, which is close to the Trinity test site in New Mexico, is the annual migration of the cranes. The crane is the Japanese symbol of happiness and long life. In the film the flight of the cranes taking off in New Mexico becomes an emblem of the flight of the wartime B-29s, the silver planes that the people of Nagasaki and other Japanese cities

called 'the Bs'. The pieces played by Otto Frisch at one of his Los
Alamos concerts, and performed by Jun in 2012, accompany the
cranes' dawn flight. The bomb dropped at Nagasaki fell from a plane
blessed by a United States Air Force chaplain, and exploded close to
Urakami Cathedral, the centre of Japanese Christianity and a refuge
for persecuted Japanese Catholics for 300 years. It killed over two-thirds
of the city's Catholic population. From these chance connections, a
narrative of loss and destruction emerged.

Nagasaki is a deep-water harbour surrounded by hills. In 1945 it was
listed as a military target because it contained a torpedo factory and a
naval dockyard. It also sheltered 13,000 Korean forced labourers and
around 200 Allied POWs. In the sixteenth century the city was a prosperous trading centre, and during the long period of Japan's isolation
from the outside world, Nagasaki remained a port where a few Dutch
traders were authorised to live and work on an island in the harbour.
Puccini set *Madame Butterfly* in Nagasaki and in the nineteenth century
a British merchant called Thomas Glover settled in the city and played
an important role in the modernisation of Japan. He built the country's
first railway and he dealt in arms. The house he built has become a
museum. It would have been destroyed if the bomb had not missed
its target since it overlooks the deep-water harbour. The harbour, and
the rivers that feed it, and the mountains that feed the rivers, make
Nagasaki a very attractive place. The mountains cluster so tightly
around the city that the airport is twenty-five miles away.

In contrast to Hiroshima, the city of Nagasaki has minimised its
commemoration of the bombing. There is one black stone pillar in
a small park that marks the hypocentre of the explosion and there is
an Atomic Bomb Museum, just as there is in Albuquerque.

During my visit the museum was crowded with school parties,
shadowed by a thin scattering of Westerners. The earnest children,
dressed like English schoolchildren of forty years ago and busy with
their notebooks, looked at the Westerners gravely, in silent enquiry.
Among the exhibits was an illustration of a human spleen swollen

by radiation damage to forty times its original size. This photograph had been supplied by the US Armed Forces Institute of Pathology. Another photograph showed the Shiroyama primary school, where at least 1,310 teachers and schoolchildren perished; the school building stood 500 yards from Ground Zero. They were among the 30,000 people who died within 3 seconds of the explosion. A large section of the Nagasaki Atomic Bomb Museum is devoted to the need for nuclear disarmament; there were no earrings or keyrings depicting Fat Man or Little Boy in the museum shop.

In his brief memoir, *What Little I Remember*, Otto Frisch recalled some of the impromptu concerts, held in the evening after a hard day in the Los Alamos laboratory. There was one good grand piano on site, and it was kept well tuned. 'I still remember', wrote Frisch after the war, 'the pleasure of starting to play on the excellent piano . . . After a while a violinist would arrive and join me in a sonata which we broke off to switch to a trio as soon as the cellist appeared . . . The party ended around eleven o'clock, with well-filled stomachs and ears full of Beethoven and Mozart.' When Los Alamos installed its own radio station, 'Otto', as Frisch was known for security reasons (his usual name was Robert), performed on air and his recitals of Scarlatti and Liszt could sometimes be picked up in Santa Fe.

Jun's performance was filmed in the Canary Concert Hall of the commune of Togitsu, a suburb of Nagasaki. For the occasion Jun wore a midnight-blue suit with a blue silk handkerchief in the breast pocket and black leather slip-on shoes with silver buckles. He also wore a distinctive white shirt with an elegant high collar. This gave him something of the style of a senior Congolese functionary in the heyday of Mobutu Sese Seko.

Just before starting the first piece Jun tripped on the steps leading down from the stage and nearly fell four steps. Had he done so his face would have struck the edge of a seat. On the train to Sendai his suitcase had crashed onto the floor from the rack above him having first bounced off the empty seat at his side. It could have broken someone's neck. But these accidents had not occurred and the concert, in an empty hall that was crowded with ghosts, took place.

The programme, originally selected by the principal ghost, Otto Frisch, consisted of the Sarabande from Bach's Partita No. 1, Beethoven's Piano Sonata No. 8 (*Pathétique*) and Chopin's Ballade No. 3 in A-flat major. Performing these three pieces for recording, with variations and repetitions, took all day, an artistic marathon. Occasionally Jun was assisted by a *tourneuse*, a young lady called Aika who looked about seventeen. In fact she was twenty-eight and had a six-year-old son. Aika was dressed in a black suit with black stockings and stiletto heels. She had long straight hair, a down-turned mouth and almond-shaped eyes that were also black. When following a conversation she rarely spoke, but very slight muscular movements in her face betrayed her reactions. The Canary Concert Hall normally seats 650 people. When empty it resembles an underground nuclear shelter. If Aika thought it odd for a five-man film crew to have flown across the world to film a concert pianist performing in an empty hall, she did not mention it.

While Jun played Chopin, I thought of some of the other ghosts in whose company I had spent so much of the previous ten years. I thought of Max Born and Lise Meitner who had condemned the bomb project from the start and of Max von Laue, who had opposed the Nazis and shunned the German bomb. I thought of Leó Szilárd, who never unpacked his suitcase when he visited Nazi Germany and who crossed the Atlantic to warn Roosevelt and became a quarry for Groves's spooks. I thought of Joseph Rotblat who had walked off the project and who, like Szilárd, abandoned physics after the war and took to biology. And then there was Harold Urey who argued in vain for atomic arms control. 'There is no defence against [these weapons],' he wrote. 'They can destroy beyond our ability to comprehend. *Fear of them will destroy our liberties.*' And there were the shades of Niels Bohr, who had been shown a sketch of a German bomb and had crossed the Atlantic to build an American one, and of Oppenheimer who proved unable to think of a plausible demonstration and who dealt with Edward Teller's hissy fit by authorising the conceited young man to work on his own far more hideous engine.

And then there was the shade of Teller himself. When Teller had finally prevailed over Harold Urey, and constructed a stockpile of 200 Fat Men and invented the H-Bomb – 1,000 times more powerful than any Fat Man – Rabi and Fermi told him that this was 'a weapon of genocide' and 'an evil thing in any light' – and Teller replied, 'Science must do the things that can be done.' He saw no impediment to conducting experiments that could lead to the annihilation of the human race, and of science, for ever.

There was no shortage of ghosts in the empty concert hall at Nagasaki.

After leaving Nagasaki we set out for the evacuation zone around Fukushima, and on the way I read an article in *The Japan Times* written by an American resident with long experience as an adviser to the Japanese government. The adviser seemed to have little respect for either the traditional values or the technical competence of the people he had chosen to live among and advise. He said that Japanese leaders had repeatedly shown unbelievable stupidity, that the national mentality was dangerously incompetent and primitive and that the country's governing class seemed unable to solve its most urgent problems. His analysis was eerily similar to Yukio Mishima's, but whereas Mishima attributed national weakness to the permanent American presence, the American adviser saw it as a consequence of the obstinate survival of Japanese traditions.

Mishima's ideas continue to resonate in Japanese politics. Nationalist leaders have called for Japan to develop its own nuclear weapons and have singled out Korean and Chinese residents as a danger to public security. Emperor-worship is still alive within some extreme right-wing groups, and there is an influential mainstream movement to revise Japanese history textbooks. Some of these books now omit references to the 1937 massacre of Nanking, when Japanese troops slaughtered thousands of Chinese civilians.

Another Japanese writer, Kenzaburō Ōe, who won the Nobel Prize in 1994 and whose ideas could hardly be further from those of Yukio Mishima, has nonetheless had a painful experience of the continuing influence of Mishima's ideas. In 1970, the year of Mishima's death, Ōe published an account of Japanese war crimes. He was particularly concerned about events on Okinawa, when the imperial army urged civilians to commit mass suicide rather than surrender to US forces in 1945. This was a phenomenon that had first been seen in June 1944, on the outlying island of Saipan, when 22,000 Japanese civilians threw themselves over sea cliffs onto rocks 80 feet below. But on that occasion the suicides had been volunteers. On Okinawa the civilians were said to have been given little choice.

In 2005 Ōe was sued for defamation by angry nationalist groups who tried to get his book pulped and it took him nearly three years to defeat them in court. During this time a right-wing government proposed to remove all mention of the Okinawa suicides from school textbooks and only backed down after mass demonstrations had taken place on Okinawa in defence of Kenzaburō Ōe's account. During the legal battle, Ōe received death threats from Mishima's disciples. In order to prepare for the case Ōe obtained and read hundreds of books written by right-wing authors such as Mishima on wartime atrocities and militarism, and when he had won the case he took the entire collection to a second-hand bookshop and left it there. He said afterwards that 'Nothing could have been as boring and painful as reading those books,' and that he had only done it in order to understand and defeat his enemies.

Mishima believed that Japan lost touch with its national soul when the emperor was deprived of his divine status. Kenzaburō Ōe, on the contrary, is convinced that the failure to abolish the imperial system in 1945 prevented the country from coming to terms with its militaristic past and transforming itself into a contented democracy.

But with the Fukushima nuclear disaster the convictions of these two writers became more difficult to distinguish.

Faced with the nuclear question Ōe has developed a theory of 'ambiguity', his word for what appears to be an impasse. For Ōe the earthquake, even at scale 9 and followed by the huge tsunami, was part of Japan's normality. But the nuclear accident was a true disaster since it was the work of man. Ambiguity is one of Ōe's recurring themes. He has always been a strong supporter of the post-war peace settlement. After the war Japan faced a new future, one that was 'made in Washington'. The country became a parliamentary democracy with pacifism written into the constitution. There would be no standing army, and no need for one, since the United States would guarantee Japan's security. And Japan embraced the 'three anti-nuclear principles' – never to possess, manufacture or use nuclear weapons. This deal gave rise to unprecedented prosperity. By the 1980s Japan was listed as the richest nation per capita in the world.

The settlement of 1945 also assured dominance of the Pacific Basin for the United States. But over the decades of the Cold War, America's Pacific empire was challenged by China – in Korea, Laos, Cambodia and Vietnam. In response Washington drew up a secret treaty which authorised the United States to stockpile nuclear warheads on Japanese soil. The Japanese armed forces, known as 'the Self-Defense Forces' were steadily increased, while American bases continued to operate all over Japan, notably on Okinawa, which remained under US administration until 1972 and where 24,000 US troops are stationed today.

At the same time Washington persuaded Japan to undertake a heavy investment in nuclear power; this was driven by US engineering firms such as General Electric, which built Fukushima on a coastline that was regularly shaken by earthquakes and drowned by tidal waves. The Fukushima nuclear power station was among the first to come on stream in Japan, in 1971. For Kenzaburō Ōe as for millions of his fellow citizens this was in clear contradiction to the three anti-nuclear principles imposed by America. The experience of living in a nation whose soil had never been invaded until 1945 and which has for the last sixty-five years become an obedient part of another nation's empire, is a further example of what Ōe calls 'ambiguity'. The value of the bargain became more questionable when Japan's economic bubble burst in the early 1990s and the country moved into ten years of recession. Twenty years after the crash, the Japanese economy has still not recovered its former prosperity.

In March 2011, in the aftermath of the tsunami, Kenzaburō Ōe gave an interview. 'When Japan was defeated,' he said,

> I was ten years old. One year later the new constitution was published and national education was redesigned so that children of my age could understand the new deal. Throughout my adolescence I frequently wondered whether constitutional pacifism really represented the post-war aspirations of the Japanese people. I think the secret treaty about stockpiling nuclear warheads and the steady build-up in the size of the army points to the answer. But we should not forget the ideals of our post-war leadership. We still remember our wartime sacrifices and the suffering caused by the atomic bombs. The dead look down and insist that we continue to respect these ideals. The memory of the victims of Hiroshima and Nagasaki should prevent us from compromising in the name of political advantage over the evil nature of nuclear weapons.

In Ōe's bitter analysis the human failure evident in the Fukushima accident is made much worse because of the disrespect it embodies towards the memory of the victims of Nagasaki. It is clear evidence that the post-war settlement has led the country into a dead end where it is incapable of assuming either its historical responsibilities or its role in the modern world. The accident at Fukushima confirmed

that the ruling elite of post-war, democratic Japan was incapable of
protecting its own people.* Fukushima has become the symbol of
'ambiguity' and of the nuclear trap; and, in a country riddled with
earthquakes, the nuclear power industry has become the symbol of
Japan's impotence and humiliation. After Fukushima, Ōe demanded
that the government terminate the arrangement on Okinawa and
abandon nuclear power. He wanted his country to identify the values
it now stood for, so that it could start to defend them. Yukio Mishima,
with his insistence on the nation's need for 'a spiritual foundation',
could hardly have put it more clearly.

The *Shinkansen* from Tokyo to Fukushima left, as usual, on the dot.
A group of retired nuclear engineers had recently volunteered to join
the rescue operation at Fukushima, saying that they already knew
exactly what to do and were too old to be at risk from long-term
radiation damage. Seated on the opposite side of the train corridor
a high-spirited party of old guys were drinking sake and beer and
noisily eating the seafood they had bought at the station. The director
thought that they looked like the B-team heading for Fukushima No.
1 to sign up for the rescue operation, but to me they seemed to have
more the air of a fishing party. It was a Sunday. They were out to
enjoy themselves and were already drinking quite fast, despite the
early start. There would be tears before bedtime. But, as the real
extent of the situation in Fukushima emerged, fast drinking – if one
was a local resident – came to seem quite a good solution.

The city of Fukushima is the provincial capital of the prefecture,
and stands about forty miles inland from Fukushima No. 1, where
the accident had occurred. When the first reactor exploded the
government evacuated a zone twelve miles deep all around the power
station. Fifty thousand families were driven out of this exclusion

* Some months before Ōe's remarks the government of North Korea, Japan's
hereditary enemy, announced that it was now in possession of its own nuclear
warheads. And on 5 April 2009 the North Koreans fired an unarmed Taepodong 2
rocket right over Japanese air space and into the Pacific to the east of Japan.

zone, which was then sealed off by the army and declared out of bounds for everyone apart from rescue workers. In an additional six-mile outer band, described as a 'Control Zone', residents were advised to leave and told that if they chose to remain they should spend as much time as possible indoors and wear a face mask when outside.

When the tsunami hit the power station on 11 March the Japanese government published a statement saying that the situation at the reactor was an emergency but that it 'posed no immediate health risk'. The government's first response was to raise the safe limit for radiation levels in school playgrounds by a factor of 20, to 3.8 microsieverts an hour. This was a level that increased the children's annual exposure to 20 mSv, the amount normally set for adults working inside nuclear power stations.

It subsequently emerged that health authorities had taken no systematic radiation measurements until 17 March, five days after a plume of radiation had started to drift across northern Japan. These measurements were not published until 24 April, when they revealed that levels of radioactivity in the 'safer' Control Zone had frequently been much higher than they were in large parts of the Evacuation Zone. At 830 mSv they were equivalent to measurements taken after the explosion at Chernobyl. But even these figures may have been unreliable. A subsequent Norwegian study showed that accurate levels of caesium-137, a radioactive element with a half-life of thirty years, were over twice as high as the level announced by the Japanese Ministry of Science and Technology.

In May, TEPCO (the Tokyo Electric Power Company), which operates the Fukushima power station, admitted that in recent years it had falsified more than 200 maintenance and safety reports. Shortly after the tsunami its chief executive retired to bed for a week, suffering from high blood pressure. When he re-emerged he issued a statement saying that his company would strive to be 'more customer oriented in the future'. In fact the company continued to minimise the risk.

On the morning our *Shinkansen* drew into Fukushima station, teachers at a nearby high school recorded radiation levels as being

fifty times higher than normal outside the school and ten times higher
inside it. Experts advised them to remove the topsoil from the school
grounds, but no one could tell them where they should dump it.

We were driven to the Control Zone by our friend Mr Watanabe,
who had made the journey from Sendai to be with us once again.
His daughter lived in Fukushima and he knew how difficult it was
to find local drivers prepared to do the job. The city's taxi drivers
had been authorised to refuse fares to the Control Zone. In the city
itself the only remaining signs of the recent disaster were the
tarpaulins stretched over some of the blue-tiled roofs, evidence of
unrepaired earthquake damage.

The region to the east of the city of Fukushima has never been
popular with tourists, but just before the earthquake it was listed as
an area of outstanding natural beauty. The fact that it has now been
emptied of most of its inhabitants has given it an additional Arcadian
charm. Quite soon the road to the eastern coast started to climb. We
left the wide flat rice paddies and passed through low hill country
that was full of streams and little farmhouses surrounded by orchards,
tall pine trees, stands of bamboo and vegetable plots. The hillsides
were terraced and irrigated and walnut trees grew thickly along the
banks of the streams. In one clearing I caught a glimpse of snow on
the mountain peaks to the west. Several of the farms advertised their
pedigree Holstein or Jersey herds. There was a smell of clover and
the alarm call of a jay. White cranes with black bills picked among
the crops. Every metre of ground seemed to be lovingly cultivated
right up to the farmhouse walls, with strawberries, leeks and beans
all ready for harvest. But the houses were empty and the crops had
been condemned and were about to rot. By 10.25 we had entered the
wind shadow of the reactor.

The prevailing wind blows from the south-east directly over this
land from Fukushima No. 1, and the radiation chart spreads out
like a plume across the map and provides a pretty accurate outline
of the wind pattern. The chart showed that there were two areas of

heavy pollution. One was around the power station and well within the Exclusion Zone. The other was to the north-west of the power station and ran from within the border of the Exclusion Zone right through the Control Zone and deep into the uncontrolled area beyond.

The first settlement we came to was Iitate, a small town twenty-five miles north-west of the power station. Here the airborne radiation figure had been measured three weeks earlier at 700 mSv a year, seven times higher than the dose normally recognised as carcinogenic.

Iitate was the scene of a tragic error in the days immediately following the explosion. Since it was outside the Control Zone it was selected as a reception centre for thousands of refugees from the coast whose villages had been destroyed by the tsunami. They remained in the commune from 13 to 19 March, which was a week of heavy winds, rain and snowfall. It was later discovered that during this period the air in Iitate was heavily polluted by iodine-131; this is a short-lived but highly toxic element, particularly dangerous for children and pregnant women. Many of the refugees had heard Fukushima No. 1 power station exploding as they fled from the tsunami and they had no idea that the remote and beautiful region in which they had taken shelter was as heavily contaminated as the area immediately around the reactor. Many others had fled from towns inside the official danger zones that were uncontaminated, into this poisoned region.

Since the prevailing wind pattern had not changed, Iitate at the time of our visit was still receiving very high levels of radiation, and 90 per cent of the population had been evacuated. A few lights were on, a few shops were open. One was a hairdresser's, with signs in three languages – 'Coiffeur, Bienvenidos, Fam. Sakamoto' – perhaps hoping to attract an international clientele. There was one old lady inside having a perm. A wizened security guard was on patrol, doing a round of the few houses that remained occupied. He said that most of those who had chosen to remain were old and lived alone. He was well past retirement age himself. He said that women of childbearing age were generally the first to leave, for fear of induced mutations.

We drove on into and right through the Control Zone and reached the border of the Exclusion Zone at Namie, a town with a population of 70,000 from which 60,000 people had been evacuated. The frontier ran through the outskirts of this town and was heavily patrolled by soldiers who had made their camp in a large, empty car park. A restaurant was open but it was only selling pre-packed sandwiches, cans of Coke and packets of crisps. Then Yuichi Matsunaga arrived, with his wife and daughter and their three large dogs, two Pyrenean Mountain Dogs and a golden retriever. The ladies wore the recommended face masks but Mr Matsunaga and his dogs went uncovered.

Matsunaga took us to see his ice-cream factory, now closed. He had specialised in red-bean flavours and used only Jersey double cream. He said his ice creams had been very popular and that he had employed 150 people. Most people he knew had lost someone in the tsunami; one of his workers had lost four family members and a neighbour had lost his entire family. His house was beside the dairy and I asked him why he had come back. It did not seem much fun, living in an empty town beside a ruined business. He said that he had been evacuated but he had only stayed away for two weeks because the apartment they had found had been rather small and there had not really been room for the dogs. The dogs, he assured us, were much happier back in Namie.

There did not seem much else to say. The ladies were too polite to go inside the house until we had finished talking to them. I asked Mr Matsunaga why his wife and daughter wore face masks while he did not and he said it was because they had been told on the radio that it made them safer. But before switching to ice creams he had been a television producer and so remained unpersuaded. Then we said goodbye to the Matsunaga family and they waved us farewell and retired swifly inside their house, with their dogs.

*

The country around Namie is noted for trout streams and the woods are full of wild boar. But the trout streams are now radioactive, fishing and hunting are banned and rice and vegetable production have been abandoned. We stopped on the edge of the Control Zone, in a deserted hamlet above Highway 115. Here several of the houses had been severely damaged by the earthquake but that was not what had driven people away three months earlier. These houses, at a height well above the tsunami, had also been abandoned in a hurry. There were children's toys, baseball gloves and bicycles left outside the front doors, and in the exterior meter box one dial was still moving, burning electrical current that would never be paid for. Radioactivity is usually at its highest in places where rainwater has been stored, in gutters, reservoirs, irrigation ditches and in patches of dried mud. Looking down I saw that ants were running through a patch of dried mud at my feet. And there were butterflies, ladybirds and quite a few spiders' webs among the irises, peonies, roses and windflowers that flourished in the abandoned gardens; no other sign of moving, sentient life. According to scientists at the University of Ryukyu the blue butterflies of Fukushima were already showing malformations of the wings, eyes and antennae. Mr Watanabe said that the ambient level of radiation was 150 mSv (twice the level at Shinkolobwe), and it was time to go.

There was one other relic of everyday normality. As we drove out of the Control Zone we repeatedly passed a roadside poster of a man in a suit and tie and the prime of life, big smile – Kameyoka of the Liberal Democrat Party! 'Second-generation representative, son of the man who graduated from army college, Policies for the State and the People.' The posters were surrounded by abandoned rice fields and I wondered whether Kameyoka would lose his seat now that he had 90,000 fewer voters.

The few people who are left living on the farms of the Control Zone still go to the woods to gather mushrooms while they wait to hear the full extent of the damage that has been done to their lives. Tōhoku farmers are forbidden to work their land, and at the time of our visit the first suicides were being discreetly reported. One man hanged himself in his barn leaving a message chalked on the door: 'The reactor cut off our hands and then our feet. To those who remain – good luck.' A national opinion poll showed that 82 per cent of those questioned wanted all fifty of Japan's nuclear power stations to be demolished. In November, with Fukushima No. 1 still out of control after 8 months of desperate efforts, 154 farms to the west of Fukushima city, over 60 kilometres from the reactor, were closed after they were found to be producing radioactive rice.

Fukushima No. 1 was designed by General Electric to run on America's spent nuclear fuel, plutonium-239, which has a half-life of 24,100 years. So the fertile lands around Namie will lie barren for rather longer than the time it takes to repair the huge amount of damage caused by the tsunami.

Among the millions of people who had to cope in March 2011 without electricity, fuel, food or water was Jun Kanno's mother, Dr Kiyo Kanno, the director of a psychiatric clinic in Shiogama, near Sendai.

Kiyo Kanno said that the earthquake of 11 March, which occurred the day after her eighty-fourth birthday, had seriously affected her work. Part of the clinic had had to be evacuated but they had managed to keep going on an emergency basis. There were sufficient stocks of most medicines, but it had taken some days to restore water, light and heat. Food supplies had taken much longer to recover. The premises of all local suppliers had been destroyed, and it was six weeks before the 1,100 railtrack 'failures', including bridges and viaducts, between Shiogama and the outside world could be repaired. The clinic got by with limited stocks of rice and beans. Dr Kanno had been interested to see that many of her patients became calmer and more rational during the emergency.

Dr Kanno is used to working under difficult conditions. She was admitted to medical school at the age of sixteen in 1943, one of the youngest, and one of the very few female medical students in Japan at that time. She studied at Tokyo Medical University and on the night before her eighteenth birthday she survived the first large-scale fire-bombing of Tokyo by the US Army Air Force. This raid, carried out by 334 B-29s on a target without air defences and containing a population of 6 million people, damaged or destroyed 267,171 buildings. It is not known how many people were killed; estimates vary between 84,000 and over 100,000. The target area, described by the USAAF as '87.4 per cent residential', was first ringed with incendiary bombs, so that it became impossible for people to escape. Then the target centre was washed down with napalm, oil and phosphorous. The bombers were flying so low that some were flipped over in the updraft from fires that were burning at just below 1000°C, and there were complaints from aircrew that at 6,000 feet the smell of roasting flesh was making them feel sick.

Dr Kanno has always believed that the city was first ringed with fire to ensure that the maximum number of people were killed, a conclusion supported by statements from USAAF commanders that the most effective way of disrupting the Japanese war effort was to maximise civilian casualties. It was General Curtis LeMay who said, 'An innocent civilian does not exist.' The B-29 – designed, according to the Albuquerque Atomic Museum as 'a hemisphere defense weapon' – only flew against Japan. By the end of July 1945, before the use of the atomic bombs, this plane had killed 900,000 people and injured 1.3 million more. The silver Bs attacked 66 cities, destroyed 43 per cent of Japan's built-up areas and rendered 8 million people homeless.* Japanese cities were largely constructed from wood, and their vulnerability to fire had first been noted by American air-force strategists in 1924.

Kiyo Kanno continued to study in Tokyo until the end of the war. She remembers that a few days after the attack on Hiroshima her teachers told her that the Americans were now using radiation bombs and as a precaution all medical students and nurses were issued with

---

* These figures can be placed beside examples of Allied civilian deaths. In the United Kingdom between 1939 and 1945 the civilian death toll was about 61,000. In the United States it was 6.

doctors' white coats which, they were assured, would reflect radiation. After the war Kiyo completed her studies and chose to specialise in psychiatry. She met her future husband, Tario Kanno, at this time.

Jun's father, Dr Tario Kanno, is also a psychiatrist, still practising and teaching at the age of ninety-two. And he provided another of Jun's links to the atomic story. Tario Kanno was born in 1919, the eighth of nine children. His father died when he was six so he was brought up by his oldest brother, a military doctor. When Japan attacked Pearl Harbor in 1941, Tario Kanno was a newly qualified teacher in a secondary school, living with his older brother in Matsue, a coastal city famous for its glorious sunsets. He was called up for military training but one morning was ordered to report to the battalion doctor. The doctor told Tario Kanno that he was being discharged on medical grounds and he was sent home. Tario Kanno said that there was nothing wrong with him, apart from haemorrhoids, and he thinks that his mother – who had always regarded him as fragile – asked his older brother to use military connections to get him invalided out of the army. A few weeks later Tario Kanno's battalion was sent overseas, to Guadalcanal, where it was wiped out.

Tario felt too ashamed to return to the school where he had been teaching so he went to Hiroshima University to study philosophy, the only subject that really interested him. In June 1945 he returned to his mother's house near Sendai for the summer vacation, and on 31 July he set out by train for the return journey to Hiroshima. The journey took two days in peacetime but communications were disrupted by the bombing and he did not want to miss a meeting with his professor scheduled for 11.15 a.m. on 6 August.

The connection with Tokyo had been cut by the American air force so he took a train across the island to Niigata, intending to travel down the west coast. Then the line was cut again when the USAAF bombed Toyama and he was diverted back inland to Nagano in the central mountains. Much of the time was spent in a train that only moved after dark. He eventually reached Matsue on 5 August. Instead of travelling on to Hiroshima that night he thought it would be more respectful to call on his brother and take an early train in the morning. In the event he just missed the early train, which arrived in Hiroshima at 8.15 a.m., 1 minute and 2 seconds before the atomic bomb exploded. Looking back on this journey now Tario Kanno says, 'The American air force saved my life.'

Tario Kanno eventually reached Hiroshima on 10 August on the first train allowed in. The stationmaster at Matsue had warned him that the city had been hit by 'a special bomb'. He got out of the train and stood on the platform. Wherever he looked he saw that there was nothing. The entire city had disappeared. There were no buildings for as far as he could see – just a few twisted metal structures. Near the station there were some survivors. They were sitting on the ground. They were naked, the skin had been stripped from their bones, and they were asking for water. His university no longer existed and everyone he knew was dead.

In Oswald Wynd's novel *The Ginger Tree*, Count Kurihama, an army officer, returns in 1904 from Japan's victorious war with Russia to recover from his wounds. While he is convalescing, he offers prayers at a Buddhist shrine, 'prayers of apology to the men under his command who had died'. He prays to the souls of these men, asking forgiveness and believing that many of them might be alive if he had given better orders.

In 2009, Tario Kanno returned to Hiroshima. Like the count in *The Ginger Tree* he wanted in his own words 'to say sorry to all my friends who died so early in their lives'. And he wanted to apologise to them because he had not fought and died in the war. After leaving Hiroshima he went to the Japanese National Shrine, 'where the chief priest was a friend of mine. There I spoke to him about what was on my mind.'

After the war Tario Kanno wanted to go to Tokyo University to continue his philosophy studies. But his brother told him that the country was in a terrible state and did not need another philosopher; he should study something that would be more useful to other people.

He switched to medicine and met Kiyo, who was already a doctor – she had qualified at the age of 21. 'It was an arranged marriage,' she said. 'There was this elderly medical student who kept proposing marriage to me. I refused him twice but the third time I agreed.'

'I note that we still appear to be married after many years,' said Tario. 'So I conclude that I must have given satisfaction.'

The tsunami of March 2011 destroyed the port of Shiogama and wrecked the centre of town. The wave stopped half a mile from the Kannos' clinic and, once order had been restored, Tario Kanno said that he wished to visit the zone. He was driven out onto the wasteland and when he got out of the car and looked around was immediately reminded of what he had seen when he stepped down onto the station platform at Hiroshima, sixty-five years earlier. 'Just nothing. Everywhere I looked. Just like Hiroshima. And I looked and I thought, "What has my life been? I do not know what my life has been."'

His life has been spent in caring for his patients, men and women who, like Aby Warburg, took refuge from the horrors of reality in the sanctuary of their delusions.

'Any average sized town can now be wiped out by a bomb the size of a football . . . Mechanical civilisation has thus reached the ultimate degree of savagery . . . (and) science has signed up in the cause of cold-blooded murder . . .'

Albert Camus, *Combat* (August 1945)

Chronology

Events leading to the first use of the atomic bomb

The official explanation for the first use of the atomic bomb is that it was built to ensure that the Nazis did not acquire a monopoly of nuclear weapons, and then used, twice, to end the war.

This explanation is still supported by many historians of the Second World War. The following chronology, drawn from the text, questions this account.

The decision to build the bomb

1939

January:	Otto Hahn announces his discovery of nuclear fission in Berlin
March:	Pierre Joliot-Curie signs a contract to build a French nuclear weapon in the Sahara Desert using uranium from the Belgian Congo
March:	German troops break Munich agreement by occupying remainder of Czechoslovakia
April:	German atomic bomb programme secretly authorised
July:	First secret delivery of Belgian uranium to warehouse in New York
August:	Nazi–Soviet Pact announced
August:	Einstein's letter to President Roosevelt warning of the danger of a Nazi atomic bomb. No effective action follows. Earlier in the year Roosevelt had ordered the construction of thousands of heavy bombers
September:	Hitler invades Poland. French bomb programme cancelled

1940

March:	Frisch–Peirls memorandum to Churchill first reveals practical possibility of an atomic bomb. Churchill appoints Maud Committee
June:	In Washington, Vannevar Bush, president of Carnegie Institute, sets up the NDRC, to direct scientific development of military research

August: Churchill sends the Tizard–Cockcroft mission to Washington,
              proposing close military co-operation

1941
May: Arthur Compton, of Chicago University, reports to President
              Roosevelt, describing atomic bomb as 'a determining factor in warfare'
July: Maud Committee's final report recommends immediate construction
              of an atomic bomb. Vannevar Bush receives a copy of this report and
              appoints Arthur Compton, Ernest Lawrence and Harold Urey as
              project directors
October: Roosevelt approves development of a weapon that 'will change the
              political organisation of the world' and promises 'unlimited funds'
6 December: President Roosevelt appoints working groups for immediate launch
              of atomic bomb programme
7 December: Japan attacks USA without warning at Pearl Harbor

1942
March: President Roosevelt and Vannevar Bush discount danger of a Nazi
              bomb, but decide to 'push' the US programme
June: In Berlin Albert Speer, on the advice of Werner Heisenberg, post-
              pones, and effectively cancels, the Nazi bomb programme
September: Brig. Gen. Leslie Groves is appointed director of Manhattan Project
October: Groves establishes his authority independently of the Joint Chiefs
              of Staff and appoints Robert Oppenheimer as director of Los Alamos
              laboratory
December: Groves obtains a monopoly of Congolese and Canadian uranium and
              ensures that United Kingdom is denied all wartime uranium supply

1943
February: Norwegian Special Forces destroy a heavy water plant essential to
              construction of a German nuclear reactor
March: Manhattan Project has grown into a top secret $2bn industry,
              employing 150,000 people on sites at Oak Ridge (Tennessee), Hanford
              (Washington State), and Los Alamos (New Mexico)
December: Twenty British scientists arrive to join the Manhattan Project

1944
January: Harold Urey, director of Oak Ridge, resigns, when he realises that
              the Manhattan Project is no longer intended to block a Nazi atomic
              bomb monopoly
March: At Los Alamos, Gen. Groves tells British physicist Joseph Rotblat
              that the new weapon is aimed at the Soviets, not the Nazis

| October: | Vannevar Bush proposes a new committee be set up, the Interim Committee, to consider post-war implications of atomic bomb |
| November: | The ALSOS team captures information in Strasbourg proving that there is no ongoing Nazi bomb programme and informs Groves |

1945

January:	First delivery of bomb-grade uranium to Los Alamos from Oak Ridge
January:	Two months after ALSOS report, Groves decides to triple production of bomb grade uranium
12 April:	Death of Franklin Delano Roosevelt. Succeeded by Vice-Pres. Harry S. Truman, who knows nothing of Manhattan Project
April:	Groves tells his superior officer, Gen. George C. Marshall, US Army Chief of Staff, that all German uranium is accounted for
25 April:	Truman first learns of the Manhattan Project
April:	New Secretary of State, James F. Byrnes, notes that possession of new weapon will enable USA to 'dictate its own terms' after the War
27 April:	First meeting of Target Committee, chaired by Groves
1 May:	Secretary of War Henry F. Stimson chairs first meeting of Interim Committee on post-war atomic policy
8 May:	Germany surrenders. Robert Oppenheimer notes that at Los Alamos scientists re-double their efforts to complete the bomb
2 July:	Uranium bomb, 'Little Boy', ready for final assembly
16 July:	'Trinity' – First atomic bomb, a plutonium device, successfully exploded in New Mexico. Scientific observers are appalled

The decision to use the bomb

1942

| May: | US cryptanalysts crack Japanese diplomatic and naval cipher. The 'Magic' intercepts enable Washington to read Japanese cabinet communications |

1944

September:	At Quebec Conference, Churchill and Roosevelt agree that the bomb might be used against Japan
September:	Japanese government first uses diplomatic channels in Stockholm, Lisbon and Bern to explore possibility of peace negotiations
October:	Battle of Leyte Gulf ensures total US Naval superiority in the Pacific
December:	President Roosevelt approves proposal to devise a demonstration use of the atomic bomb

1945

| 5 April: | US forces land on Okinawa. Japanese 'war party' govt. falls. New prime minister Suzuki known to be in favour of peace |

May:	Early in the month Truman informed through Bern and Lisbon that Tokyo wishes to negotiate a conditional surrender
17 June:	Under chairmanship of Oppenheimer, Scientific Panel informs Target Committee that it can think of no effective demonstration of the bomb, short of dropping it on a living target
22 June:	Fall of Okinawa renders Japan indefensible. New Japanese cabinet orders further moves towards surrender through Moscow embassy
16 July:	Following Trinity, Gen. Groves agrees that the war will be over 'after we have dropped two bombs on Japan'
20 July:	At Los Alamos and in Chicago, Manhattan Project scientists petition Washington to authorise technical demonstration of the bomb. Oppenheimer suppresses the petition
22 July:	US decodes instruction to Japan's Moscow embassy to negotiate 'unconditional surrender' provided Imperial House is preserved
24 July:	At Potsdam Conference in Berlin, Truman tells Stalin of existence of a powerful new weapon. Stalin announces he will be ready to attack Japan on 11 August
26 July:	Final Potsdam Declaration demands 'unconditional surrender' Truman endorses order to drop the bomb after 3 August
28 July:	Stalin tells Truman and Attlee that Japan has requested Moscow's assistance in immediate peace negotiations. It is agreed that Moscow will reject this request
31 July:	In five months of heavy bombing the USAAF has destroyed 66 cities, including Tokyo, killed 900,000 people and rendered millions more homeless. Japan has no industry or anti-aircraft defences left. USAAF commander Gen. Curtis LeMay says that with conventional bombing the war will be over in two weeks
6 August:	Uranium bomb dropped on Hiroshima
9 August:	Plutonium bomb dropped on Nagasaki
12 August:	Washington accepts continuation of Imperial rule
15 August:	Japan surrenders

Notes

ABBREVIATIONS USED IN THE NOTES

AJPT: Taylor; Bernst.: Bernstein, Oppenheimer; Bernst. Farm: Bernstein Farm Hall; Br. Lies: Brown A. C.; Camb. Encyl: Oliver; Chern.: Chernow; Cornv: Cornevin; D.Tel.: Daily Telegraph; DHL Mex.: Lawrence; DLB: Dictionary of Literary Biography; DR: Marnham, A Life of Diego Rivera; FT: Financial Times; GO'K: Hassrick; Gomb.: Gombrich; Hist. Tdy: History Today; HobsCap: Hobsbawm Capital; HobsEmp: Hobsbawm Empire; Hochs.: Hochschild; HoD: Conrad, Heart of Darkness; IHT: International Herald Tribune; Jap.T.: Japan Times; Kenn.: Kennedy; LeM.: Le Monde; Longm.: Longman Handbook; McCull.: McCullough; McSw.: McSweeney; Medw: Medawar; NatLamp: National Lampoon Bicentennial Calendar 1976; Neill.: Neillands; Nostr.: Conrad, Nostromo; NTr Handb.: National Trust Handbook; NY'er: New Yorker; NYRB: New York Review of Books; NYT: New York Times; OneWorld: Masters; Rhd: Rhodes; Schweb.: Schweber; Seng.: Sengier; Simm.: Simmons; Steinbg: Warburg; Steng.: Stengers; Stim.: Stimilli; ST: Sunday Times; Szasz: Szasz, Sun; Sz.Br.: Szasz British; Thomp.: Thompson; Times: Barraclough; Tuch.: Tuchman; Wrng: Wrong; Zoelln.: Zoellner

FOREWORD

p. v   Their Ghost Dance ended (Zinn. 22)

CHAPTER 1

p. 5   Auckland (*Auckland Star* 9.vi.1901 p.13)

CHAPTER 2

p. 9   shot himself (Meyers 33–4)
p. 10   African cake (Steng. 40)
p. 13   the wretched people of the earth (Steng. 58–9)
p. 18   well-kept alley (*HoD* Ev. 104)

CHAPTER 3

p. 19   that would last for three years (Meyers 97)
p. 31   the railway was rebuilt (Hochs. 279)
P. 32   routine attention (Wrng 256)
         MONUC is currently termed MONUSCO

CHAPTER 4

p. 49   National Atomic Museum – now called the National Museum of Nuclear
             Science and History
         'the gimmick' (Beser 79)
         ex-tail gunner in a B-29 (Rovere 95). [Like other claims made by Senator
             McCarthy this was incorrect. During the Pacific War he occasionally
             occupied the tail gunner's seat as a passenger in a B-29. He once fired
             4,700 rounds from a tail gun in a single day, but the aircraft was on the
             ground and he was aiming at coconut trees.]
p. 52   Coronado stormed (Simm. 20–1)
         Spider Woman (Simm. 22)
p. 54   who has been flayed (Paz 29)
p. 55   coloured races (Simm. 133)

CHAPTER 5

p. 60   antiquity for modern civilisation (Gomb. 87, 307–8)
p. 61   Fifth Avenue (Chern. 47–50)
p. 61   Warburg's line of research (Gomb. 85–7)
p. 62   conscience of the Eastern States (Gomb. 88)
         snuffling riff-raff (Roeck 165–6)
p. 66   the office of the Governor (Thomp. 31)

CHAPTER 6

p. 68   A Confederate Veteran (Miller 192)
         90 million survivors (HobsEmp 47)

CHAPTER 15

p. 192   two émigré Berlin physicists (Rhd 321–5)
         not technically possible (Rhd 319–20)
         to the cost of the war (Wilson J. quoted Rhd 323)
p. 193   a three-page memorandum (Medw 243)
         Burlington House, Piccadilly (Medw 220)
         MAUD - Military Application of Uranium Detonation (A widely-accepted
         alternative is that the chosen name was due to a muddle over the identity
         of a woman living in Kent) (Gowing. 34)
p. 194   Canada at the time (Medw 221)
         with the use of U-235 (Szasz 5)
p. 195   British nuclear research (Szasz 7)
         Advisory Committee on Uranium (Rhd 315)
         and unimpressive man (Rhd 368, 372)
p. 197   bankers, politicians, Money (Bird 87)(DR 248)
         a summary of the Maud report (Rhd 368)
         under the Briggs committee (Rhd 360)
p. 198   its applications multiply (Rhd 365)
         at that meeting Roosevelt (Aczel 129–30)
         organisation of the world (Rhd 379)
         overview of the possibilities (Rhd 386–7)
p. 200   words, to be pushed (Rhd 405–6)
         attacking his lungs or skin (Rhd 358)
         for a single night since (Rhd 356)

CHAPTER 16

p. 203   specific duties required (Groves xi)
         so did everybody else (Rhd 427)
         stunningly vast enterprises (Kenn. 664)
p. 204   Oppenheimer's ambition (Bird 185)
p. 205   his handsome private income (Schweb. 209). [This could be as much as
         $15,000 a year – or $500,000 today.]
         drive towards an atomic bomb (Bird 177)
p. 206   lucky escape in November 1942 (Rhd 450)
p. 207   to build a laboratory (Seidel 45)
         Fn. For a shorter period (Church 52, 63)
p. 208   failed his Army medical (Bird 210–11)
p. 209   Harvard two years later (NYT 10.xi.99)
         Rome with Fermi (Schweb. 87)
p. 210   Nobel Prize winners (Bernst. 80)(Szasz 18–21)
         working on a British bomb (Szasz xix)
p. 211   an even higher loyalty (York 165). [Fuchs was originally transferred to Los

Alamos, as one of a theoretical team, because of Edward Teller's refusal to
calculate implosion compression figures.]
Dachau concentration camp (Rhd 257, 263)
Physics was almost a vocation (Schweb. 13)
idyllic and leisurely (Schweb. 100)
feels that his responsibility lies (Rhd 425)
a wicked enterprise (Medw 86, 88)

p. 212   weapons of destruction (Szasz 58)
three centuries of physics (Rhd 452)
Hitler the only national leader (Rhd 312)

p. 213   the war had become completely hopeless (Cornv. 427) (Rose 301-2)
cancelled in June 1942 (Rhd 405)(Bernst. Farm 39–41)
Norwegian special forces in 1943 (Br. *Lies* 372–3)
grounds of the city hospital (Rhd 606)
supplies were accounted for (Rhd 613)

p. 214   Jewish physics (Kenn. 666–7)
On 19 February President Roosevelt (Kenn. 753)

p. 215   the north of New Mexico (Wilson 311)
Policy Committee in June 1943 (Rhd 500)

p. 216   signed in December 1942 (Brion 235)
Sengier to inform them (Brion 237)
the mine, $13m. (Zoelln. 63)
valuable resources of the mine (Cornv. 289)
commissioner turned historian (Wrng 37)

p. 217   Minière's mines in Katanga (Camb. Encyl 205)
400 Africans were killed (Camb. Encyl 189)
higher than the safe maximum (*NY'er* 13.ix.2010)
from radioactive materials (*LeM.* 13.xii.09)
Special Cobalt (Cornv. 288)
at Port-Franqui [now Ilebo]

p. 218   employing 150,000 people (Kenn. 664–5)
Fat Man, the plutonium bomb (Kenn. 665)
known to show nuclear fission (Rhd 460–1)

p. 219   uranium by February 1946 (Rhd 486–96; 600–02)
major effort of espionage (Rhd 605)

p. 220   not to bomb civilian populations (Rhd 309-10)
American military casualties [PMS Blackett (p. 78) noted that US casualty
figures were 'very light'. Total US battle deaths during the war were only
three times higher than road deaths during the same period.]
for the consequent bloodshed (Rhd 335-3)

CHAPTER 17

p. 221   with Roosevelt's death [According to Alexander Sachs, the bearer of Einstein's
         original letter, President Roosevelt had given 'a general acquiescence' in
         December 1944 to Sachs's plan to invite national and religious leaders to
         observe Trinity. (Szasz 153)]

p. 222   the time of our lives (Szasz 18)
         were considered too valuable (Rhd 418)

p. 223   our chief enemy, the Russians (Szasz 57)
         Los Alamos as a mechanic (Szasz 85–6)(*NatLamp.* 19.vi)
         scientists on the Town Council (Rhd 566)

p. 224   a battle of wits (Rhd 564–70)
         attention to our hi-jinks (Rhd 453)
         when they were young men (Rhd 601–2)

p. 225   arrive one month later (Rhd 604–5)
         California and Arizona (Rhd 605)
         after the German surrender (Szasz 25)

p. 226   When he was told (McCull. 376, 378). [Truman later said that at this
         meeting Stimson had been just as positive about the weapon's proactive
         role as its capacity to shorten the war.]
         dictate our own terms (Rhd 618)
         have given them a chance (Rhd 690)

p. 227   with one dismissive sentence (Rhd 428)
         report directly to him (Rhd 626)

p. 229   distances of 10,000 yards (Rhd 653)

p. 230   hell's wrong with the weather (Rhd 653)

p. 231   a very scary time (Rhd 675)

p. 232   a foul and awesome display (Rhd 675)
         since 1942 (Sz.Br. 93)
         two days before the Trinity test (Rhd 662)

p. 234   began to howl in triumph (Szasz 90)
         a very large munitions dump (Groves 433–4)

p. 235   a short vacation (Szasz 128)
         Here in 1945 (Szasz 84)

CHAPTER 18

p. 238   not leaving one stone (Neill. 380)
         killed enough they stop fighting (Kenn. 845)

p. 239   Following the invasion of Okinawa (Kenn. 834–7)
         warn the Japanese about the atomic bomb (Kenn. 835)
         spare the civilian population wherever (Rhd 640)
         Battle of the Somme (Horne 293–4)

p. 240   one of pure evil (Rhd 630, 632)
       As far as degradation went (Rhd 647)
       would run out within the city (Groves 272)

p. 241   wisdom of Henry Stimson (Groves 257)
       in some uninhabited place (Medw 138)
       and never seen again (Bird 297)

p. 242   international control unrecorded (Rhd 620–4, 651)
       by 155 scientists (Bird 302)

p. 243   harmless but effective demonstration (Kenn. 840)
       no . . . alternative to direct military use (Rhd 696–7)
       they could keep their Emperor on July 24 (Rhd 684, 689)
       Fn.between Roosevelt and Churchill (Rhd 537)

p. 244   with a very long airstrip (Rhd 554)
       as soon as made ready (Rhd 691)
       Fn.Gen. Spaatz had insisted (Neill. 381) (Zinn. 39)

p. 245   a pot of boiling black oil (Rhd 704–11)

p. 246   a further 130,000 survivors (Rhd 733–4)
       Commanding General over there (Rhd 734)

p. 247   James Salter (conversation with the author – July 2009)
       War suspends morality (AJPT 601)

p. 248   the death of 39 million (Rhd 630)
       a little boy on a toboggan (Cochran 174)(Szasz 155)

p. 249   for a day and maybe longer (Rhd 736–7)
       a junior Los Alamos physicist (Rhd 737–8)
       just enough fuel left (Beser 133)
       Fn. on an inhabited area (Neill. 381)

p. 250   70,000 people had died (Akizuki 52–3)

p. 251   decided to surrender (Kenn. 851). [When the news reached US military
       personnel, on 15 August, celebrations broke out and thousands of automatic
       weapons were fired into the air. Seven US servicemen were killed as a result.]

p.252   spina bifida (Sz.Br. 40)
       12 lb. metal weight (Conant 339)
       honorary citizen of the state (De Groot 104)
       the duty before God and the world (Schweb. 5)

p. 253   Five senior American commanders (Zinn 47, 49)(Rhd 687)(Bird 300–1)
       The Japanese were ready to surrender (Rhd 688)
       arms race had begun (Szasz 148). [Patrick Blackett, Oppenheimer's old
       tutor and a member of the Maud Committee, took the same view. Writing
       as early as 1948, he described the bombing of Hiroshima and Nagasaki as

'a highly successful move in power politics'.]
I don't hesitate to call a crime (*IHT*)

EPILOGUE

CHRONOLOGY

Select Bibliography

Aczel Amir D., *Uranium Wars* (USA 2009)

Akizuki Tatsuichiro, *Nagasaki 1945* (London 1981)

Allbright Joseph and Kunstel Marcia, *Bombshell: the Secret Story of America's Unknown Spy Conspiracy* (USA 1997)

Alperowitz Gar, *The Decision to Use the Atomic Bomb* (USA 1996)

Anders Gunther, *Hiroshima est partout* (Paris 2008)

– *Burning Conscience* (USA 1962)

Andrew Christopher and Mitrokhin Vasili, *The Mitrokhin Archive: the KGB in Europe and the West* (London 1999)

Anscombe GEM, *Ethics, Religion and Politics Vol. III* (London 1981)

Ascherson Neal, *The King Incorporated: Leopold II in the Age of Trusts* (London 1963)

Attali Jacques, *Un homme d'influence: Sir Siegmund G. Warburg 1902-82* (Paris 1985)

Bacher Robert F., *Robert Oppenheimer 1904-1967* (USA 1999)

Barraclough G. ed., *Times Atlas of World History* (London 1979)

Beevor Antony, *The Second World War* (London 2012)

Bernstein Jeremy, *Oppenheimer: Portrait of an Enigma* (USA 2004)

– *Hitler's Uranium Club: the secret recordings at Farm Hall* (USA 1996)

Beser Jacob, *Hiroshima and Nagasaki Revisited* (USA 1988)

Best Geoffrey, *Churchill and War* (London 2005)

Bird Kai and Sherwin Martin J., *American Prometheus: The triumph and tragedy of J. Robert Oppenheimer* (USA 2006)

Blackett PMS, *Fear, War and the Bomb: Military and Political Consequences of Atomic Energy* (London 1948)

Brion René and Moreau Jean-Louis, *De la mine à Mars: la genèse d'Umicore* (Brussels 2004)

Brown Andrew, *Keeper of the Nuclear Conscience: The life and work of Joseph Rotblat* (London 2012)

Brown Anthony Cave, *Bodyguard of Lies: The Vital Role of Deceptive Strategy in World War II* (London 1976)

Brown Dee, *The American West* (USA 1994)

Bundy McGeorge, *Danger and Survival* (USA 1988)

Carson Cathryn and Hollinger David A. eds., *Reappraising Oppenheimer: centennial studies and reflections* (USA 2005)

Cassidy David C., *Uncertainty: The Life and Science of Werner Heisenberg* (USA 1992)
- *J. Robert Oppenheimer and the American Century* (USA 2005)

Chernow Ron, *The Warburgs: a family saga* (London 1993)

Chevalier Haakon, *Oppenheimer: the Story of a Friendship* (USA 1965)

Church Fermor S. and Pond Peggy, *When Los Alamos was a Ranch School* (USA 1998)

Cochran Bert, *Harry Truman and the Crisis Presidency* (USA 1973)

Cohen Avner, *Israel and the Bomb* (USA 1998)

Cornet Anne and Gillet Florence, *Congo Belgique 1955-1965* (Brussels 2010)

Cornwell John, *Hitler's Scientists: Science, War and the Devil's Pact* (London 2003)

Conant Jennet, *109 East Palace* (USA 2005)

Conrad Joseph, *Heart of Darkness* (London 1902, Everyman edition 1967)
- *Nostromo* (London 1904)
- *Personal Record* (London 1912)

Cornevin Robert, *Le Zaire des origines à nos jours* (Brussels 1989)

Davis Nuel Pharr, *Lawrence and Oppenheimer* (USA 1968)

De Boeck Filip and Plissart Marie-Francoise, *Kinshasa: Tales of the Invisible City* (Ghent 2004)

De Groot G.J., *The Bomb: a Life* (USA 2004)

Deitch Kenneth M. ed., *The Manhattan Project: a Secret Wartime Mission* (USA 1995)

Delpech Thérèse, *L'Ensauvagement: le retour de la barbarie au XXIe siècle* (Paris 2005)

Dowden Richard, *Africa: Altered States, Ordinary Miracles* (London 2008)

Dyson Freeman, *Weapons and Hope* (New York 1984)

Elliot Gil, *Twentieth Century Book of the Dead* (London 1972)

Endo Shusaku, *Samurai* (London 1982)

Fermi Rachel and Samra Esther, *Picturing the Bomb* (USA 1995)

Frayn Michael, *Copenhagen* (London 1998)

Frisch Otto, *What Little I Remember* (London 1979)

Geeraerts Jeff, *Gangrene* (London 1974)

Gilpin Robert, *American Scientists and Nuclear Weapons Policy* (USA 1962)

Giroud Françoise, *Une femme honorable: Marie Curie, une vie* (Paris 1981)

Glasstone Samuel ed., *The Effects of Nuclear Weapons* (USA 1957)

Glover Jonathan, *Humanity: A Moral History of the 20th Century* (London 1999)

Glynn Paul, *A Song for Nagasaki* (Sydney 1988)

Goldschmidt Bertrand, *Le Complexe atomique* (Paris 1980)

Gombrich E.H., *Aby Warburg: an intellectual biography* (London 1970)

Gowing Margaret, *Britain and Atomic Energy: 1939-1945* (London 1964)

Groves Leslie, *Now It Can Be Told: the story of the Manhattan Project* (USA 1964)

Hamby Alonzo L., *Man of the People: the Life of Harry S. Truman* (London 1995)

Harris Jonathan, *Hiroshima: a study in Science, Politics and the Ethics of War* (USA 1970)

Harris Richard, *National Trust Guide – Santa Fe* (USA 1997)

Hassrick Peter H. ed., *The Georgia O'Keeffe Museum* (USA 1997)

Hastings Lord 'Max', *Nemesis: the Battle for Japan, 1944-45* (London 2007)

Heisenberg Werner, *Physics and Beyond: Memories of a Life in Science, trans. A.J. Pomerans* (London 1971)

Herken Gregg, *Brotherhood of the Bomb: the Tangled Lives and Loyalties of Robert Oppenheimer, Ernest Lawrence and Edward Teller* (USA 2002)

Hersey John, *Hiroshima* (USA 1946)

Hoard Dorothy, *Historic Roads of Los Alamos* (USA 2009)

Hobsbawm Eric, *The Age of Capital 1848-1875* (London 1975)

– *The Age of Empire 1875-1914* (London 1987)

Hochschild Adam, *King Leopold's Ghost* (USA 1998)

Horne Alistair, *The Price of Glory: Verdun 1916* (London 1962)

Houston Douglas, *Valley of the Simonsberg* (Cape Town 1981)

Howard Michael, *Peace and War: the Fifth Athenaeum Lecture* (unpubl. 2002)

Irving David, *The Virus House: Germany's Atomic Research and Allied Countermeasures* (London 1967)

Jungk Robert, *Brighter than a Thousand Suns* (London 1958)

Kahn Herman, *On Thermonuclear War* (USA 1960)

Keegan John, *The Second World War* (London 1989)

– *Intelligence in War* (London 2003)

Kennedy David M., *Freedom From Fear: the American People 1929-1945* (London 1999)

Kingsley Mary, *Travels in West Africa* (London 1897)

Kinvig Clifford, *Churchill's Crusade: The British Invasion of Russia, 1918-20* (London 2006)

Kunetka James, *City of Fire: Los Alamos and the Birth of the Atomic Age, 1943-45* (USA 1978)

– *Oppenheimer: the Years of Risk* (USA 1982)

Lamb Richard, *Churchill as War Leader: Right or Wrong?* (London 1991)

Lawrence D. H., *The Plumed Serpent* (London 1926)

– *Mornings in Mexico* (London 1927)

Le Fur Yves ed., *Masques: chefs-d'oeuvres des collections du quai Branly* (Paris 2008)

Levi-Strauss Claude, *L'autre face de la lune* (Paris 2011)

Longman Handbook of Modern European History, 1763-1985 (London 1989)

Mabille Xavier, Tulkens Charles-X. and Vincent Anne, *La Société Générale de Belgique 1822-1997* (Brussels 1997)

McCullough David, *Truman* (USA 1992)

McMillan Priscilla J., *The Ruin of J. Robert Oppenheimer and the Birth of the Modern Arms Race* (USA 2005)

Macé Francois and Mieko, *Le Japon d'Edo* (Paris 2006)

Marnham Patrick, *Fantastic Invasion: Dispatches from Africa* (London 1980)
– *Dreaming with His Eyes Open: A Life of Diego Rivera* (London 1998)

Masters Dexter and Way Katherine eds., *One World or None* (USA 1946)

Mead Walter Russell, *American Foreign Policy and How It Changed the World* (USA 2001)

Medawar Jean and Pyke David, *Hitler's Gift: Scientists who fled Nazi Germany* (London 2000)

Meyers Jeffrey, *Joseph Conrad: a Biography* (London 1991)

Miller William, *A New History of the United States* (USA 1968)

Mishima Yukio, *La mort en été* (Paris 1983)

Monk Ray, *The Life of J. Robert Oppenheimer* (London 2012)

Moorehead Alan, *The Traitors: the Double Life of Füchs, Pontecorvo and Nunn May* (London 1952)

Morgan K.O., *Labour in Power: 1945-1951* (London 1984)

Muggeridge Malcolm, *Tread Softly for You Tread on my Jokes* (London 1966)

Murray Jocelyn ed., *Cultural Atlas of Africa* (London 1981)

Nagai Takashi, *The Bells of Nagasaki* (London 1987)

Neillands Robin, *The Bomber War: Arthur Harris and the Allied Bomber Offensive 1939-1945* (London 2001)

Ōe Kenzaburo, *Hiroshima Notes* (USA 1995)

Oliver Roland and Crowder Michael eds., *Cambridge Encyclopedia of Africa* (London 1981)

Oppenheimer J.R., *Science and the Common Understanding* (USA 1954)
– 'On Albert Einstein', from *The Company They Kept* (USA 2006)

Pais Abraham, *Niels Bohr's Times* (London 1991)

Paz Octavio, *The Labyrinth of Solitude* (USA 1950)

Powers Thomas, *Heisenberg's War* (USA 1993)

Quinlan Michael, *Thinking About Nuclear Weapons* (London 2009)

Raish Carol and McSweeney Alice M., *Land Grants and the US Forest Service* (Natural Resources Journal, University of New Mexico 2008)

Read Piers Paul, *Ablaze: the Story of Chernobyl* (London 1993)

Reader John, *Africa: a Biography of the Continent* (USA 1998)

Rhodes Richard, *The Making of the Atomic Bomb* (USA 1986)

Roberts J.M., *A History of the World* (USA 1976)

Roeck Bernd, *Florence 1900: the Quest for Arcadia* (USA 2009)

Rose Paul Lawrence, *Heisenberg and the Nazi Atomic Bomb Project: A Study in German Culture* (USA 1998)

Rovere Richard H., *Senator Joe McCarthy* (USA 1959)

Russell Bertrand, *Has Man a Future?* (London 1961)

Sando Joe S., *Pueblo Nations: Eight Centuries of Pueblo Indian History* (USA 1998)

Schweber S. S., *In the Shadow of the Bomb: Bethe, Oppenheimer and the Moral Responsibility of the Scientist* (USA 2000)

Seidel Robert W., *Los Alamos and the development of the atomic bomb* (USA 1995)

Sengier E., *Notes biographiques* (Brussels unpubl.)

Simenon Georges, *A la recherche de l'homme nu* (Paris 1976)

Simmons Marc, *New Mexico: an Interpretative History* (USA 1988)

Smith Alice Kimball and Weiner Charles eds., *Robert Oppenheimer: Letters and Recollections* (USA 1980)

Soudoplatov Pavel and Soudoplatov Anatoli, *Missions Speciales* (Paris 1994)

Stearns Jason K., *Dancing in the Glory of Monsters: the Collapse of the Congo and the Great War of Africa* (USA 2011)

Stengers Jean, *Congo: Mythes et réalités* (Brussels 2007)

Stimilli Davide ed., *La Guérison infinie: Histoire clinique d'Aby Warburg* (Paris 2007)

Stokes, Henry Scott, *The Life and Death of Yukio Mishima* (London 1975)

Stoff Michael B., Fanton Jonathan F. and Williams R. Hal, *The Manhattan Project: a documentary introduction to the Atomic Age* (USA 1991)

Stone Norman, *Europe Transformed* (London 1983)

Szasz F.M., *The Day the Sun Rose Twice: the story of the Trinity Site nuclear explosion, July 16, 1945* (USA 1984)

– *British Scientists and the Manhattan Project: the Los Alamos Years* (London 1992)

Tawada Yoko, *Journal des jours tremblants: Après Fukushima* (Paris 2012)

Taylor AJP, *English History: 1914-1945* (London 1965)

Thompson Waite and Gottlieb Richard M., *The Santa Fe Guide* (USA 1993)

Tuchman Barbara W., *The Proud Tower: a Portrait of the World before the War - 1890-1914* (USA 1966)

Turconi Angelo and Neyt Francois, *Infini Congo* (unpubl., Lubumbashi 2010)

Turnbull Colin, *The Forest People* (London 1961)

– *Man in Africa* (London 1976)

United States Strategic Bombing Survey: Part 4 and 5 (USA 1946)

US Atomic Energy Commission, *In the matter of J. Robert Oppenheimer; transcript of hearing before Personnel Security Board, Washington D.C., April-May 1954* (USA 1954)

Van Reybrouck David, *Congo: une Histoire* (Amsterdam 2010)

Volpi Jorge, *A la recherche de Klingsor* (Paris 2001)

Vonnegut Kurt, *Slaughterhouse Five* (USA 1969)

Warburg Aby, trans. Steinberg Michael P., *Images from the Region of the Pueblo Indians of North America* (USA 1995)

Weigle Marta, *The Penitentes of the Southwest* (USA 1970)

Weinstein Allen and Vassiliev Alexander, *The Haunted Wood* (USA 1999)

West Nigel, Venona, *The Greatest Secret of the Cold War* (London 2000)

West Rebecca, *The Meaning of Treason* (London 1949)

White Michael, *Rivals: Conflicts as the Fuel of Science* (London 2001)

Williams Francis, *A Prime Minister Remembers* (London 1961)

Wilson Chris, *The Myth of Santa Fe: Creating a Modern Regional Tradition* (USA 1997)

Wilson Jane, ed., *All in Our Time: Bulletin of the Atomic Scientists* (USA 1975)

Wrong Michela, *In the Footsteps of Mr Kurtz* (London 2000)

Wynd Oswald, *The Ginger Tree* (London 1977)

York Herbert F., *The Advisors: Oppenheimer, Teller and the Superbomb* (USA 1976)

Zeilig Leo, *Patrice Lumumba: Africa's Lost Leader* (London 2008)

Zinn Howard, *La Bombe: De l'inutilité des bombardements aériens* (Quebec 2011)

Zoellner Tom, *Uranium: War, Energy and the Rock that Shaped the World* (USA 2009)

Acknowledgements

The subject was first suggested by Toby Eady in London and to him and to Dan Frank and Joy de Menil in New York my grateful thanks are due. I would also like to thank Steve Westheimer and Candace Kern in Santa Fe who have provided so much support and friendship over the years. In addition I am grateful for the encouragement of the late Angus Cameron, who recalled his personal experience of being blacklisted during the McCarthy years, and to Liz Calder who introduced me to Bruce Robinson, director of *Withnail and I* and author of the original (censored) screenplay of the Hollywood film *Fat Man*.

Bruce Robinson held strong views on Lieutenant-General Leslie Groves, some of which he was kind enough to share with me over supper in the King's Road on 9 May 2001.

I concede that the subject of this book became an obsession while I was writing it. I tried not to think about it outside working hours. Not thinking about the atomic bomb is most people's default position, naturally enough.

My particular thanks are due to Steve Hawes who first introduced me to Manu Riche, and to Manu Riche who revived this project when it was quietly expiring. Special thanks also to Jun Kanno in Paris and to Major Jean-Marc Hubot, formerly of Belgian Military Intelligence, last seen somewhere in the Ardennes. My thanks as well to those who read all or part of the work in progress, including Professor George

Huxley, Dr Claudia Wedepohl, Steve Westheimer, Manu Riche, Jun Kanno, Sarah Nisbet, Polly Coles, Silvia Crompton and Jamie Coleman. I must also thank:

In the DRC
His Excellency Moïse Katumbi Chapwe the Governor of Katanga, Dr Bernard Blanpain, Hendrik De Witt, Laurent de Calion, Franz Couttenier, Walter Couttenier, Martine Deru, Paul Fransen, Georges Forrest, Dirk Van Hoeymissen, Major Gilbert, Professor Chaim Goris, Philip Heuts, Colonel Simba, Renaat Lambeets, Luc Cuveele, Wouter Dewilde, Paul Kaboba, Jean-Marie Dikanga Kazadi, General Jean-Claude Kifwa, Soeur Marie-Françoise, Bernard Lamby, Professor Joseph Ibongo, Hubert Maheux, Jean-Pierre Neyrinck, Lionel Ngondo, Ilunga Ley Ngwej Privato, Dr Christian Ramaekers, Jacques Somville, Benoit Standart, Eric de Lamotte, Major Patrick Van Alphen and in South Africa the late Jimmy Nisbet

In New Mexico
Patty Allalunis, Ann Beyer, JoAnn Butler, Dr Don Coates, Judy Klinger, Alice M. McSweeney, Bill McSweeney, Joseph M. Talachy, Jacob Viarrial, Judy and Philip Tuwaletstiwa, Carlos Valdez, Keith Vizcarra, C. C.Wood, Ryan Bushman, Randy David

In New York
Lucretia Stewart, Ben Sonnenberg, Ted Morgan, Sherry Stanton

In Paris
Pierre Braillard, Geneviève Dupuy, Laure de Gramont

In Brussels
Eric Van Zuylen, Philippe Van Meerbeeck, Geneviève De Bauw, Paul Heymans, Eric Goosens, Michel De Certeau, Etienne Denis, Michèle Hubinon, Vincent Bribosia, Harold Mechlynck, Geneviève Planchard

In Switzerland
Dr Gerhard Dammann and the staff and patients of the Psychiatric Clinic at Munsterlingen

In Japan
Dr Tario Kanno, Dr Kiyo Kurosawa, Michiko Shoji, Madame Kiomi Yamamoto

Libraries and Archives
The New York Public Library, the Library of Congress, the State Library of New Mexico, the National Atomic Museum at Albuquerque, the Los Alamos Historical Museum, the Rockefeller Archive, National Archives and Records in Washington D.C., the Massachusetts Institute of Technology Archives and Special Collections, the Niels Bohr Library at the American Institute of Physics, the Warburg Insitute, the London Library, the British Library, the Bodleian Library, the fellow librarian of Corpus Christi College, Oxford, the Musée Royale de l'Afrique Centrale at Tervuren, the Musée Nationale de la République Democratique du Congo at Kinshasa

I have made every effort to trace copyright holders. If there have been any inadvertent errors or omissions the publishers will correct these in future editions. My thanks are due to the following holders of material which is in copyright: the Warburg Institute in London for permission to quote from Aby Warburg's lecture "Images from the Region of the Pueblo Indians of North America"; the Cornell University Press NYC, for Michael P. Steinberg's translation of Aby Warburg's lecture; the Georgia O'Keeffe Museum of Abiqui NM, for the writing of Georgia O'Keeffe; Simon and Schuster Inc. NYC, for *The Making of the Atomic Bomb* by Richard Rhodes; the Harry S. Truman Library, Independence MO, for the diary of Harry S. Truman.

I would also like to thank Mildred Marney of Rowan Script who has read and typed this book in more versions than any sane person should have been asked to do. I owe a great deal to my editors at Chatto, Penny Hoare and Poppy Hampson. For the opinions expressed and for any errors I remain entirely responsible.

Index

DRC indicates Democratic Republic of Congo.

programme secretly authorised
185–6, 287; Einstein's letter to
President Roosevelt warning of the
danger of a Nazi atomic bomb. No
effective action follows 186–7, 287;
Pierre Joliot-Curie signs a contract
to build a French nuclear weapon in
the Sahara Desert using uranium
from the Belgian Congo 189, 287;
first secret delivery of Belgian
uranium to warehouse in New York
189–90, 287; Hitler invades Poland.
French bomb programme cancelled
189, 287; Frisch-Peierls memorandum to Churchill first reveals
practical possibility of an atomic
bomb. Churchill appoints Maud
Committee 192–3, 210, 287;
Churchill sends atomic bomb contd.
the Tizard-Cockcroft mission to
Washington, proposing close military
co-operation 195, 288; Vannevar
Bush, president of Carnegie
Institute, sets up the NDRC, to
direct scientific development of military research 196, 287; Maud
Committee's final report recommends immediate construction of an
atomic bomb. Vannevar Bush
receives a copy 197, 288; Arthur
Compton, of Chicago University,
reports to President Roosevelt,
describing atomic bomb as 'a deter-
mining factor in warfare' 198, 288;
Roosevelt approves development of a
weapon that 'will change the political organisation of the world' and
promises 'unlimited funds' 198, 288;
President Roosevelt appoints
working groups for immediate
launch of atomic bomb programme
198–9, 288; President Roosevelt and
Vannevar Bush discount danger of a
Nazi bomb, but decide to 'push' the
US programme 199–200, 288; Brig.
Gen. Leslie Groves is appointed
director of Manhattan Project 203–4,

288; Groves establishes his authority
independently of the Joint Chiefs of
Staff 203, 288; Robert Oppenheimer
appointed director of Los Alamos
laboratory 204–5, 288; twenty British
scientists arrive to join the
Manhattan Project 210–11, 288;
Albert Speer, on the advice of
Werner Heisenberg, postpones, and
effectively cancels, the Nazi bomb
programme 213, 288; the ALSOS
team captures information proving
that there is no ongoing Nazi bomb
programme and informs Groves 213,
289; at Los Alamos, Groves tells
British physicist Joseph Rotblat that
the new weapon is aimed at the
Soviets, not the Nazis 213, 288;
Groves tells his superior officer,
Gen. George C. Marshall, US Army
Chief of Staff, that all German
uranium is accounted for 213, 289;
Norwegian Special Forces destroy a
heavy water plant essential to
construction of a German nuclear
reactor 213, 288; Groves obtains a
monopoly of Congolese and
Canadian uranium and ensures that
United Kingdom is denied all
wartime uranium supply 213–14,
288; Manhattan Project has grown
into a top secret $2bn industry,
employing 150,000 people on sites at
Oak Ridge (Tennessee), Hanford
(Washington State), and Los Alamos
(New Mexico) 218, 288; Harold
Urey, director of Oak Ridge, resigns,
when he realises that the Manhattan
Project is no longer intended to
block a Nazi atomic bomb monopoly
218–19, 288; death of Franklin
Delano Roosevelt. Succeeded by
Vice-Pres. Harry S. Truman, who
knows nothing of Manhattan Project
219, 289; two months after ALSOS
report, Groves decides to triple
production of bomb grade uranium

219, 289; first delivery of bomb grade uranium to Los Alamos from Oak Ridge 224–5, 289; Germany surrenders. Robert Oppenheimer notes that at Los Alamos scientists re-double their efforts to complete the bomb 225, 289; Truman first learns of the Manhattan Project 226, 289; new Secretary of State, James F. Byrnes, notes that possession of new weapon will enable USA to 'dictate its own terms' after the War 226, 289; Vannevar Bush proposes a new committee be set up, the Interim Committee, to consider post-war implications of atomic bomb 227–8, 289; first meeting of Target Committee, chaired by Groves 227, 289; Secretary of War Henry F. Stimson chairs first meeting of Interim Committee on post-war atomic policy 227–8, 289; uranium bomb, 'Little Boy', ready for final assembly 228, 289; first atomic bomb, a plutonium device, successfully exploded 228–32, 289; following Trinity, Gen. Groves agrees that the war will be over 'after we have dropped two bombs on Japan' 232, 290; in five months of heavy bombing the USAAF has destroyed 66 cities, including Tokyo, killed 900,000 people and rendered millions more homeless. Japan has no industry or anti-aircraft defences left. USAAF commander Gen. Curtis LeMay says that with conventional bombing the war will be over in 2 weeks 238–40, 290; at Los Alamos and in Chicago Manhattan Project scientists petition Washington to authorise technical demonstration of the bomb. Oppenheimer suppresses the petition 242, 290; under chairmanship of Oppenheimer, Scientific Panel informs Target Committee that it can think of no effective demonstration of the bomb, short of dropping it on a living target 242–3, 290; at Potsdam Conference in Berlin, Truman tells Stalin of existence of a powerful new weapon. Stalin announces he will be ready to attack Japan on 11 August 243, 290; Churchill and Roosevelt agree that the bomb will be used against Japan, once, after a warning has been issued 243n, 288; final Potsdam Declaration demands 'unconditional surrender'. Truman endorses order to drop the bomb after 3 August 243–4, 290; Japanese surrender talks and decision to drop bomb 243, 244, 247, 248, 249, 251, 252–3, 254, 259, 267, 289, 290; uranium bomb dropped on Hiroshima 244–7, 290; plutonium bomb dropped on Nagasaki 247–51, 290; Washington accepts continuation of Imperial rule 251, 290; Japan surrenders 251, 290; chronology of events leading to the first use of 287–90 see also atom; nuclear fission and Manhattan Project

Atomic Bomb Museum, Nagasaki 268–9

Austro-Hungarian Army 182

Aztecs 52, 66, 68–9, 163

B-29 Superfortress (WWII bomber) 48, 49, 50, 238–9, 240, 244–5, 249, 256, 267–8, 282

Bainbridge, Kenneth 232

Bandelier, Adolph 63, 65, 66, 166

barium 179, 180

Becknell, William 71

Beernaert, Auguste 42

Belgian Congo: uranium exported from used in Manhattan Project xvii, 10, 40, 138–9, 148, 189–90, 198, 215–18, 224, 255, 287; annexed by Belgium, 1908 146; German use of uranium from 186, 189; Belgian investment in following First World

New Mexico xviii, 47–59, 60–7,
68–81, 82–91, 127–9, 161–4, 165,
167, 170, 230; map of xiv; author in
47–51, 55–9; National Atomic
Museum in 49–51; Spanish Empire
in 52–5, 58, 68–71, 82–3, 89; Native
Americans/Indians in 53–6, 58–9,
62–7, 69–78, 80, 82–91, 162, 163–8,
170–1; Warburg in 60–7, 82, 84–8,
109–18; United States/Anglo settling
of 71–8, 88–91, 162, 164–8, 170–1;
Oppenheimer visits 127–9, 161–2,
168–73; Trinity test in 228–37, 238;
impact of atom bomb on 252 *see also*
Los Alamos *and under individual area
and place name*
New Spain 52, 58, 71
New York Times 186, 234
Newton, Isaac 124
Nichols, Lieu. Col. Kenneth 203
Nimitz, General 253
9/11 176
NKVD 135
Nobel Prize 102, 120, 121, 121n, 122,
123, 134, 138, 184, 197, 204, 210,
218,   258, 272
Norway: heavy water production in
193, 213
Nostromo (Conrad) 116–17
Now It Can Be Told (Groves) 203, 221
nuclear fission: developments in
research, February 1932–January
1939 177; potential dangers well
known 178; Chadwick 'discovers'
existence of neutron 178; first artificial transmutation of a nucleus 179;
Fermi shows neutrons more effective
at smashing atoms if slowed down by
passing through a material barrier
179; Hahn discovers nuclear fission
179–80; Meitner–Frisch verification
180; Szilárd's reaction to 180–1 *see
also* Szilárd, Leó
nuclear reactors: Congolese 37–40;
building of first 189, 193, 199, 218,
224, 288; Fukushima 275–6, 277,
278, 281

O'Keeffe, Georgia 69, 70, 76, 77,
162–3
Ōe, Kenzaburō 272, 273–5, 275n
Office of Secure Transportation 51
Okinawa Island, Japan 239, 247, 251,
272, 273, 275, 289, 290
OKW (German Supreme Command)
185, 193
Oliphant, Max 193, 195–6
On the Edge of the Primeval Forest
(Schweitzer) 6
Oppenheimer, Ella 129
Oppenheimer, Frank 134, 205
Oppenheimer, Julius 128, 129, 130,
132
Oppenheimer, Julius Robert: travels to
Hamburg, 1921 95–6; visits
Joachimsthal and nearly dies from
'trench dysentery', 1921 96, 120,
127, visits New Mexico with Herbert
Smith, 1922 127, 128–9, 130, 164,
167; family background 128; education and intellectual talent 128–9,
130, 132–3, 135–6, 204; emotional
fragility 129, 132; attends Harvard
130–1; Whitehead and 130–1;
Oppenheimer, Julius Robert contd.
Cavendish Laboratory 131, 132,
133–4; return visit to Sangre de
Cristo 131–2; mental collapse,
1925–6 132–3, 204; Corsica, visits
132; meets Dirac and Bohr 133;
meets Born 134; Göttingen, studies
at 134–6; studies with Ehrenfest in
Leiden 136; studies in Zurich 136,
137, 161; returns from Europe to
California 137, 161; Perro Caliente
('Hot Dog') cabin, New Mexico,
visits 161, 162; traces of in New
Mexico 168–70, 172, 173; author's
proposed biography of 168–9; reaction to Hahn's breakthrough 181;
importance of to building of atom
bomb 191; Berkeley and 197, 204;
Ernest Lawrence and 197, 205;
Groves appoints as scientific director
of Manhattan Project and head of

www.vintage-books.co.uk

Jiang Zilong

All the Colours of
the Rainbow

Translated by Wang Mingjie

Panda Books